COLLECTION EDITS BY
JUSTIN EISINGER & ALONZO SIMON

COLLECTION DESIGN BY
JEFF POWELL

WINTERWORLD CREATED BY
CHUCK DIXON AND JORGE ZAFFINO

ISBN: 978-1-63140-256-2

18 17 16 15 1 2 3 4

IDW®
www.IDWPUBLISHING.com
IDW founded by Ted Adams, Alex Garner, Kris Oprisko, and Robbie Robbins

Ted Adams, CEO & Publisher
Greg Goldstein, President & COO
Robbie Robbins, EVP/Sr. Graphic Artist
Chris Ryall, Chief Creative Officer/Editor-in-Chief
Matthew Ruzicka, CPA, Chief Financial Officer
Alan Payne, VP of Sales
Dirk Wood, VP of Marketing
Lorelei Bunjes, VP of Digital Services
Jeff Webber, VP of Digital Publishing & Business Development

Facebook: **facebook.com/idwpublishing**
Twitter: **@idwpublishing**
YouTube: **youtube.com/idwpublishing**
Instagram: **instagram.com/idwpublishing**
deviantART: **idwpublishing.deviantart.com**
Pinterest: **pinterest.com/idwpublishing/idw-staff-faves**

Originally published as WINTERWORLD issues #5–7 and WINTERWORLD #0.

WINTER WORLD

THE STRANDED

WRITTEN BY
CHUCK DIXON

THE STRANDED

ILLUSTRATED BY
TOMAS GIORELLO

COLORED BY
DIEGO RODRIGUEZ

LETTERED BY
ROBBIE ROBBINS

WYNN'S TALE

ILLUSTRATED BY
TOMMY LEE EDWARDS

LETTERED BY
JOHN WORKMAN

COVER BY
TOMMY LEE EDWARDS

SERIES EDITED BY
DAVID HEDGECOCK

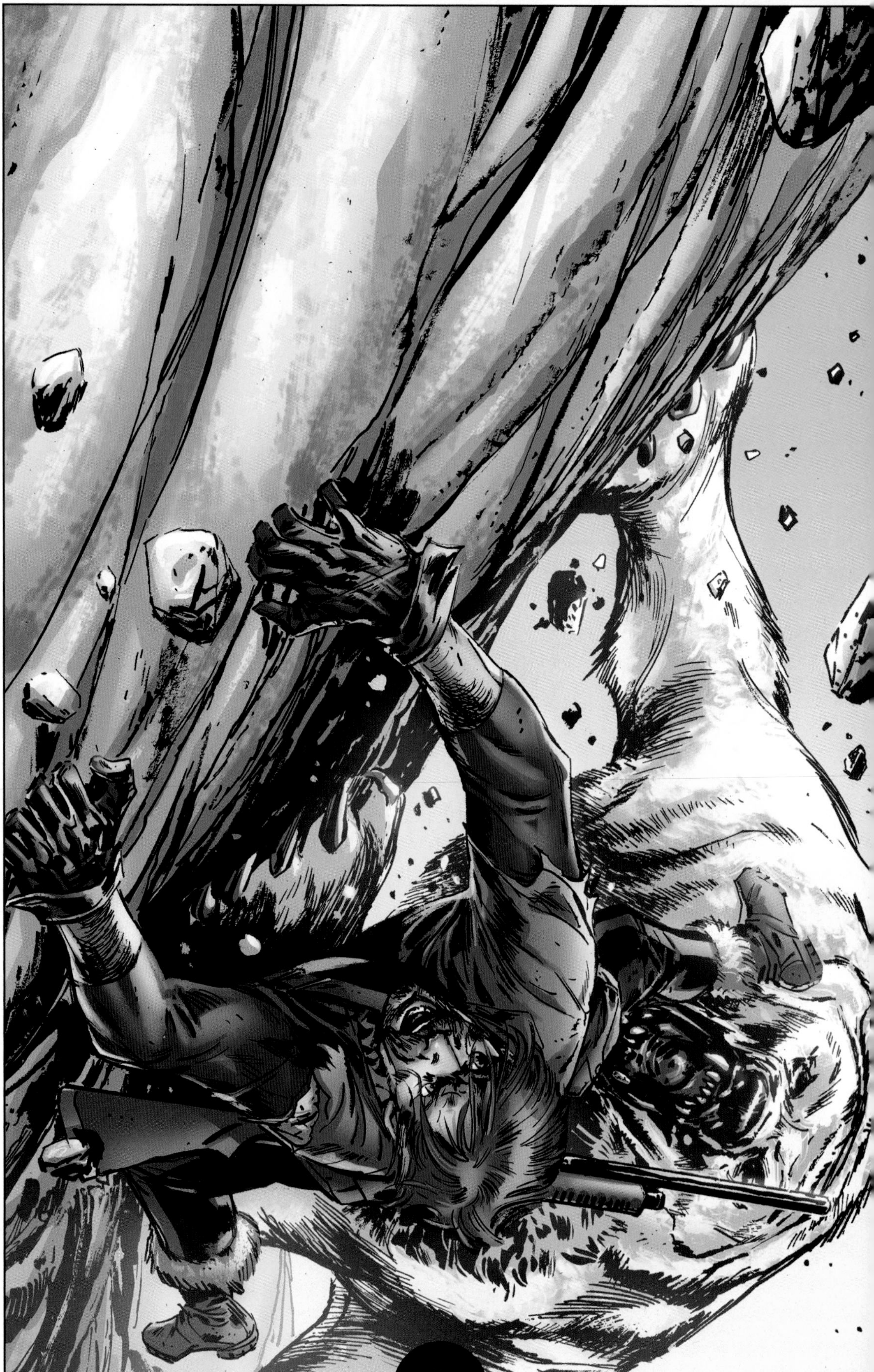

1

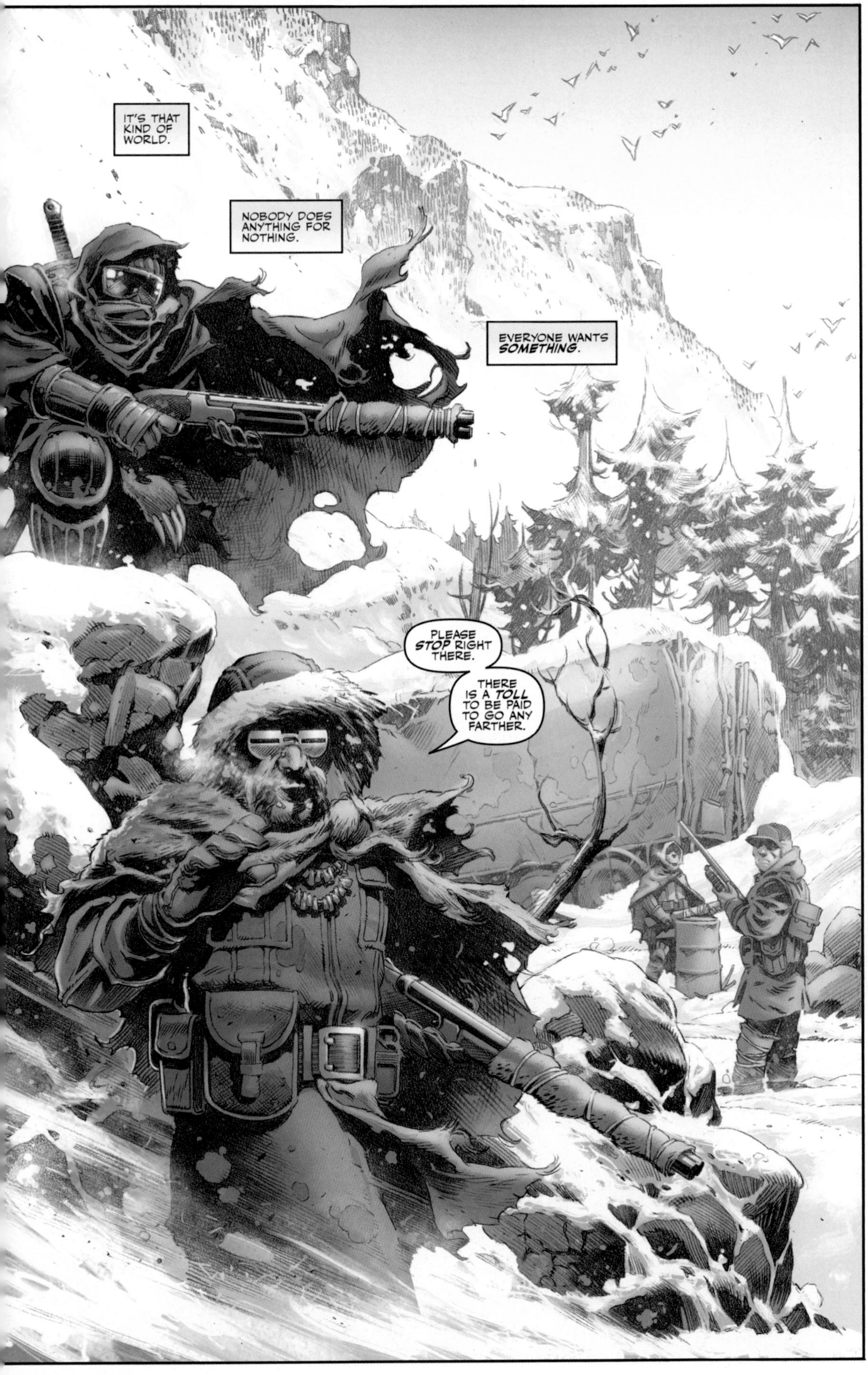
IT'S THAT KIND OF WORLD.
NOBODY DOES ANYTHING FOR NOTHING.
EVERYONE WANTS SOMETHING.
PLEASE STOP RIGHT THERE.
THERE IS A TOLL TO BE PAID TO GO ANY FARTHER.

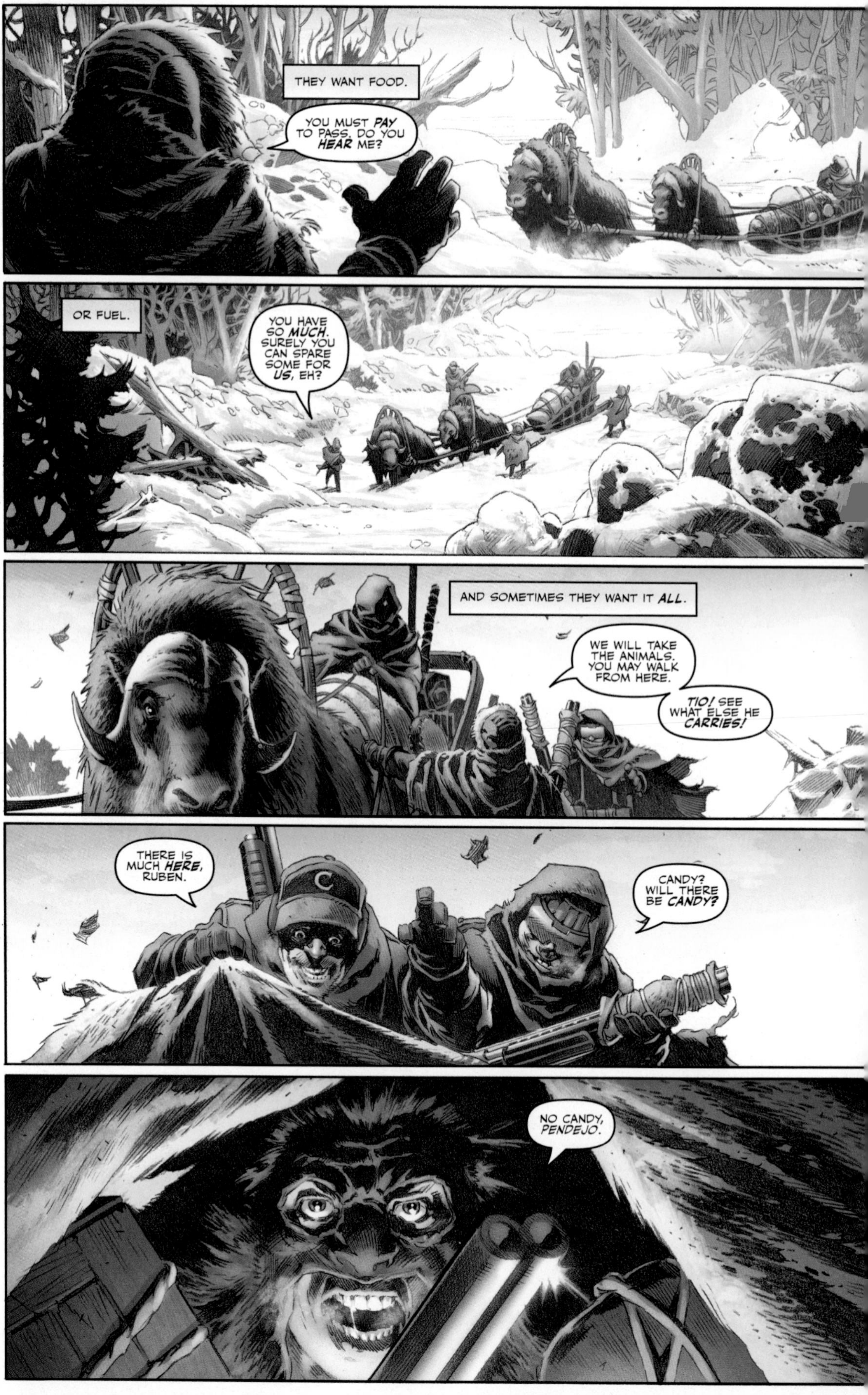
THEY WANT FOOD.
YOU MUST PAY TO PASS. DO YOU HEAR ME?
OR FUEL.
YOU HAVE SO MUCH. SURELY YOU CAN SPARE SOME FOR US, EH?
AND SOMETIMES THEY WANT IT ALL.
WE WILL TAKE THE ANIMALS. YOU MAY WALK FROM HERE.
TIO! SEE WHAT ELSE HE CARRIES!
THERE IS MUCH HERE, RUBEN.
CANDY? WILL THERE BE CANDY?
NO CANDY, PENDEJO.

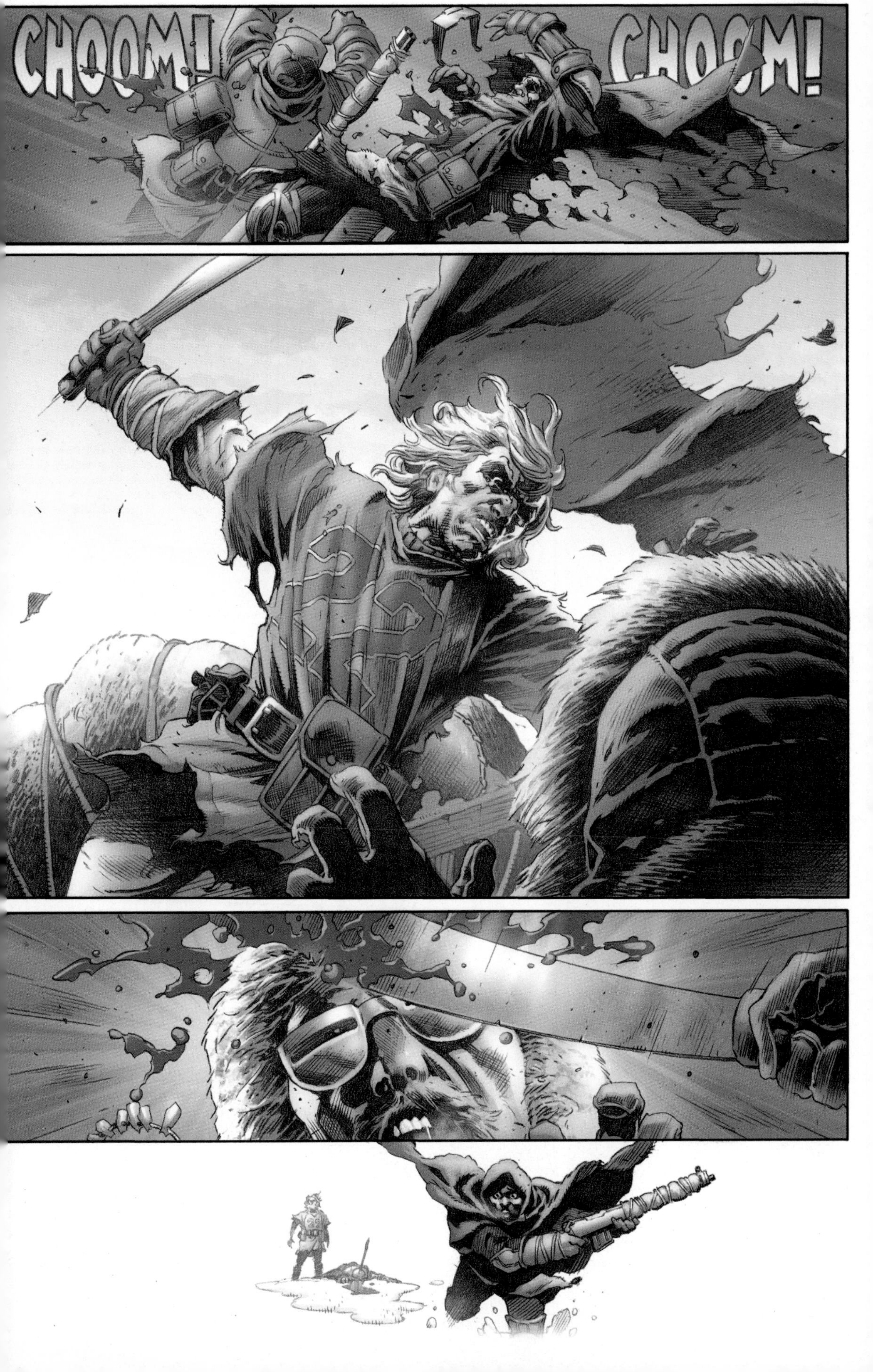
CHOOM!
CHOOM!

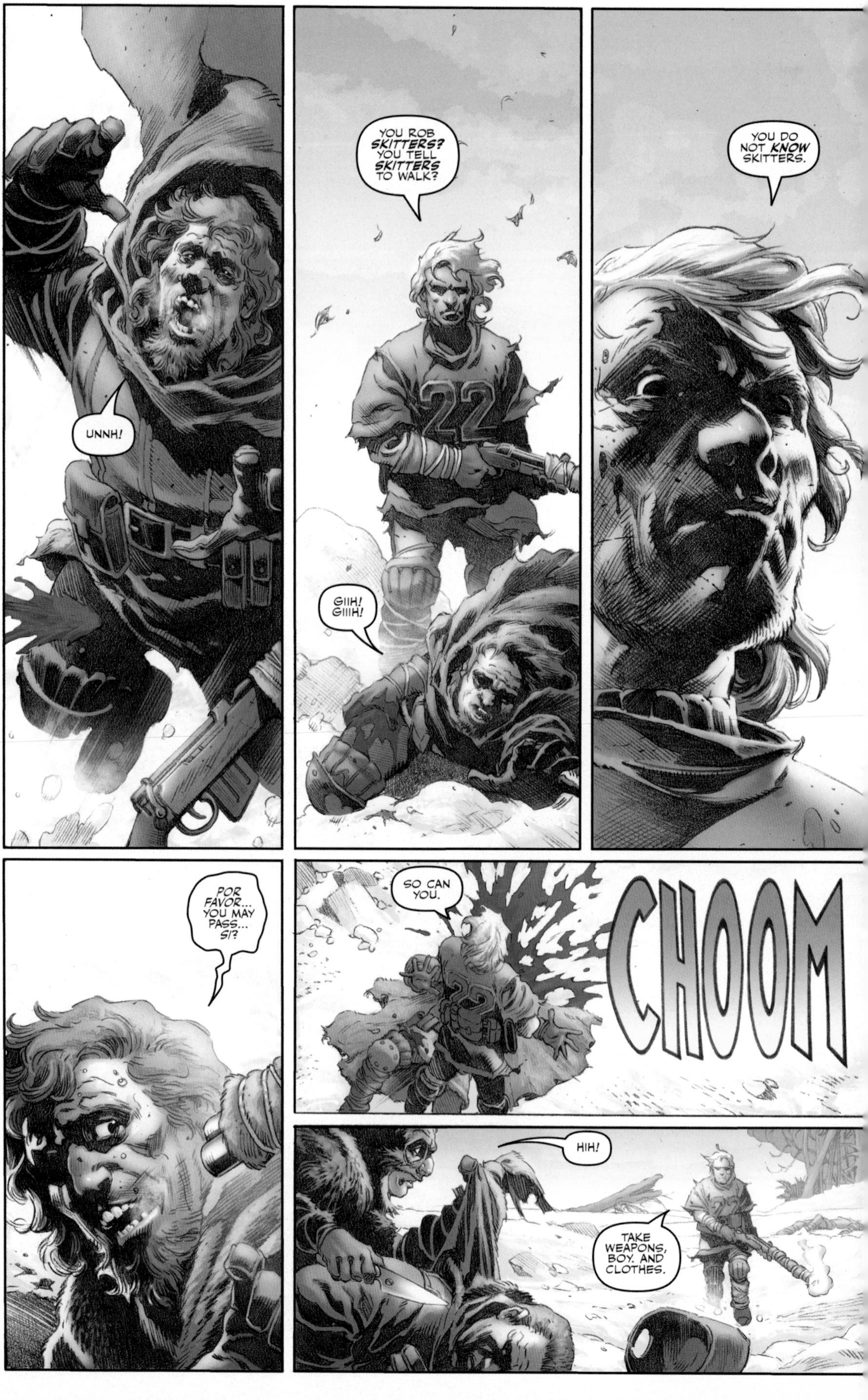
UNNH!
YOU ROB SKITTERS? YOU TELL SKITTERS TO WALK?
GIIH! GIIIH!
YOU DO NOT KNOW SKITTERS.
POR FAVOR... YOU MAY PASS... SI?
SO CAN YOU.
CHOOM
HIH!
TAKE WEAPONS, BOY. AND CLOTHES.

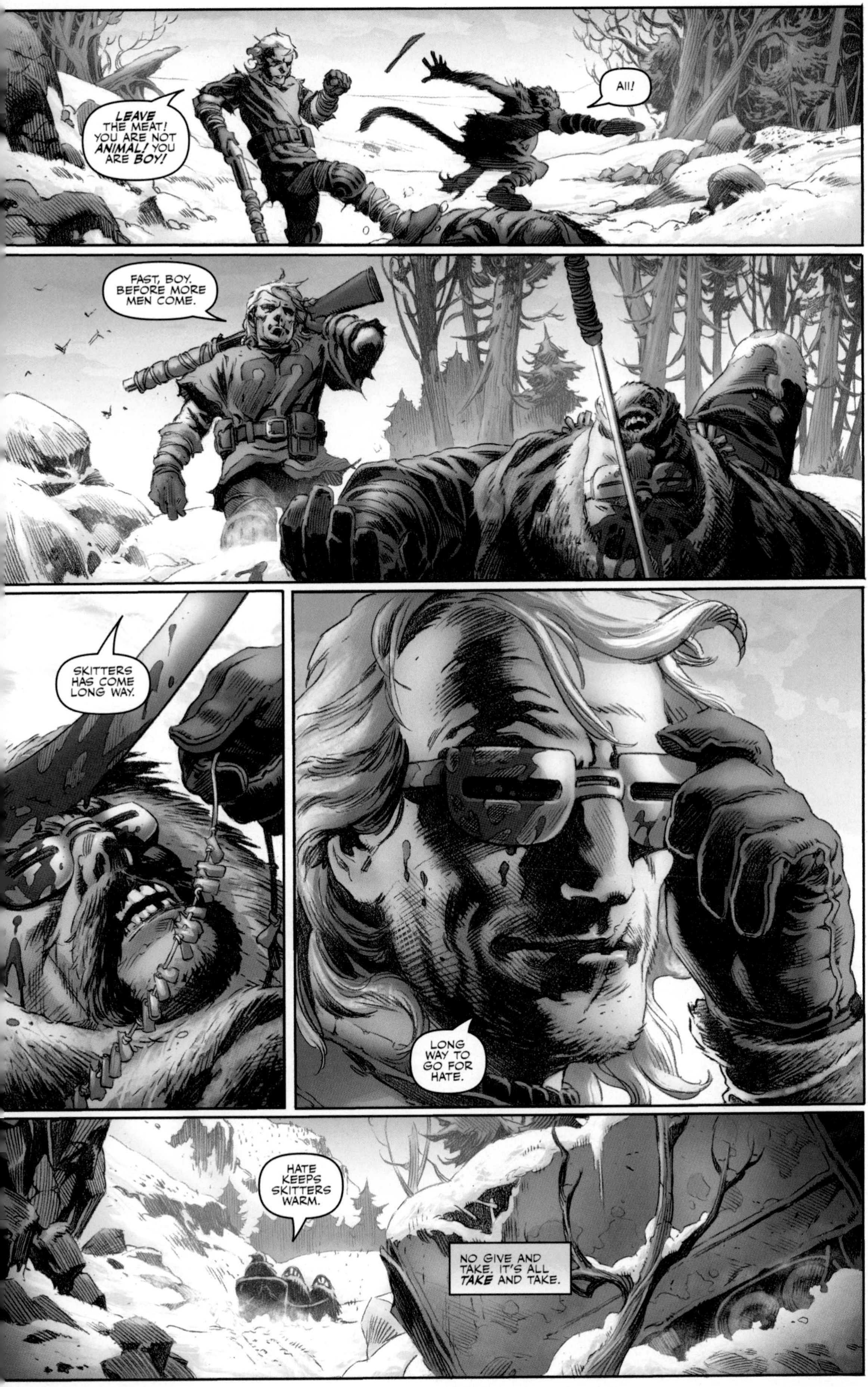
LEAVE THE MEAT! YOU ARE NOT ANIMAL! YOU ARE BOY!
AII!
FAST, BOY. BEFORE MORE MEN COME.
SKITTERS HAS COME LONG WAY.
LONG WAY TO GO FOR HATE.
HATE KEEPS SKITTERS WARM.
NO GIVE AND TAKE. IT'S ALL TAKE AND TAKE.

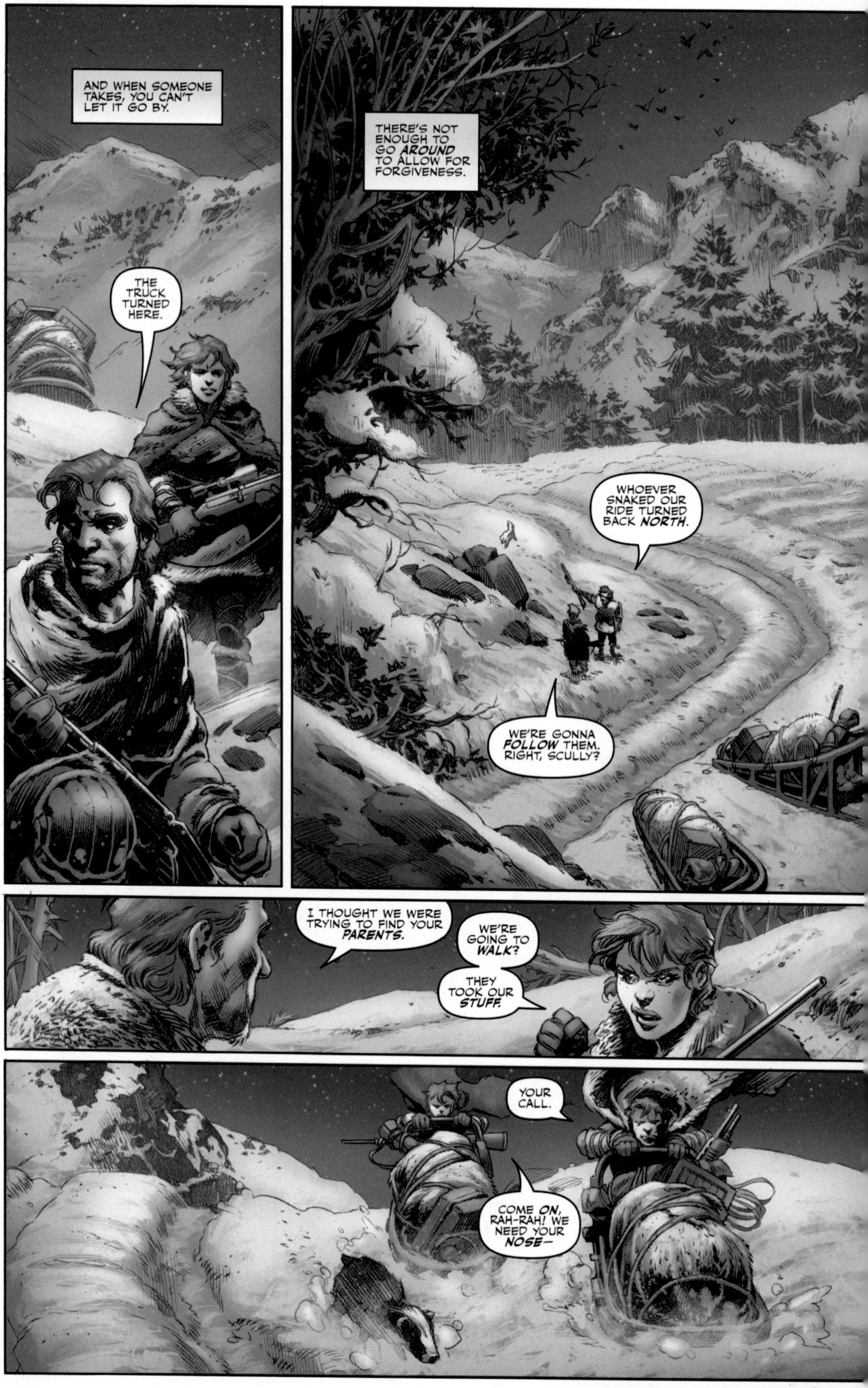
AND WHEN SOMEONE TAKES, YOU CAN'T LET IT GO BY.
THE TRUCK TURNED HERE.
THERE'S NOT ENOUGH TO GO AROUND TO ALLOW FOR FORGIVENESS.
WHOEVER SNAKED OUR RIDE TURNED BACK NORTH.
WE'RE GONNA FOLLOW THEM. RIGHT, SCULLY?
I THOUGHT WE WERE TRYING TO FIND YOUR PARENTS.
WE'RE GOING TO WALK?
THEY TOOK OUR STUFF.
YOUR CALL.
COME ON, RAH-RAH! WE NEED YOUR NOSE—

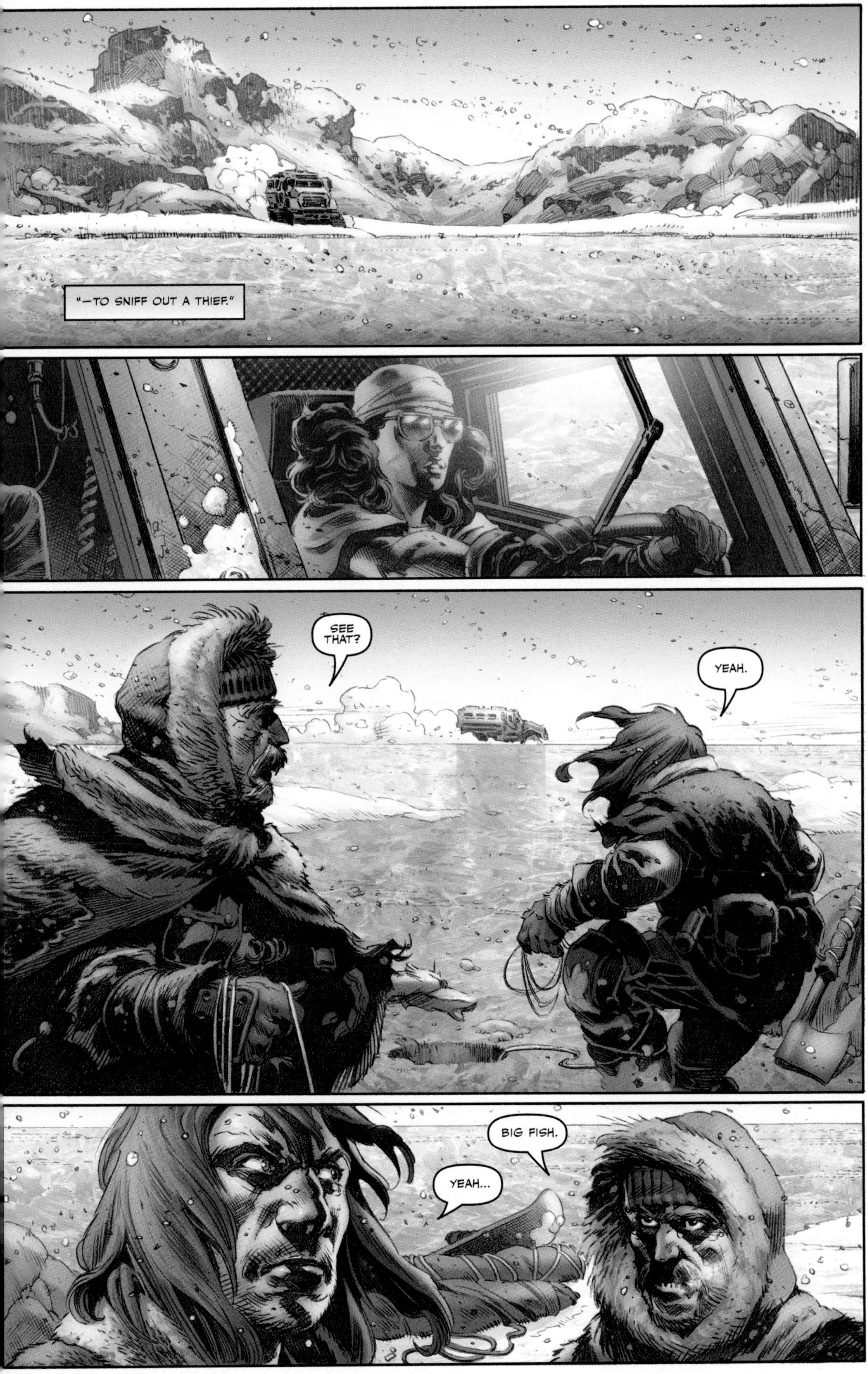
"—TO SNIFF OUT A THIEF."
SEE THAT?
YEAH.
BIG FISH.
YEAH...

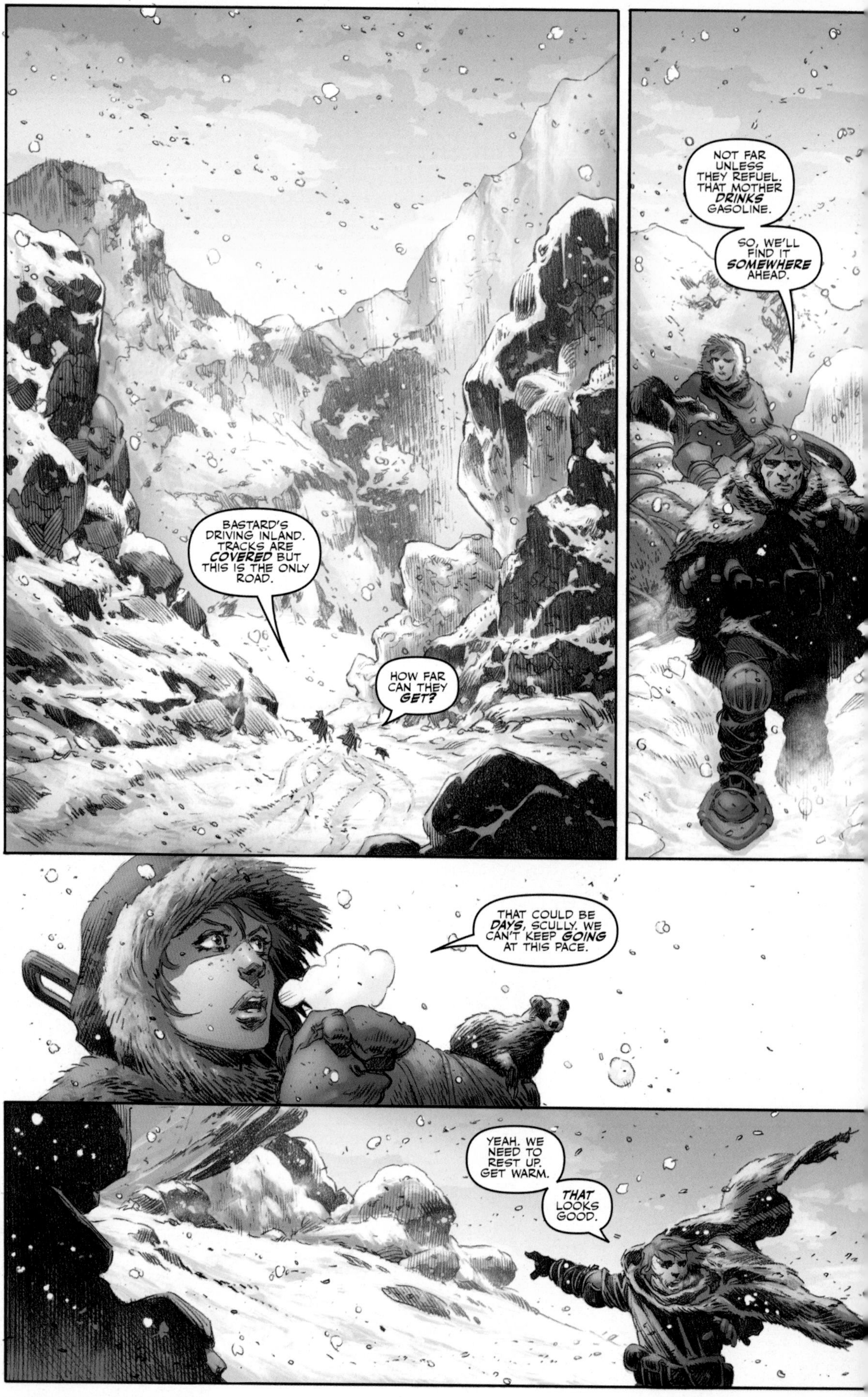
BASTARD'S DRIVING INLAND. TRACKS ARE COVERED BUT THIS IS THE ONLY ROAD.
HOW FAR CAN THEY GET?
NOT FAR UNLESS THEY REFUEL. THAT MOTHER DRINKS GASOLINE.
SO, WE'LL FIND IT SOMEWHERE AHEAD.
THAT COULD BE DAYS, SCULLY. WE CAN'T KEEP GOING AT THIS PACE.
YEAH. WE NEED TO REST UP. GET WARM.
THAT LOOKS GOOD.

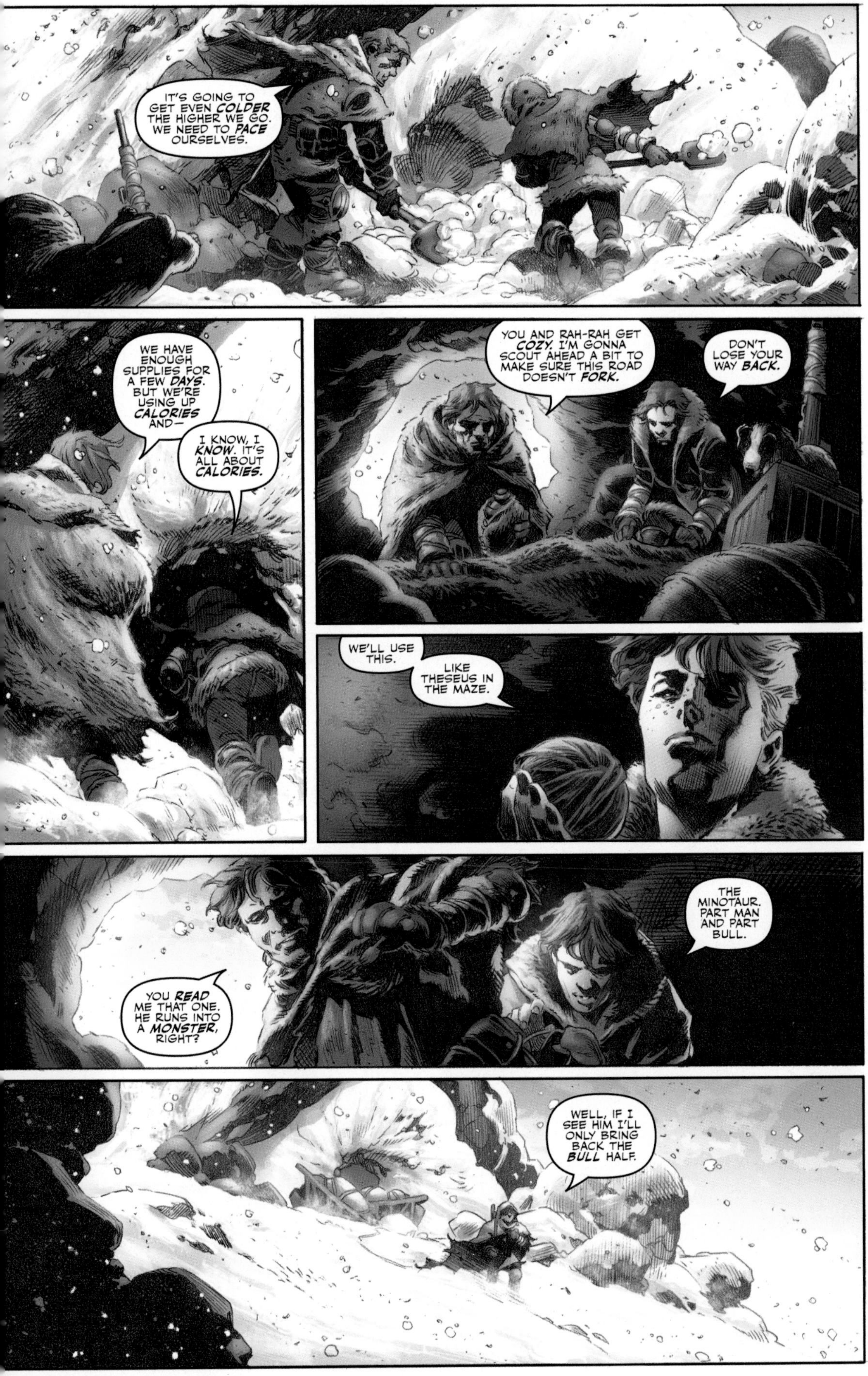
IT'S GOING TO GET EVEN COLDER THE HIGHER WE GO. WE NEED TO PACE OURSELVES.
WE HAVE ENOUGH SUPPLIES FOR A FEW DAYS. BUT WE'RE USING UP CALORIES AND—
I KNOW, I KNOW. IT'S ALL ABOUT CALORIES.
YOU AND RAH-RAH GET COZY. I'M GONNA SCOUT AHEAD A BIT TO MAKE SURE THIS ROAD DOESN'T FORK.
DON'T LOSE YOUR WAY BACK.
WE'LL USE THIS.
LIKE THESEUS IN THE MAZE.
YOU READ ME THAT ONE. HE RUNS INTO A MONSTER, RIGHT?
THE MINOTAUR. PART MAN AND PART BULL.
WELL, IF I SEE HIM I'LL ONLY BRING BACK THE BULL HALF.

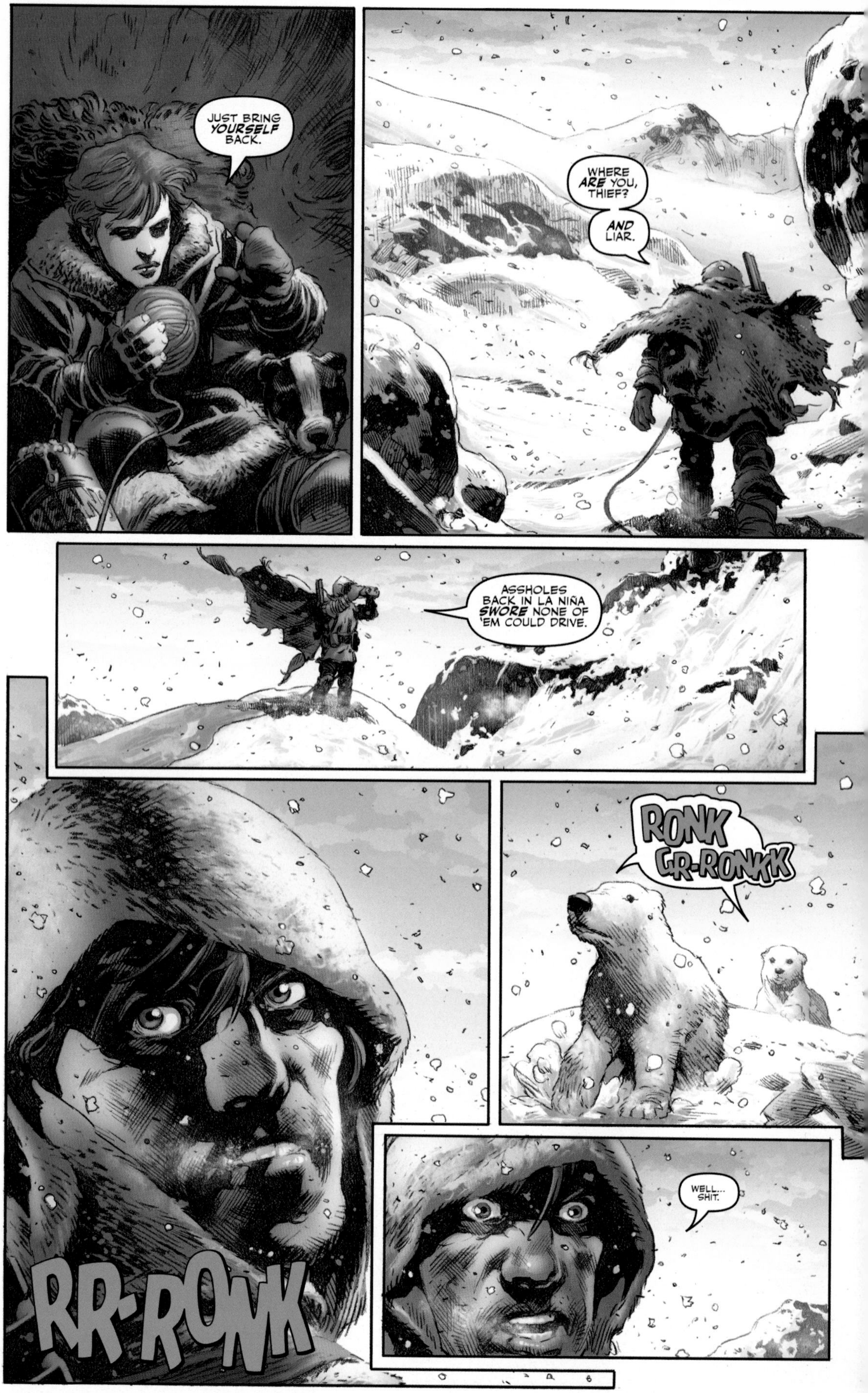
JUST BRING *YOURSELF* BACK.
WHERE *ARE* YOU, THIEF?
AND LIAR.
ASSHOLES BACK IN LA NIÑA *SWORE* NONE OF 'EM COULD DRIVE.
RONK GR-RONKK
RR-RONK
WELL... SHIT.

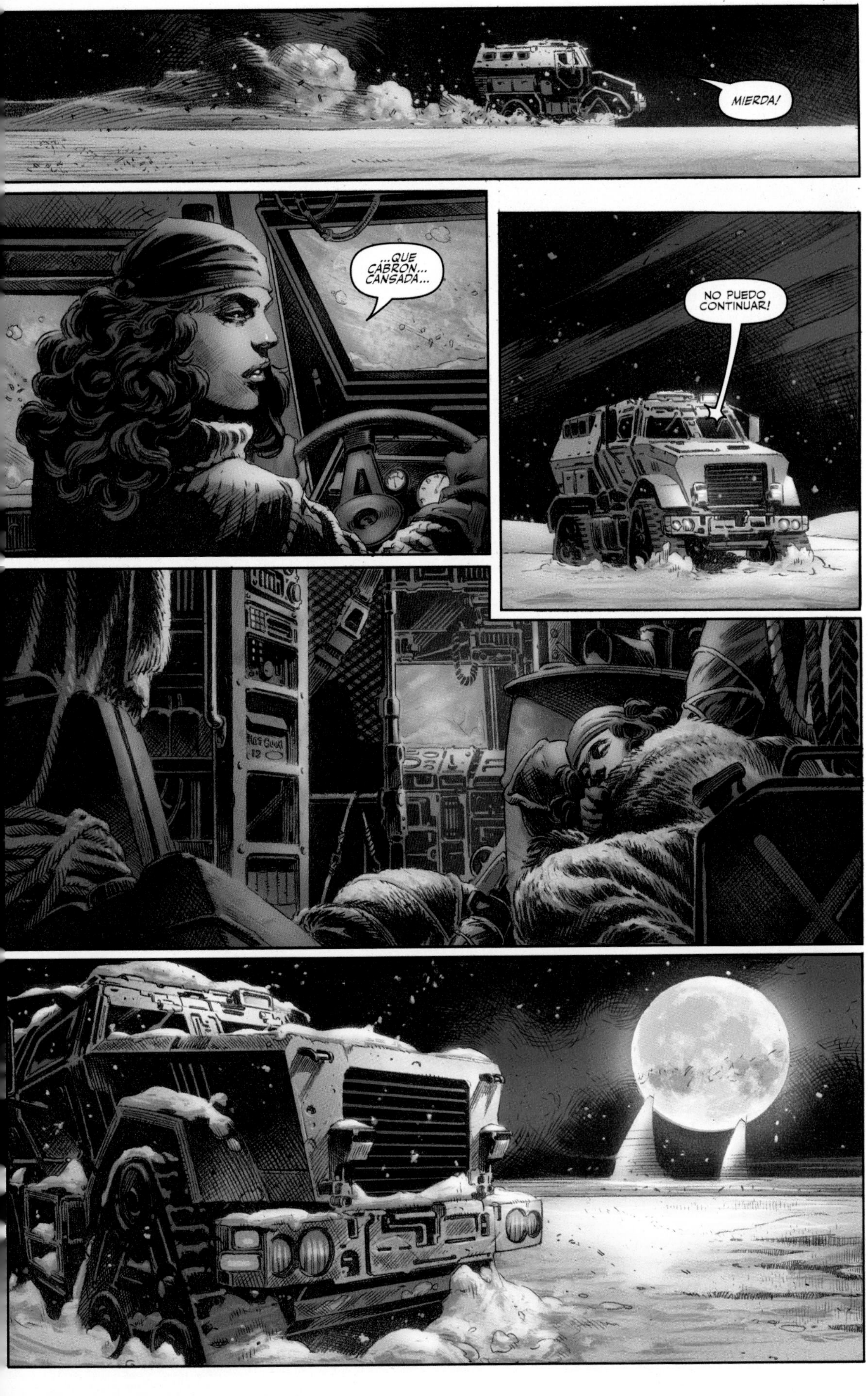
MIERDA!
...QUE CABRON... CANSADA...
NO PUEDO CONTINUAR!

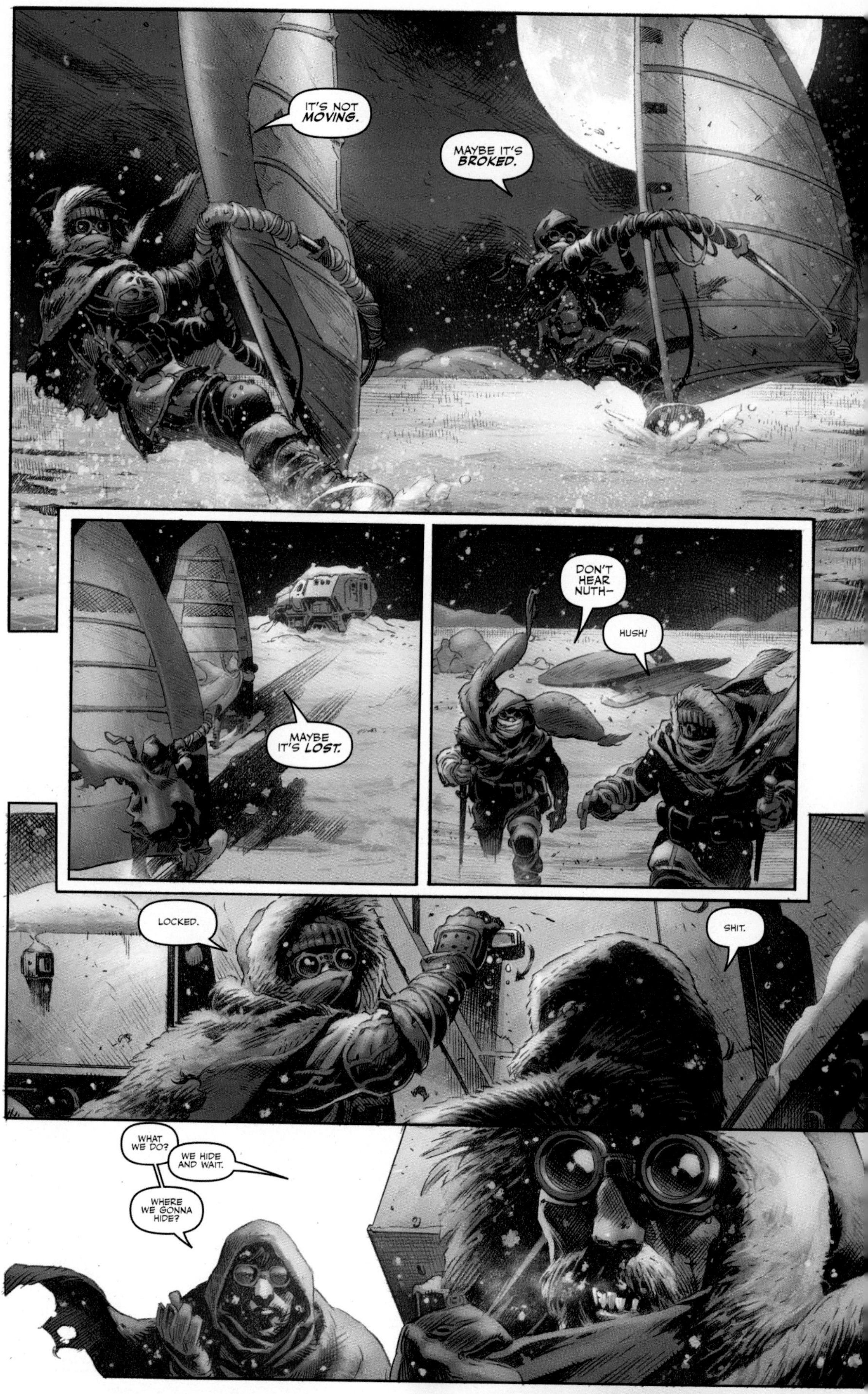
IT'S NOT MOVING.
MAYBE IT'S BROKED.
MAYBE IT'S LOST.
DON'T HEAR NUTH–
HUSH!
LOCKED.
SHIT.
WHAT WE DO?
WE HIDE AND WAIT.
WHERE WE GONNA HIDE?

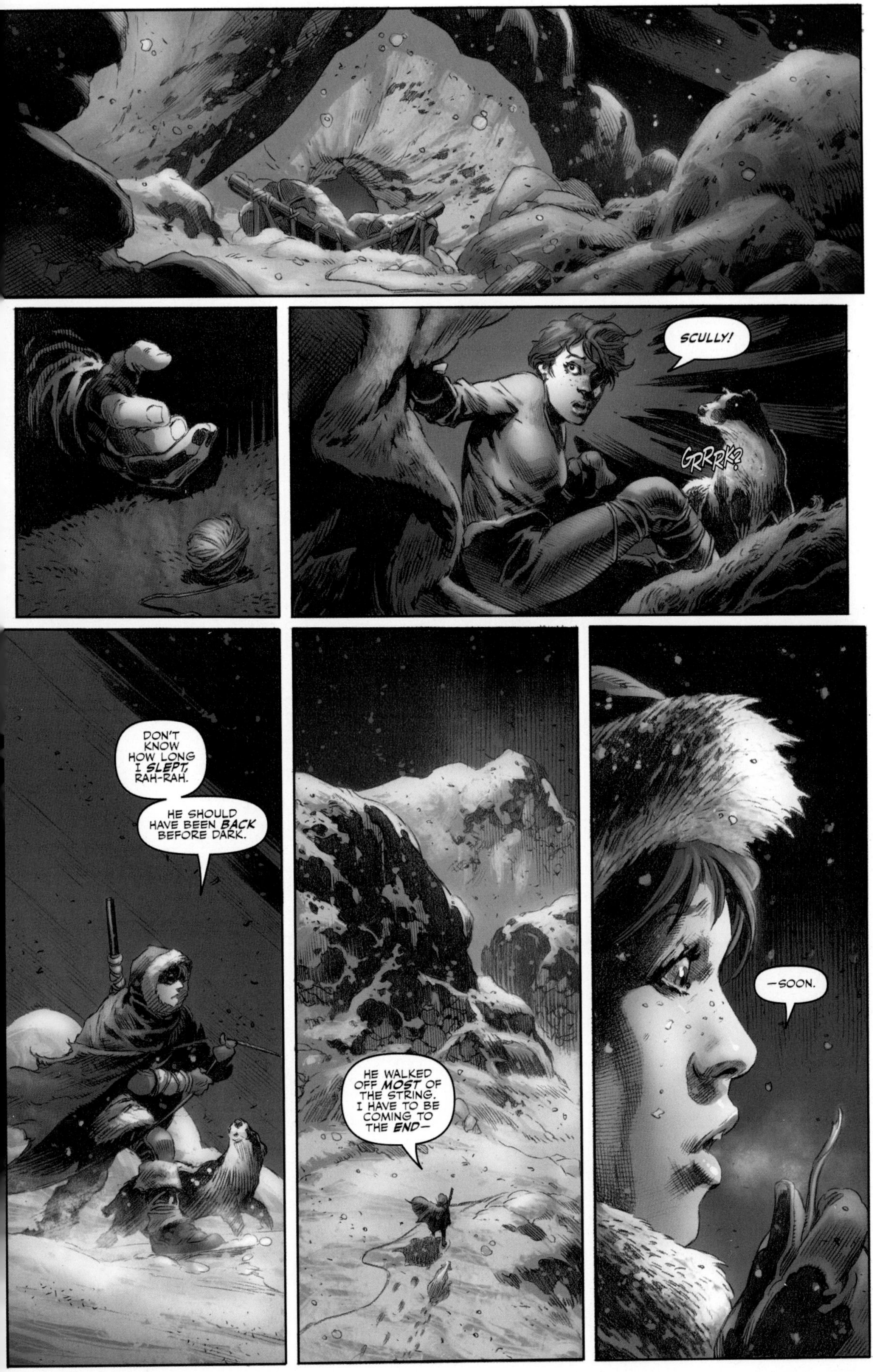
SCULLY!
GRRRK?
DON'T KNOW HOW LONG I SLEPT, RAH-RAH.
HE SHOULD HAVE BEEN BACK BEFORE DARK.
HE WALKED OFF MOST OF THE STRING. I HAVE TO BE COMING TO THE END—
—SOON.

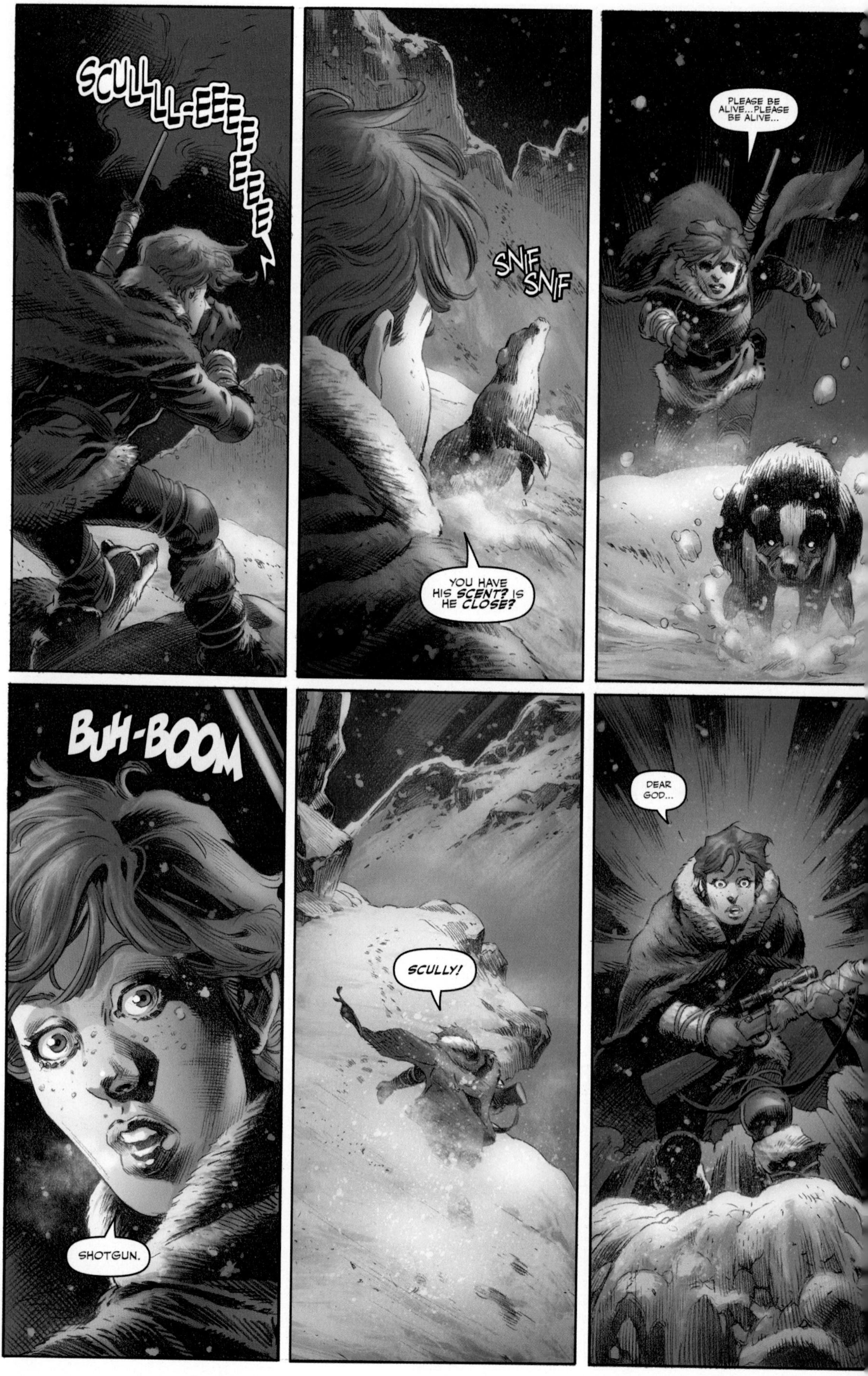
SCULL-LL-EEEEEEEEE
SNIF SNIF
YOU HAVE HIS SCENT? IS HE CLOSE?
PLEASE BE ALIVE...PLEASE BE ALIVE...
BUH-BOOM
SHOTGUN.
SCULLY!
DEAR GOD...

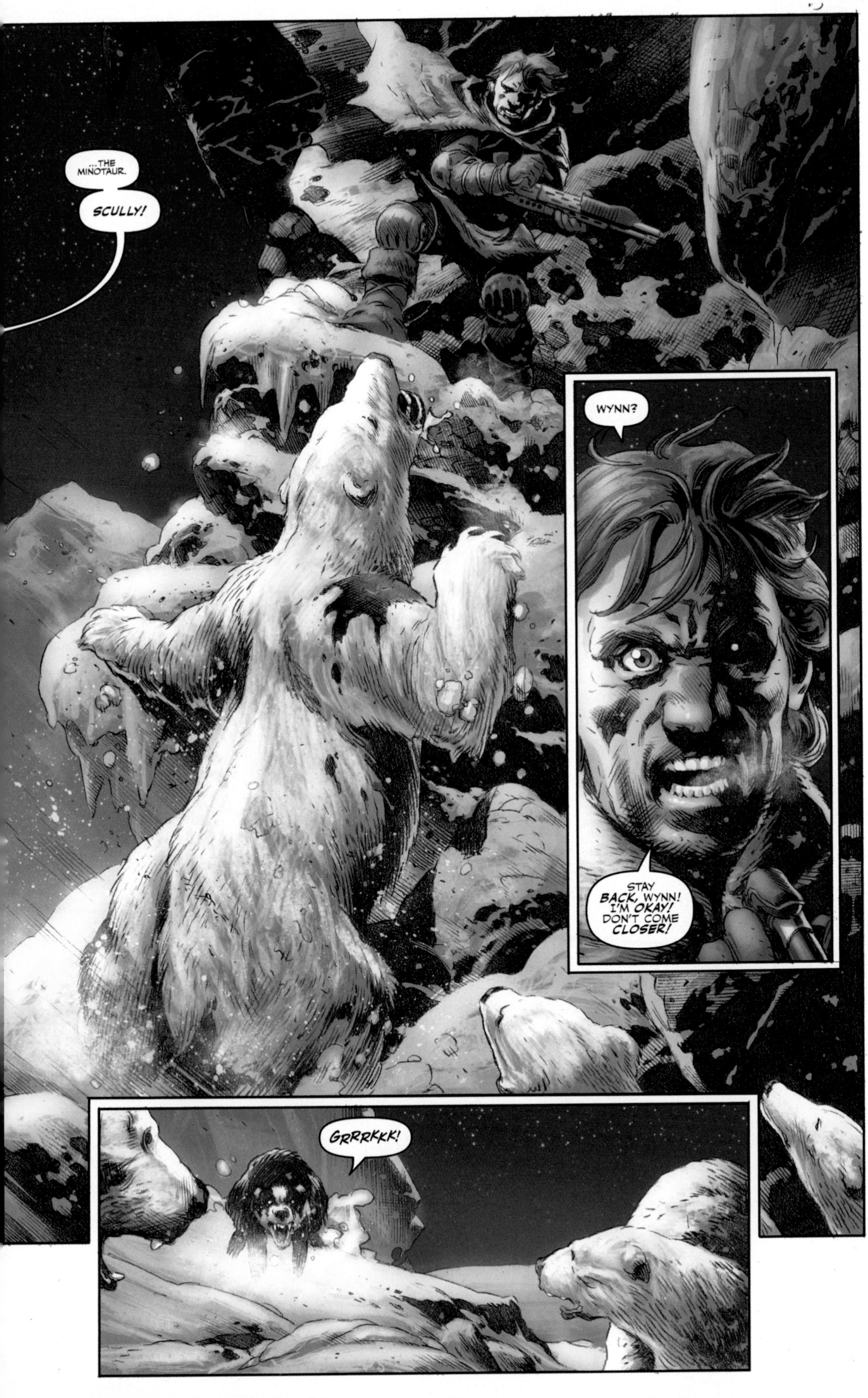

...THE MINOTAUR.
SCULLY!
WYNN?
STAY BACK, WYNN! I'M OKAY! DON'T COME CLOSER!
GRRRKKK!

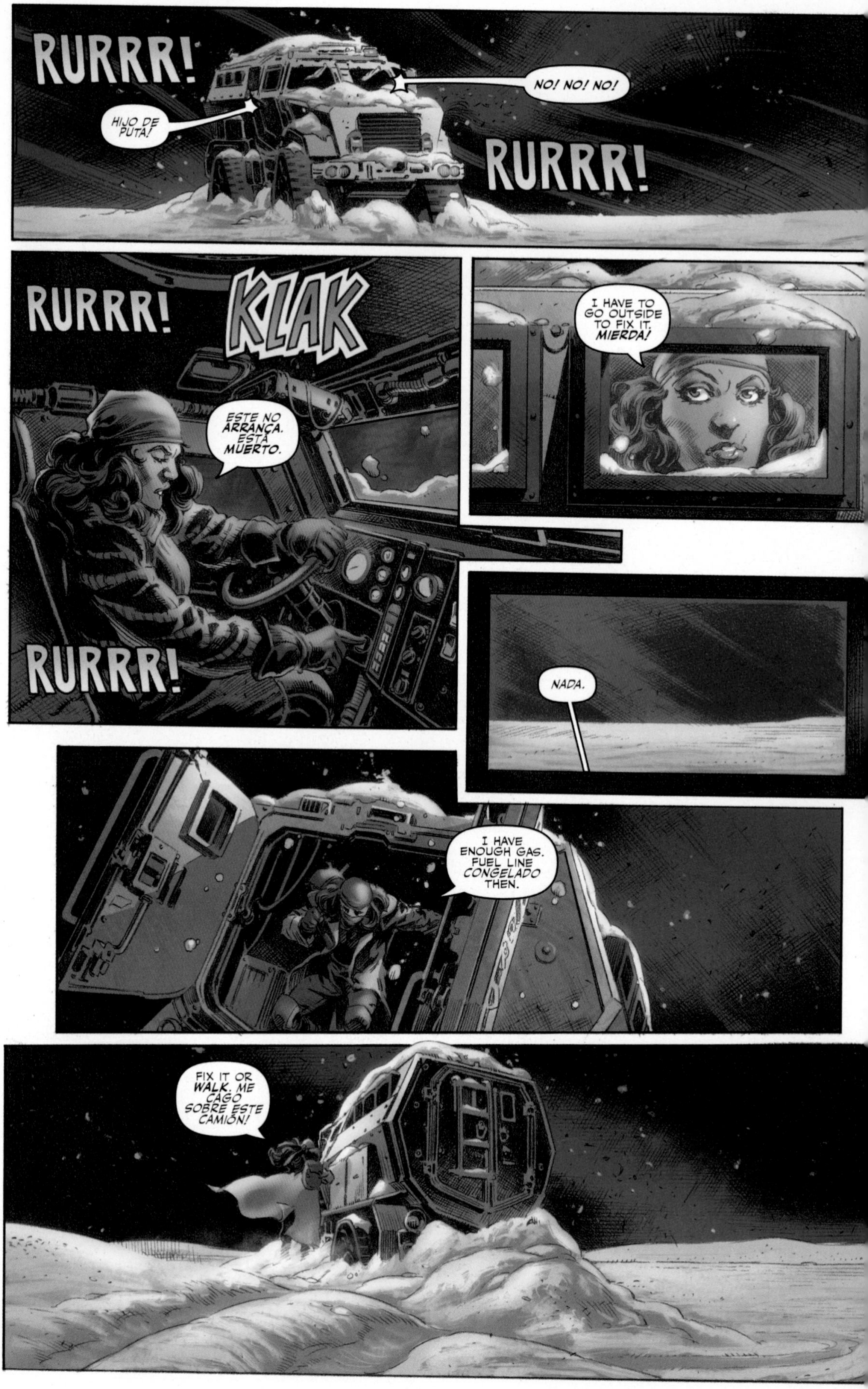

RURRR!
HIJO DE PUTA!
NO! NO! NO!
RURRR!
RURRR!
KLAK
ESTE NO ARRANCA. ESTÁ MUERTO.
RURRR!
I HAVE TO GO OUTSIDE TO FIX IT. MIERDA!
NADA.
I HAVE ENOUGH GAS. FUEL LINE CONGELADO THEN.
FIX IT OR WALK. ME CAGO SOBRE ESTE CAMIÓN!

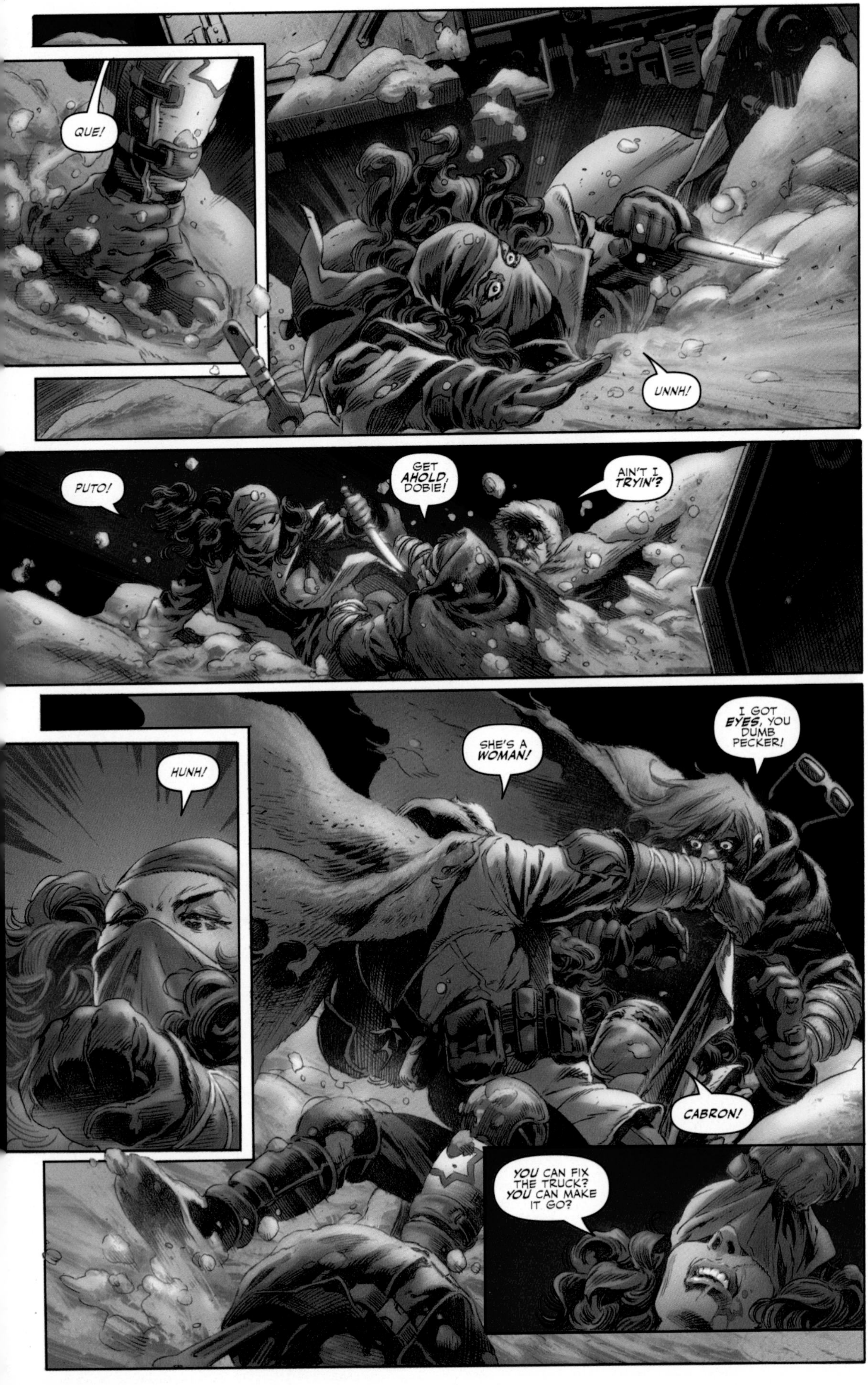
QUE!
UNNH!
PUTO!
GET AHOLD, DOBIE!
AIN'T I TRYIN'?
HUNH!
SHE'S A WOMAN!
I GOT EYES, YOU DUMB PECKER!
CABRON!
YOU CAN FIX THE TRUCK? YOU CAN MAKE IT GO?

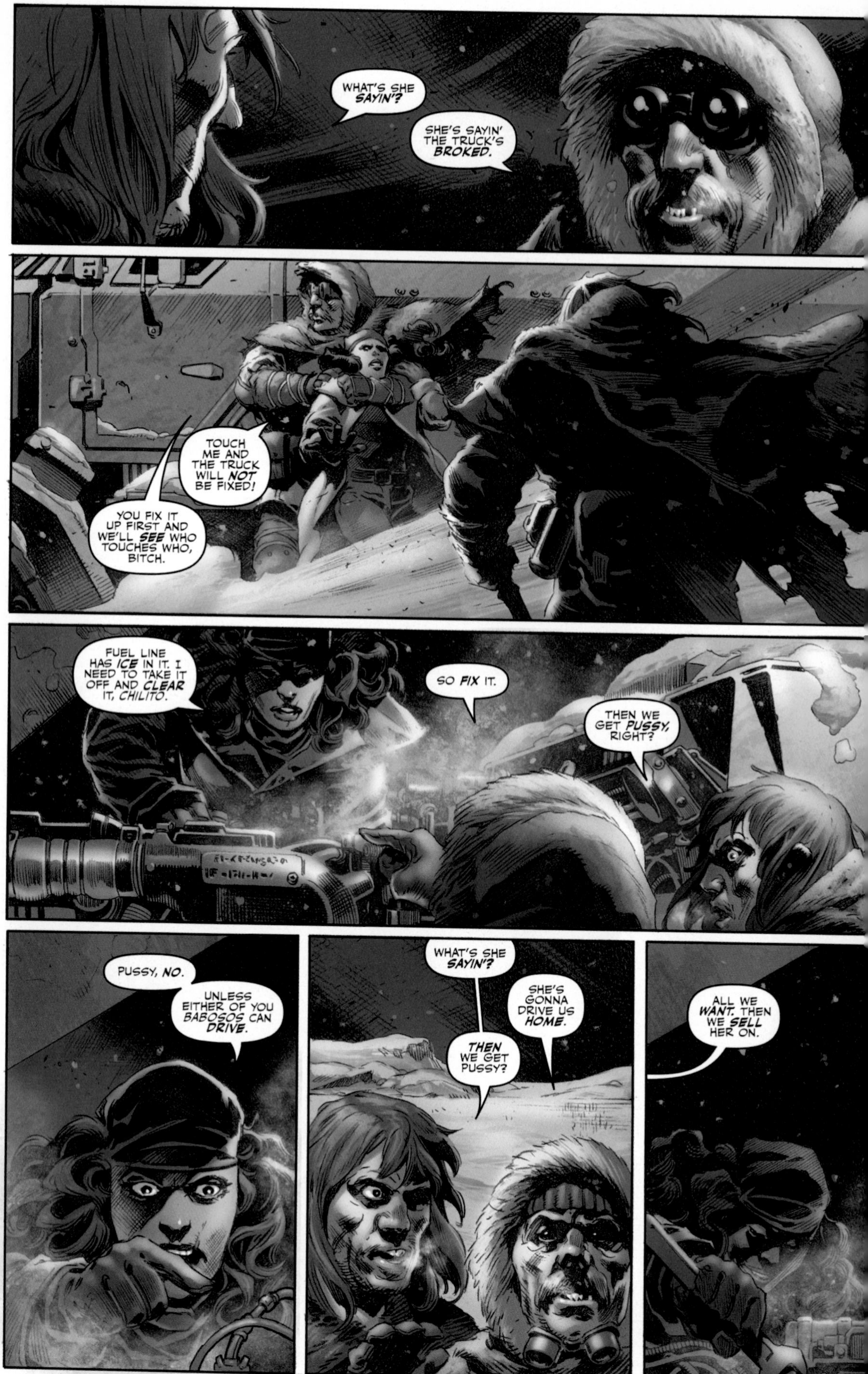
WHAT'S SHE SAYIN'?
SHE'S SAYIN' THE TRUCK'S BROKED.
TOUCH ME AND THE TRUCK WILL NOT BE FIXED!
YOU FIX IT UP FIRST AND WE'LL SEE WHO TOUCHES WHO, BITCH.
FUEL LINE HAS ICE IN IT. I NEED TO TAKE IT OFF AND CLEAR IT, CHILITO.
SO FIX IT.
THEN WE GET PUSSY, RIGHT?
PUSSY, NO.
UNLESS EITHER OF YOU BABOSOS CAN DRIVE.
WHAT'S SHE SAYIN'?
SHE'S GONNA DRIVE US HOME.
THEN WE GET PUSSY?
ALL WE WANT. THEN WE SELL HER ON.

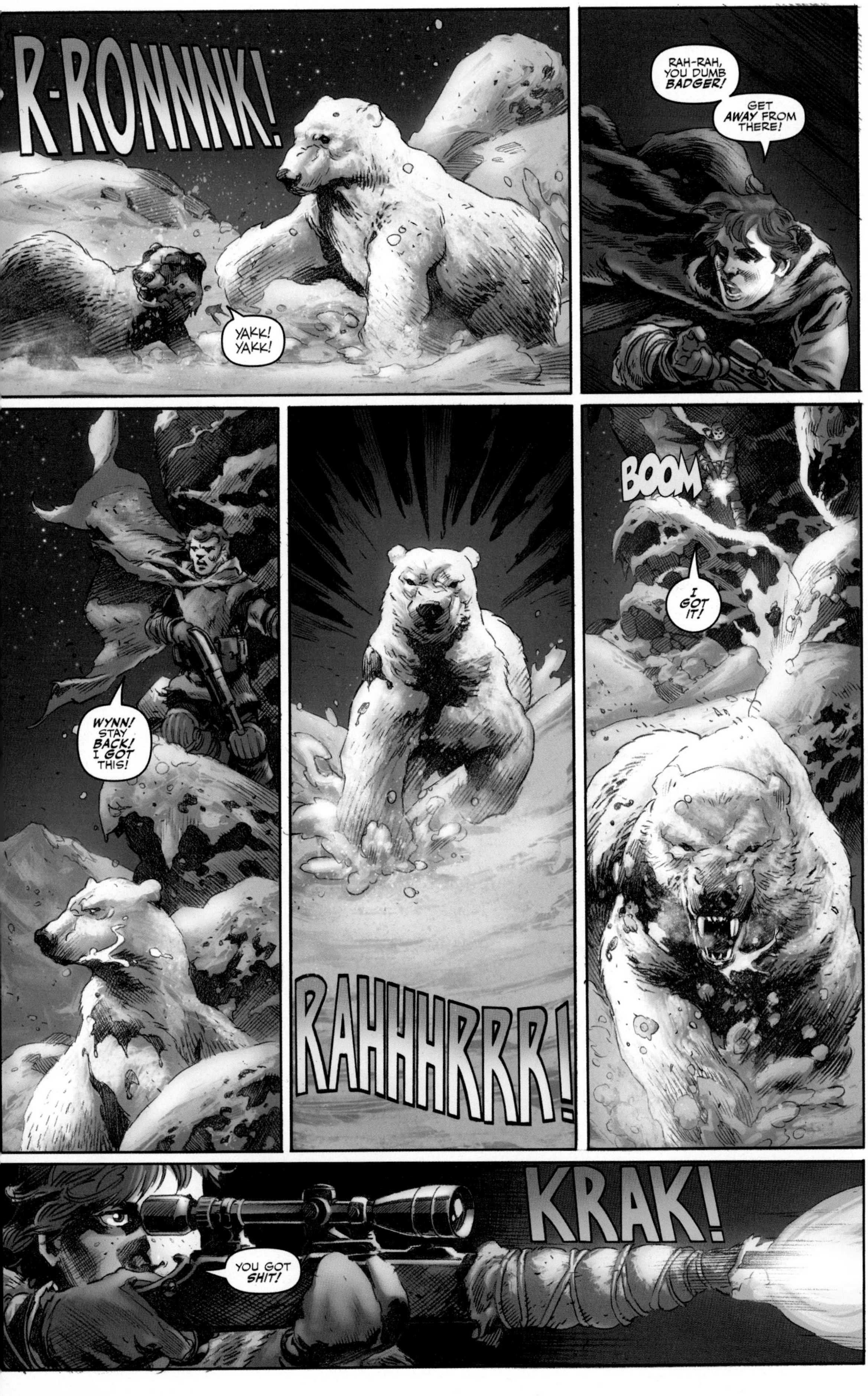
R-RONNNK!
YAKK! YAKK!
RAH-RAH, YOU DUMB BADGER!
GET AWAY FROM THERE!
WYNN! STAY BACK! I GOT THIS!
RAHHHRRR!
BOOM
I GOT IT!
KRAK!
YOU GOT SHIT!

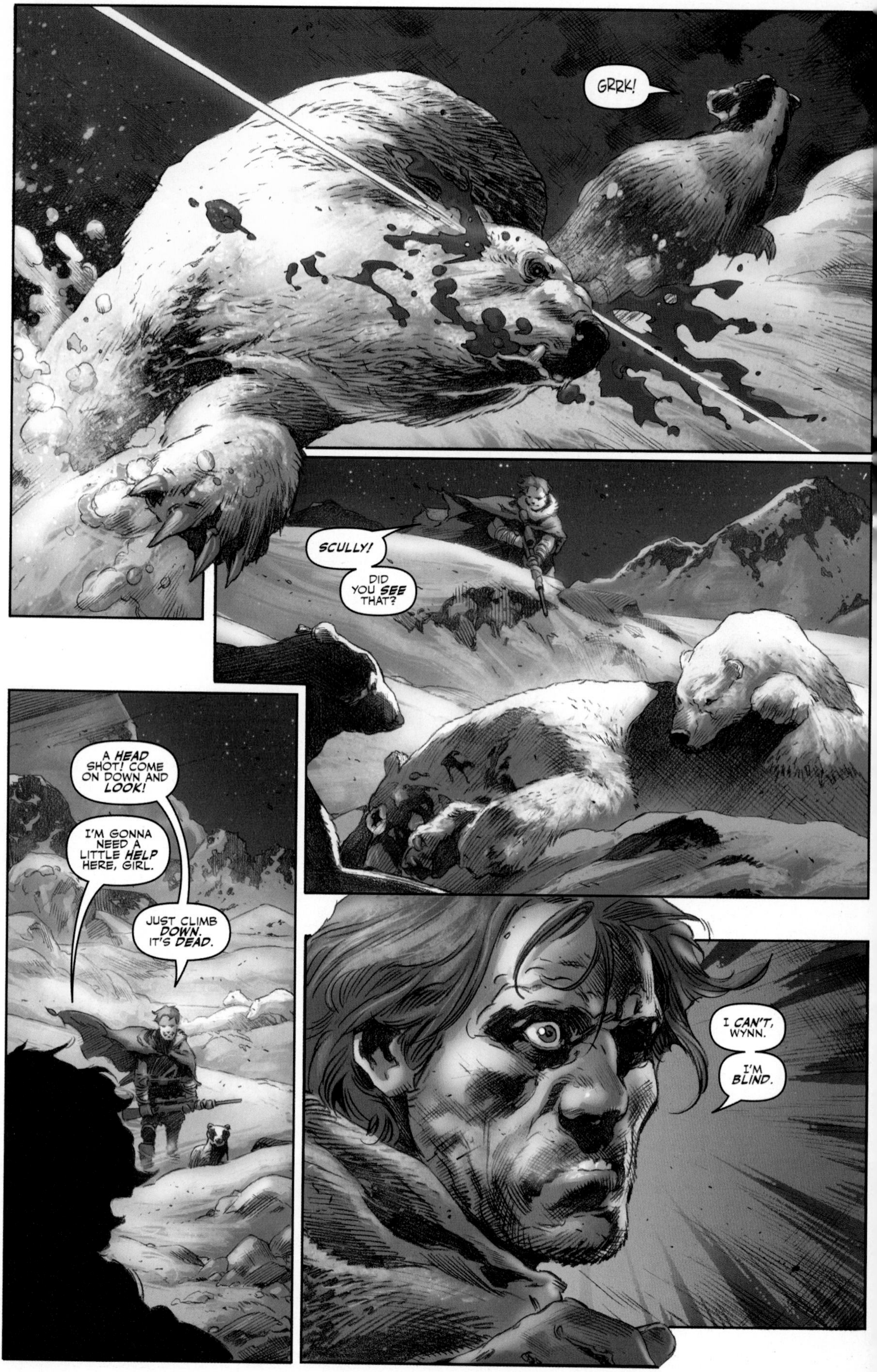

GRRK!
SCULLY!
DID YOU SEE THAT?
A HEAD SHOT! COME ON DOWN AND LOOK!
I'M GONNA NEED A LITTLE HELP HERE, GIRL.
JUST CLIMB DOWN. IT'S DEAD.
I CAN'T, WYNN.
I'M BLIND.

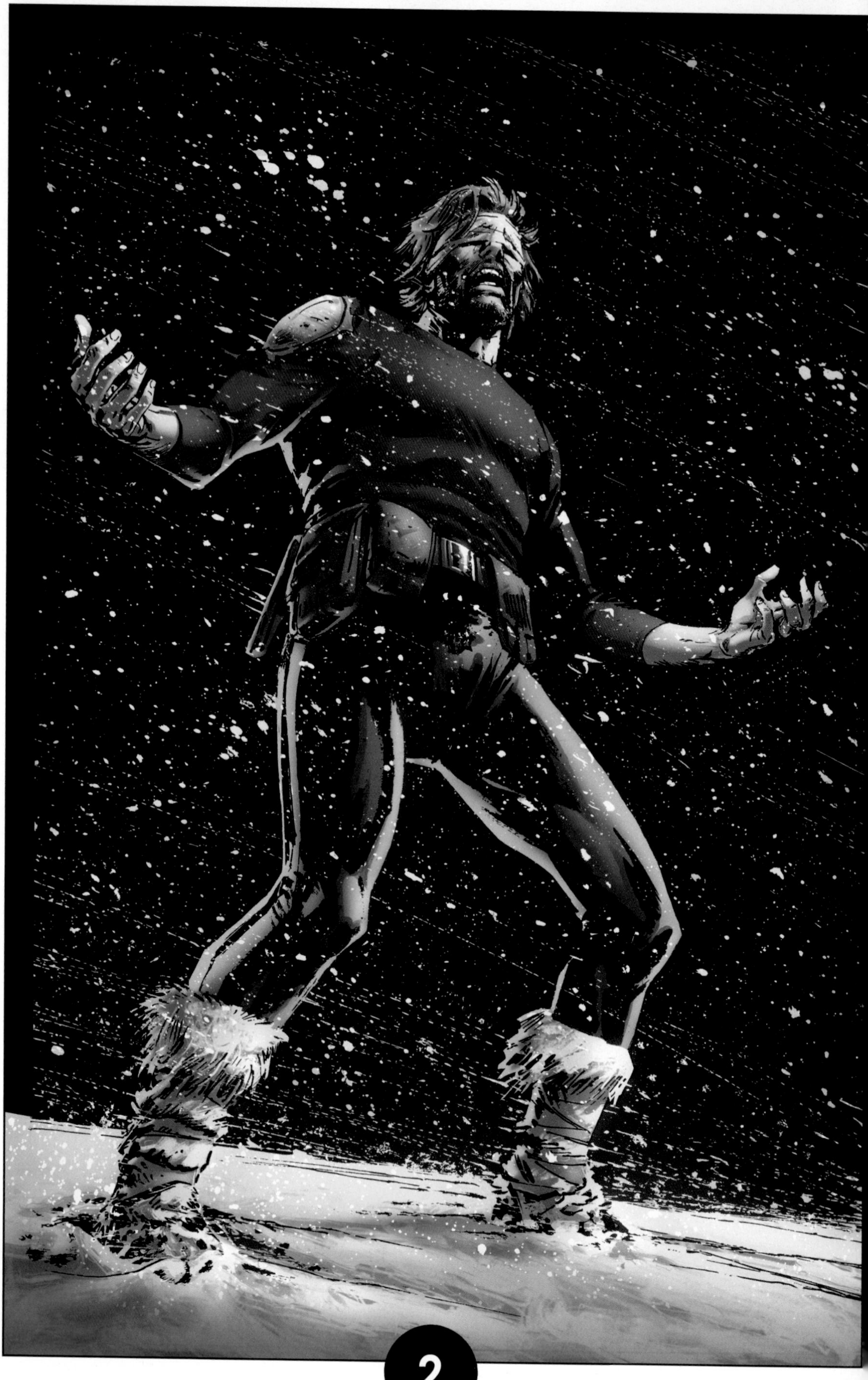

2

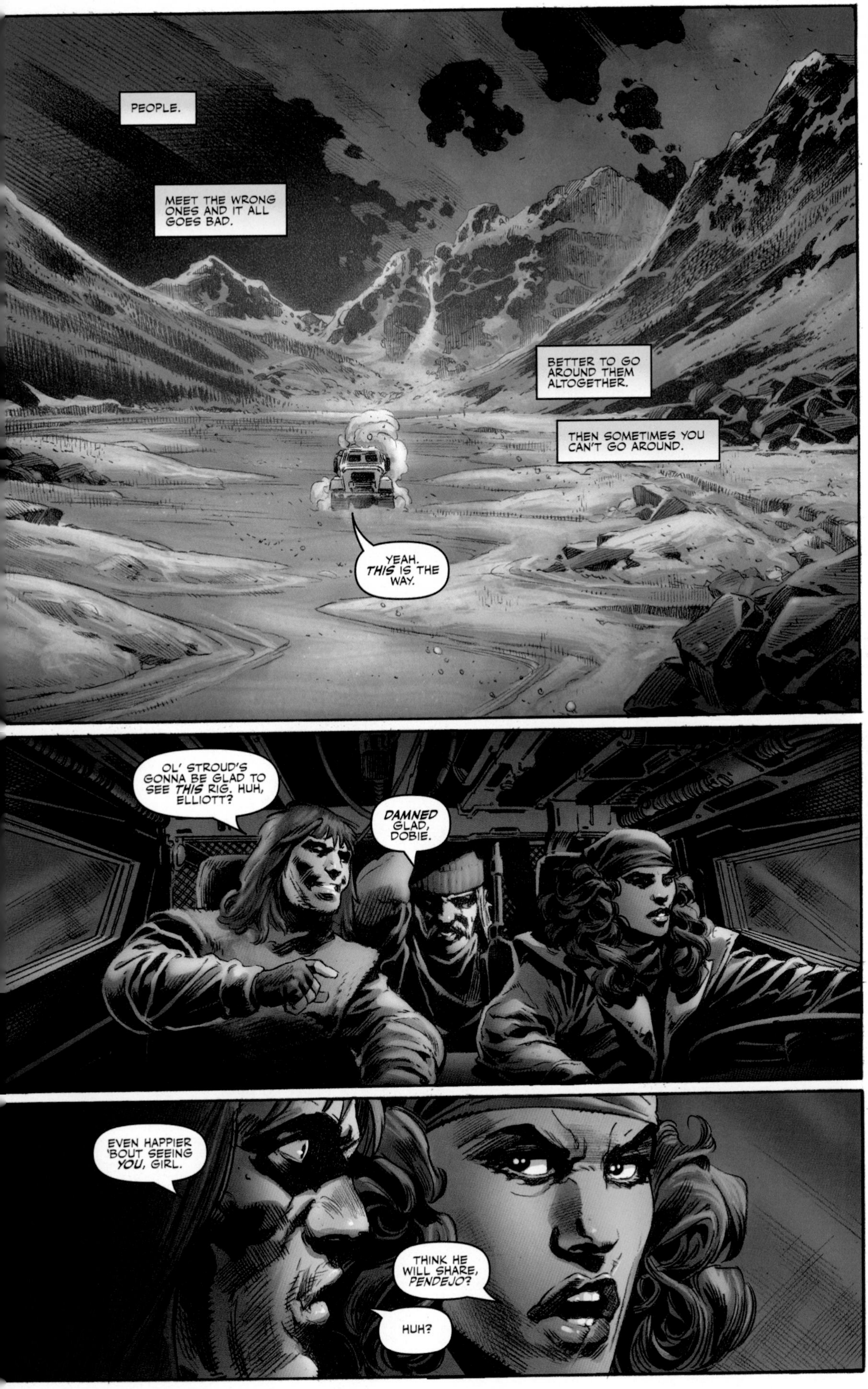
PEOPLE.
MEET THE WRONG ONES AND IT ALL GOES BAD.
BETTER TO GO AROUND THEM ALTOGETHER.
THEN SOMETIMES YOU CAN'T GO AROUND.
YEAH. THIS IS THE WAY.
OL' STROUD'S GONNA BE GLAD TO SEE THIS RIG. HUH, ELLIOTT?
DAMNED GLAD, DOBIE.
EVEN HAPPIER 'BOUT SEEING YOU, GIRL.
THINK HE WILL SHARE, PENDEJO?
HUH?

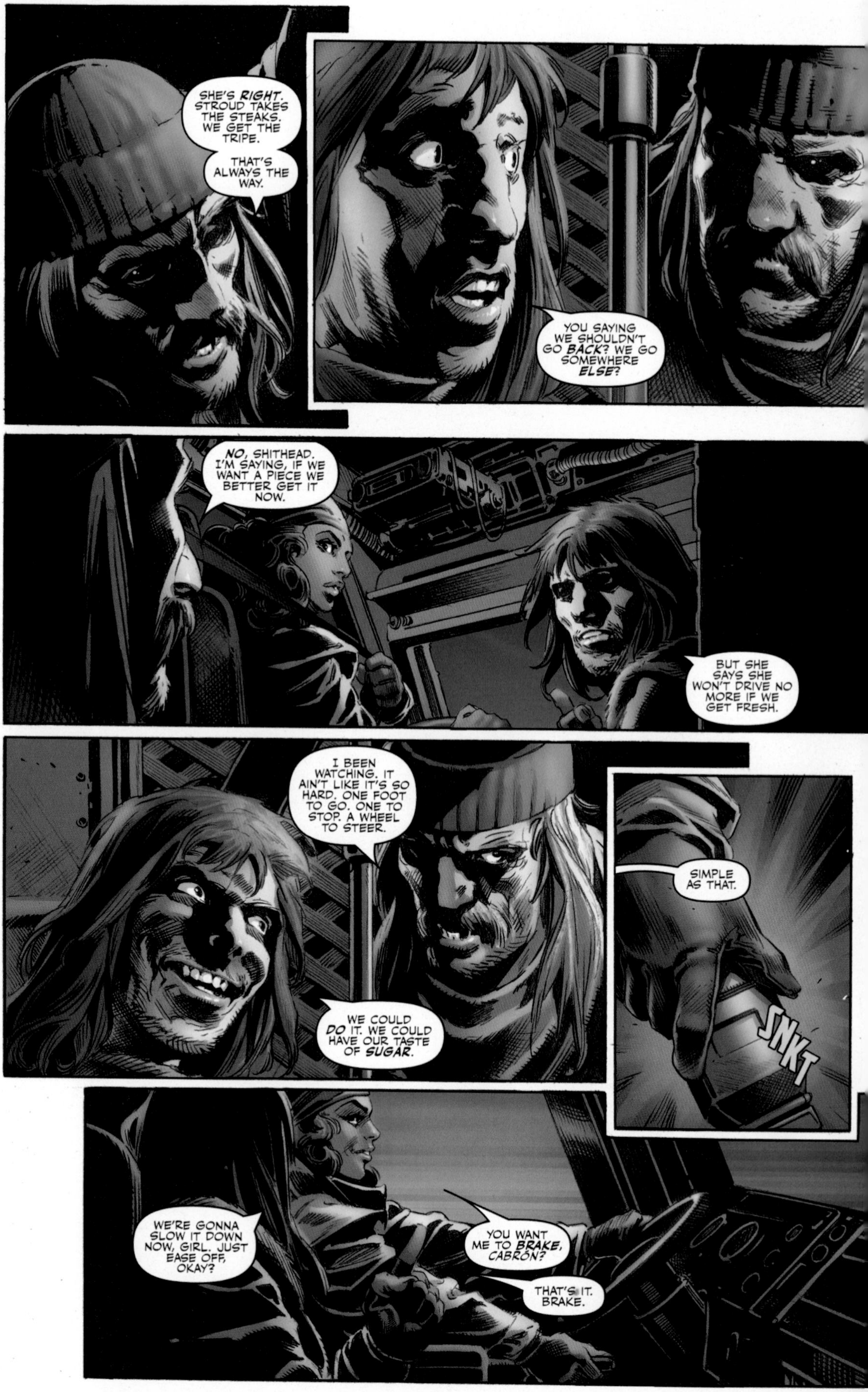
SHE'S RIGHT. STROUD TAKES THE STEAKS. WE GET THE TRIPE.
THAT'S ALWAYS THE WAY.
YOU SAYING WE SHOULDN'T GO BACK? WE GO SOMEWHERE ELSE?
NO, SHITHEAD. I'M SAYING, IF WE WANT A PIECE WE BETTER GET IT NOW.
BUT SHE SAYS SHE WON'T DRIVE NO MORE IF WE GET FRESH.
I BEEN WATCHING. IT AIN'T LIKE IT'S SO HARD. ONE FOOT TO GO. ONE TO STOP. A WHEEL TO STEER.
WE COULD DO IT. WE COULD HAVE OUR TASTE OF SUGAR.
SIMPLE AS THAT.
SNKT
WE'RE GONNA SLOW IT DOWN NOW, GIRL. JUST EASE OFF, OKAY?
YOU WANT ME TO BRAKE, CABRÓN?
THAT'S IT. BRAKE.

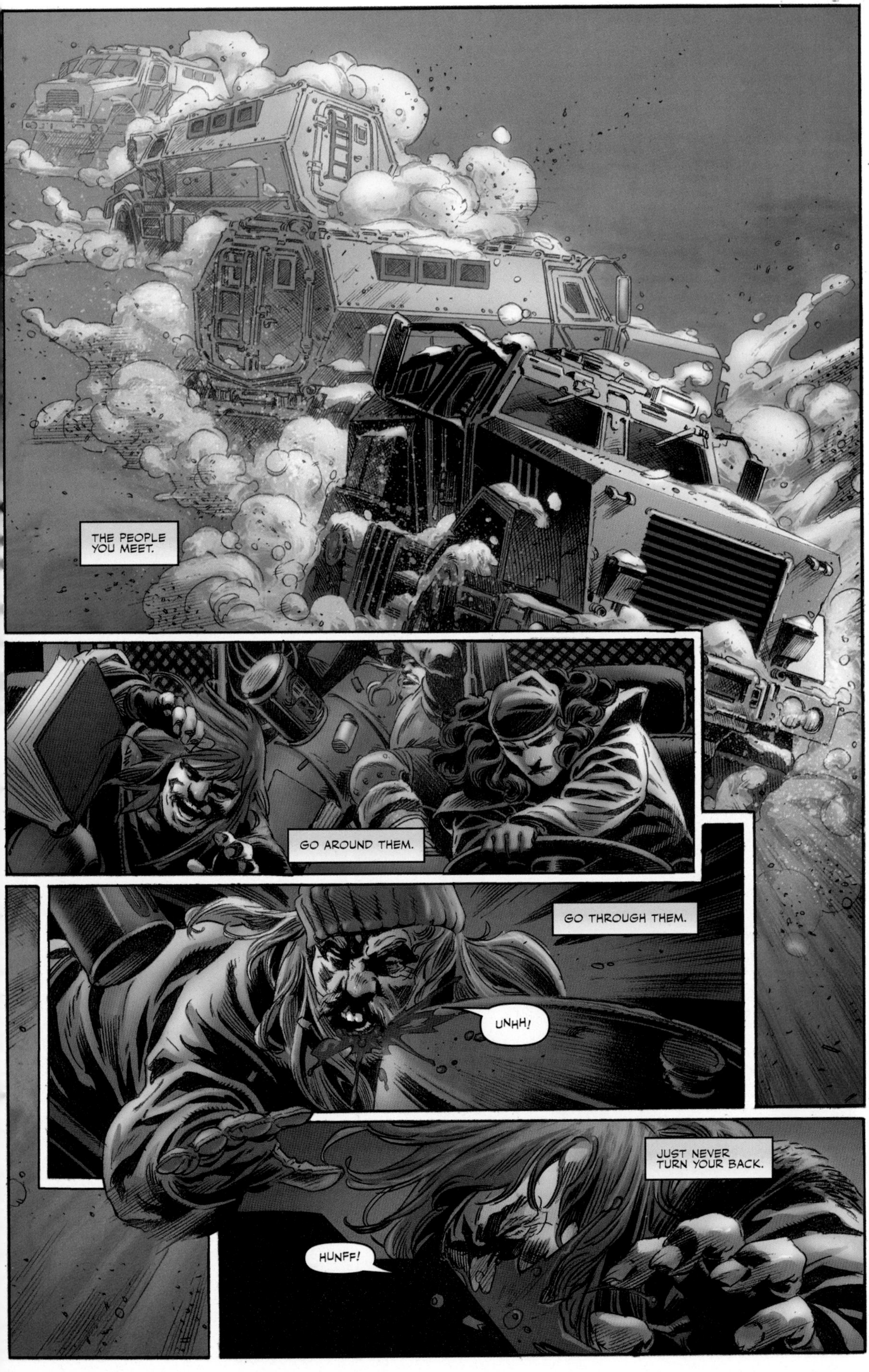
THE PEOPLE YOU MEET.
GO AROUND THEM.
GO THROUGH THEM.
UNHH!
JUST NEVER TURN YOUR BACK.
HUNFF!

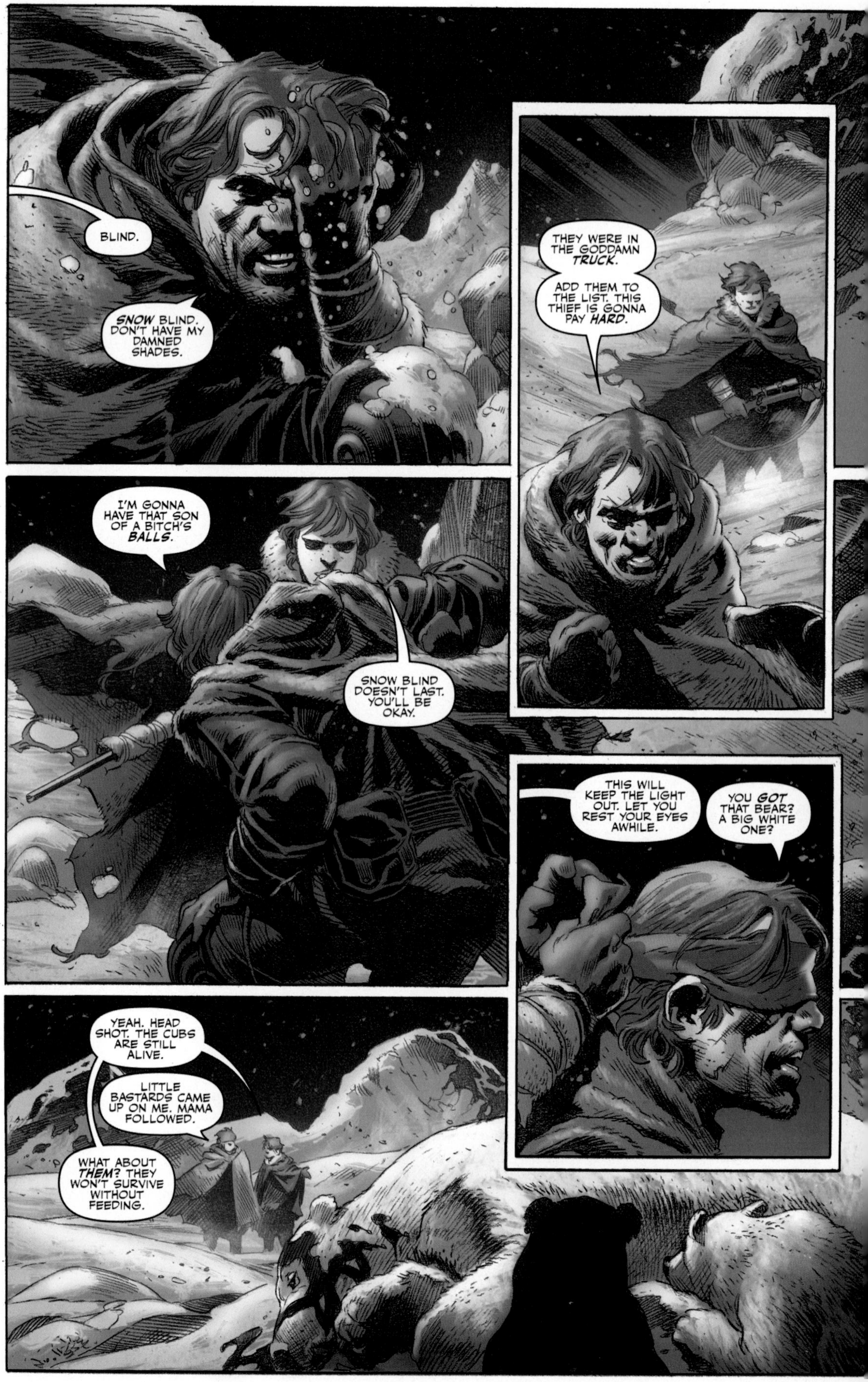
BLIND.
SNOW BLIND. DON'T HAVE MY DAMNED SHADES.
THEY WERE IN THE GODDAMN TRUCK.
ADD THEM TO THE LIST. THIS THIEF IS GONNA PAY HARD.
I'M GONNA HAVE THAT SON OF A BITCH'S BALLS.
SNOW BLIND DOESN'T LAST. YOU'LL BE OKAY.
THIS WILL KEEP THE LIGHT OUT. LET YOU REST YOUR EYES AWHILE.
YOU GOT THAT BEAR? A BIG WHITE ONE?
YEAH. HEAD SHOT. THE CUBS ARE STILL ALIVE.
LITTLE BASTARDS CAME UP ON ME. MAMA FOLLOWED.
WHAT ABOUT THEM? THEY WON'T SURVIVE WITHOUT FEEDING.

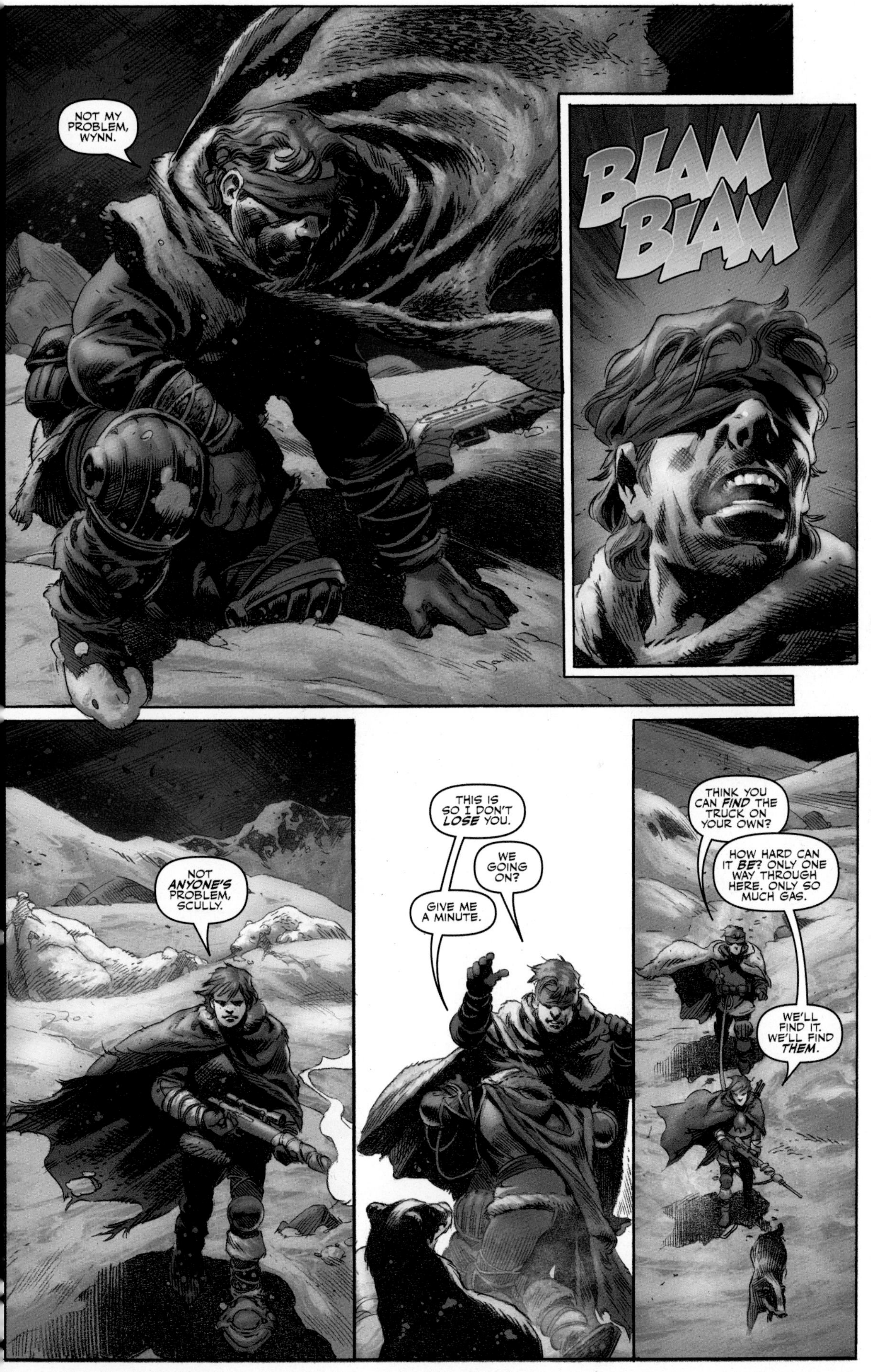
NOT MY PROBLEM, WYNN.
BLAM BLAM
NOT ANYONE'S PROBLEM, SCULLY.
THIS IS SO I DON'T LOSE YOU.
WE GOING ON?
GIVE ME A MINUTE.
THINK YOU CAN FIND THE TRUCK ON YOUR OWN?
HOW HARD CAN IT BE? ONLY ONE WAY THROUGH HERE. ONLY SO MUCH GAS.
WE'LL FIND IT. WE'LL FIND THEM.

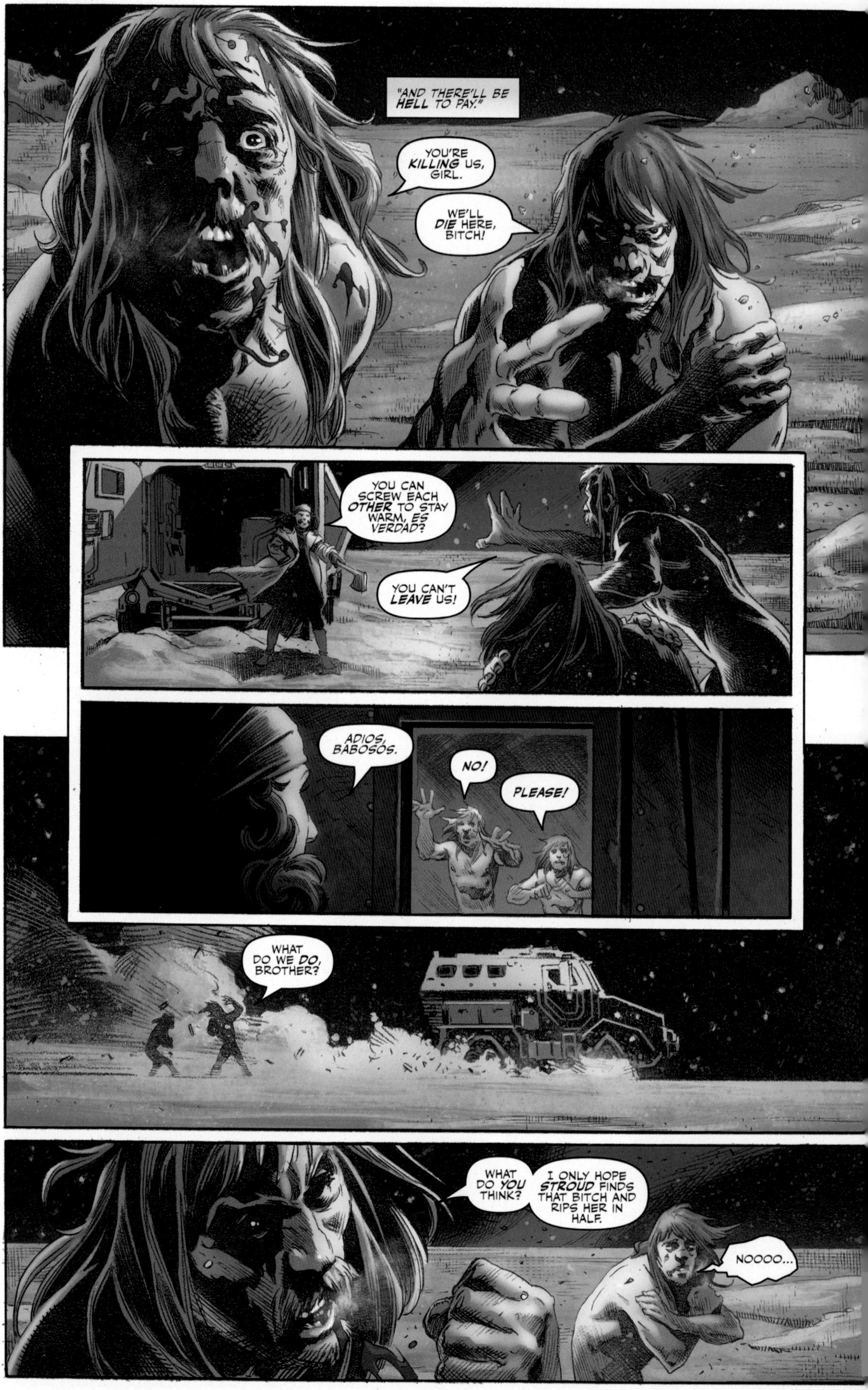
"AND THERE'LL BE HELL TO PAY."
YOU'RE KILLING US, GIRL.
WE'LL DIE HERE, BITCH!
YOU CAN SCREW EACH OTHER TO STAY WARM, ES VERDAD?
YOU CAN'T LEAVE US!
ADIOS, BABOSOS.
NO!
PLEASE!
WHAT DO WE DO, BROTHER?
WHAT DO YOU THINK?
I ONLY HOPE STROUD FINDS THAT BITCH AND RIPS HER IN HALF.
NOOOO...

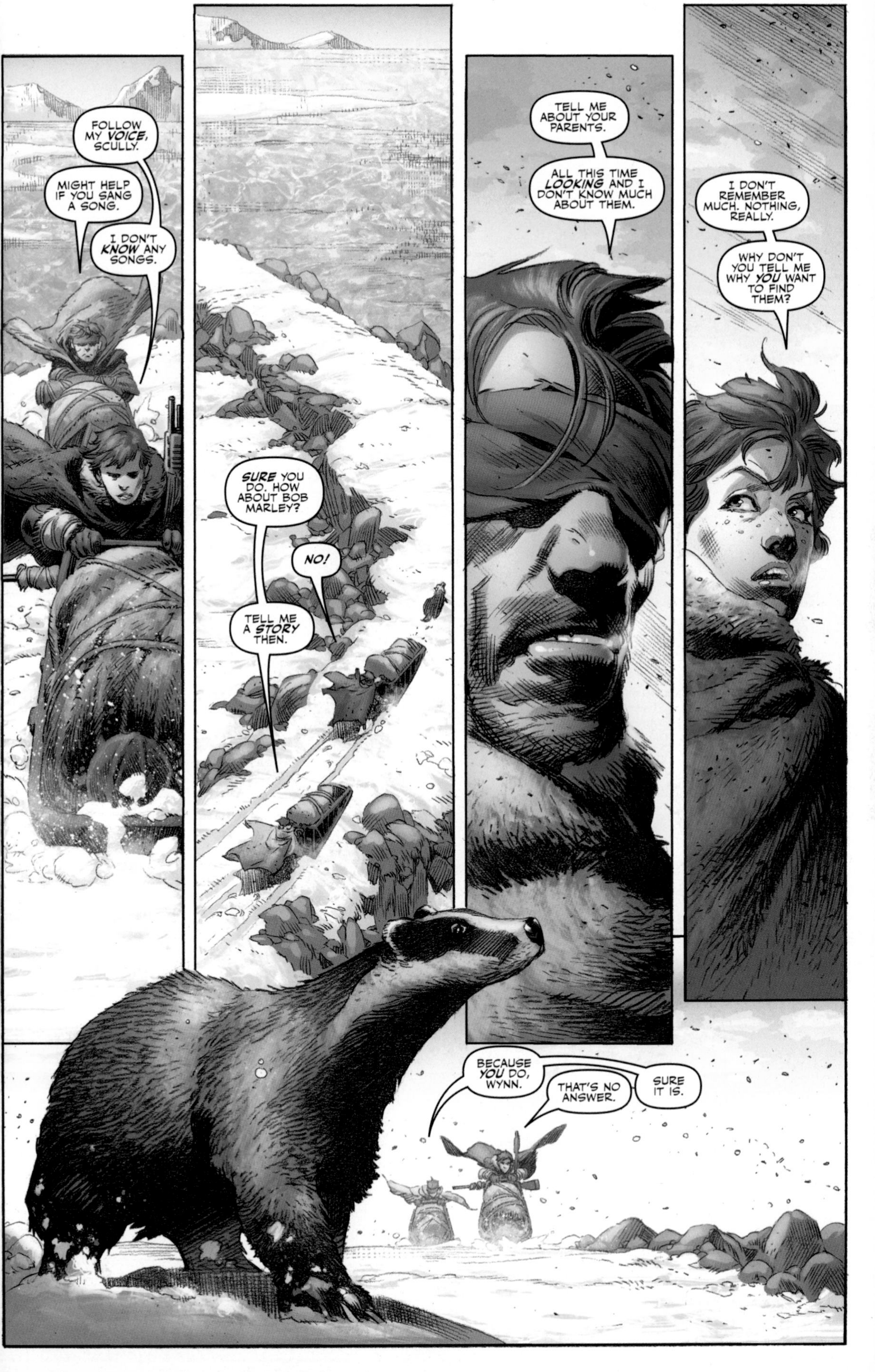
FOLLOW MY *VOICE*, SCULLY.
MIGHT HELP IF YOU SANG A SONG.
I DON'T *KNOW* ANY SONGS.
SURE YOU DO. HOW ABOUT BOB MARLEY?
NO!
TELL ME A *STORY* THEN.
TELL ME ABOUT YOUR PARENTS.
ALL THIS TIME *LOOKING* AND I DON'T KNOW MUCH ABOUT THEM.
I DON'T REMEMBER MUCH. NOTHING, REALLY.
WHY DON'T YOU TELL ME WHY *YOU* WANT TO FIND THEM?
BECAUSE *YOU* DO, WYNN.
THAT'S NO ANSWER.
SURE IT IS.

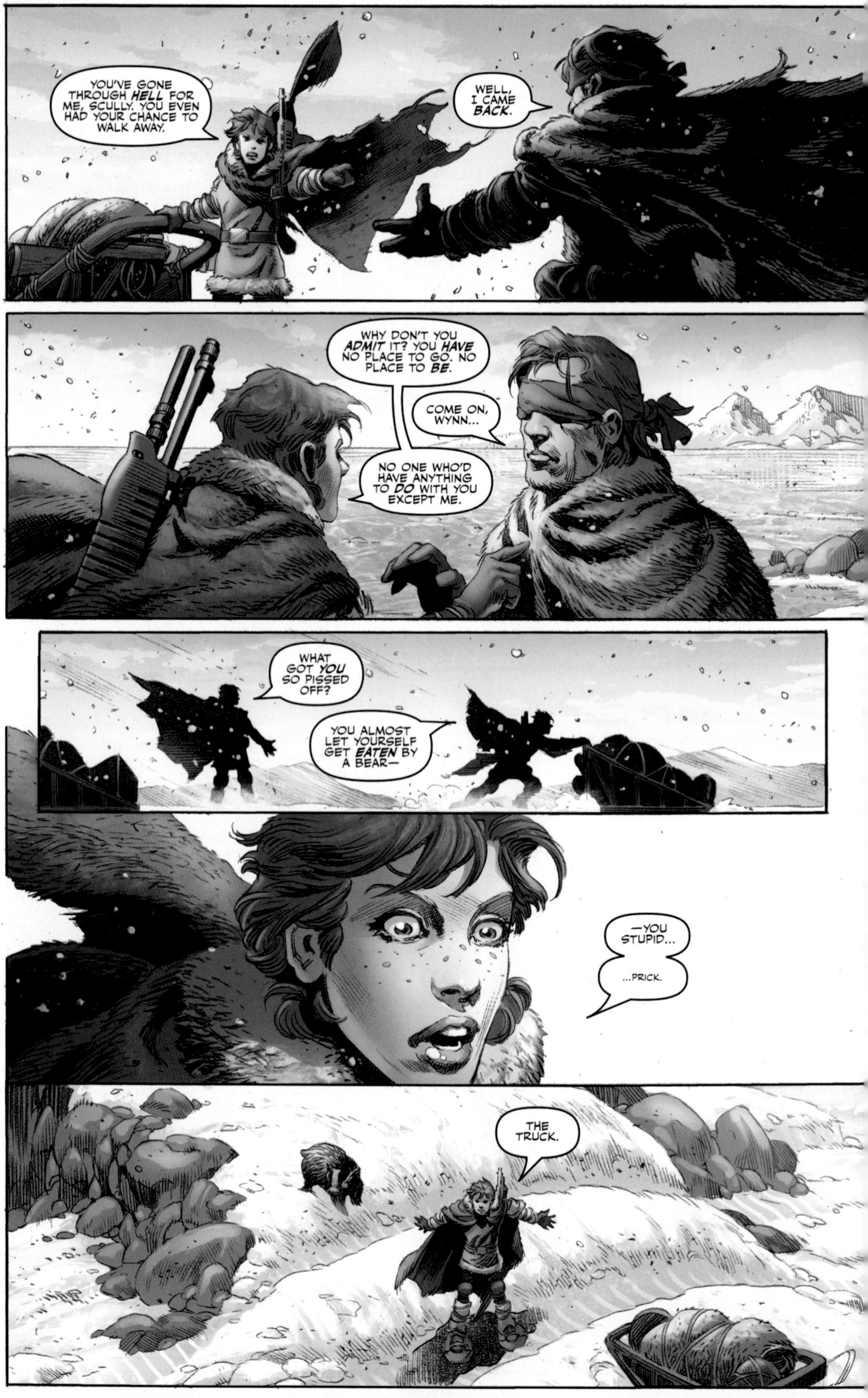
YOU'VE GONE THROUGH HELL FOR ME, SCULLY. YOU EVEN HAD YOUR CHANCE TO WALK AWAY.
WELL, I CAME BACK.
WHY DON'T YOU ADMIT IT? YOU HAVE NO PLACE TO GO. NO PLACE TO BE.
COME ON, WYNN...
NO ONE WHO'D HAVE ANYTHING TO DO WITH YOU EXCEPT ME.
WHAT GOT YOU SO PISSED OFF?
YOU ALMOST LET YOURSELF GET EATEN BY A BEAR—
—YOU STUPID...
...PRICK.
THE TRUCK.

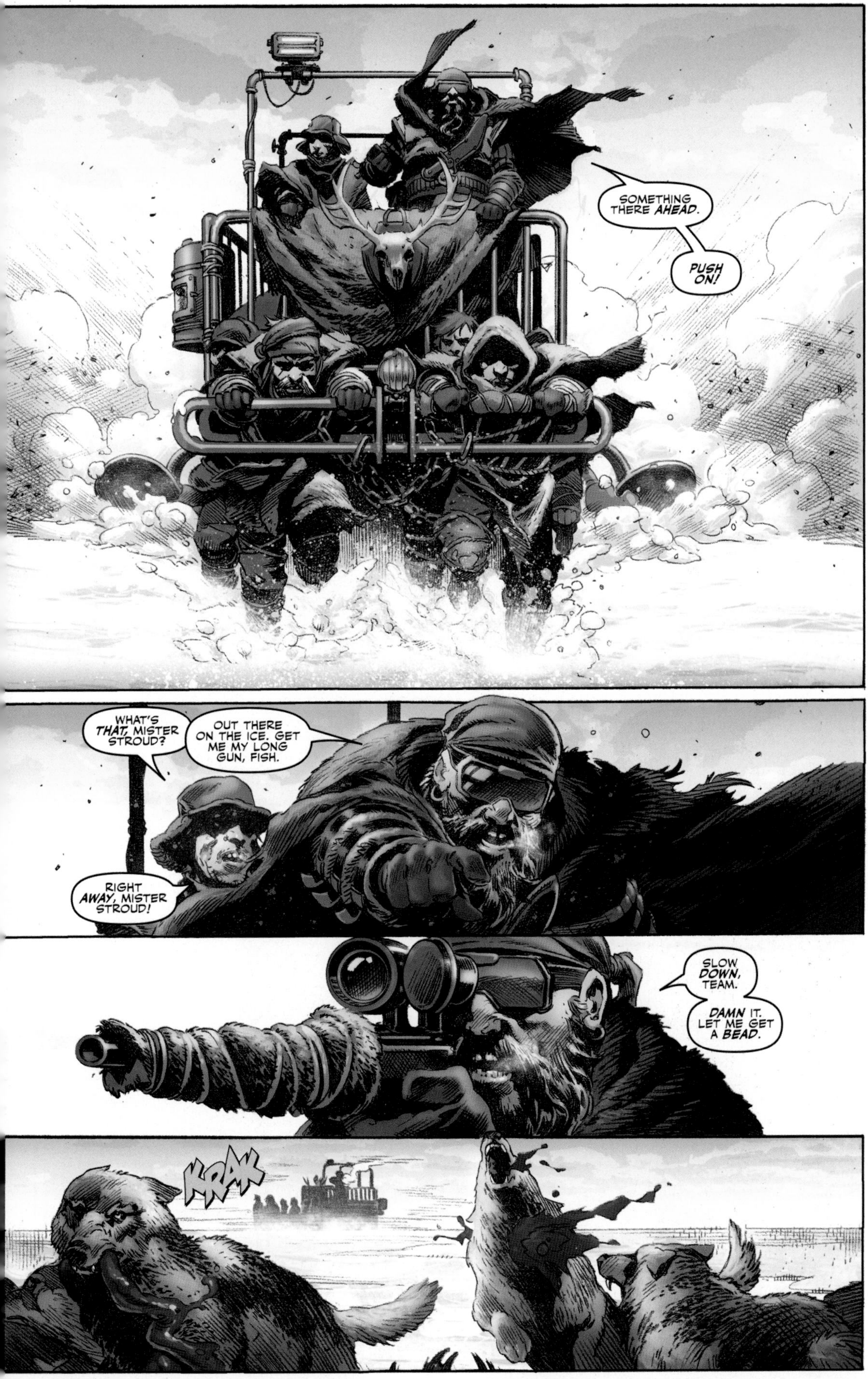
SOMETHING THERE *AHEAD*.
PUSH ON!
WHAT'S *THAT,* MISTER STROUD?
OUT THERE ON THE ICE. GET ME MY LONG GUN, FISH.
RIGHT *AWAY,* MISTER STROUD!
SLOW *DOWN,* TEAM.
DAMN IT. LET ME GET A *BEAD*.
KRAK

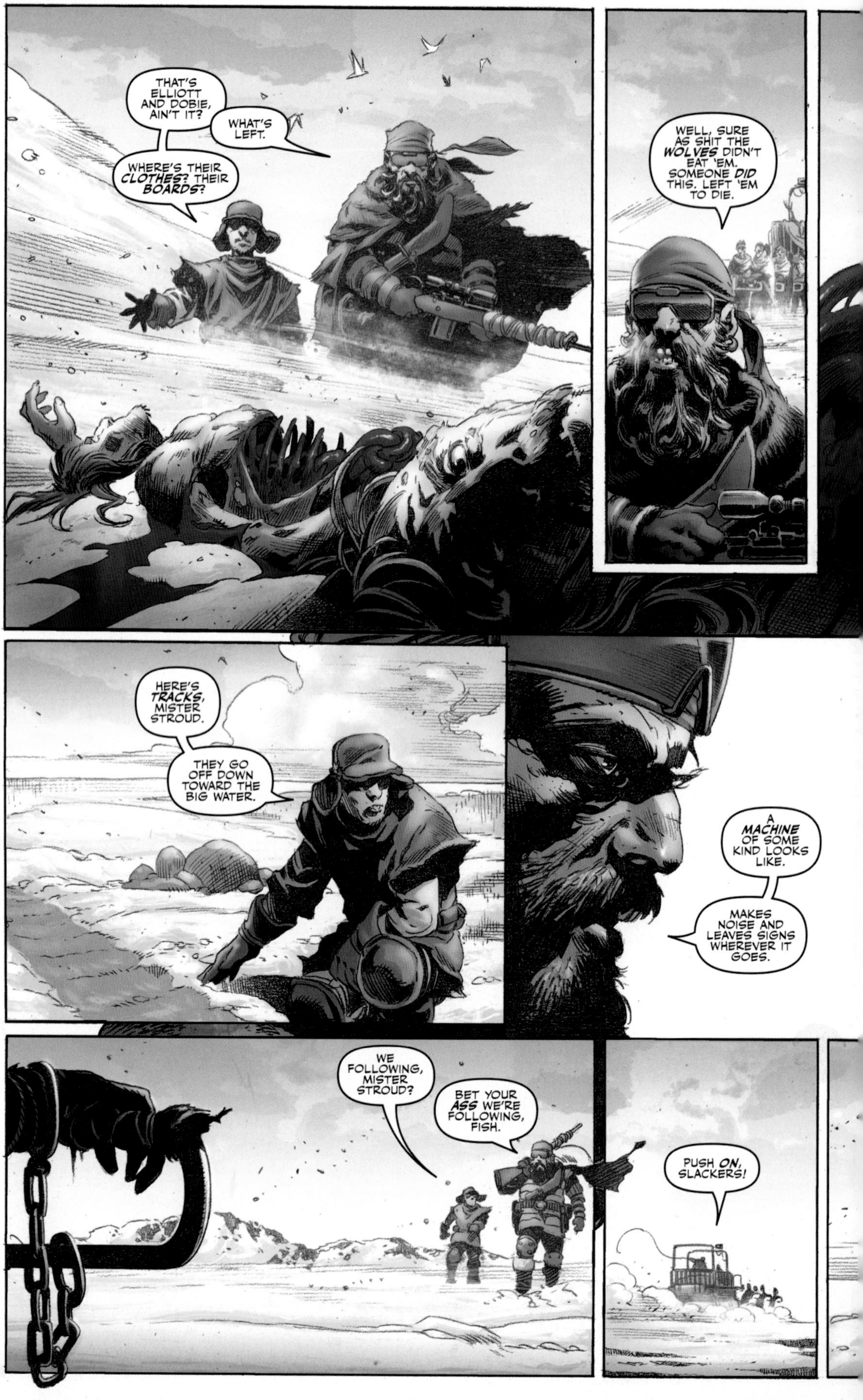
THAT'S ELLIOTT AND DOBIE, AIN'T IT?
WHAT'S LEFT.
WHERE'S THEIR CLOTHES? THEIR BOARDS?
WELL, SURE AS SHIT THE WOLVES DIDN'T EAT 'EM. SOMEONE DID THIS. LEFT 'EM TO DIE.
HERE'S TRACKS, MISTER STROUD.
THEY GO OFF DOWN TOWARD THE BIG WATER.
A MACHINE OF SOME KIND LOOKS LIKE.
MAKES NOISE AND LEAVES SIGNS WHEREVER IT GOES.
WE FOLLOWING, MISTER STROUD?
BET YOUR ASS WE'RE FOLLOWING, FISH.
PUSH ON, SLACKERS!

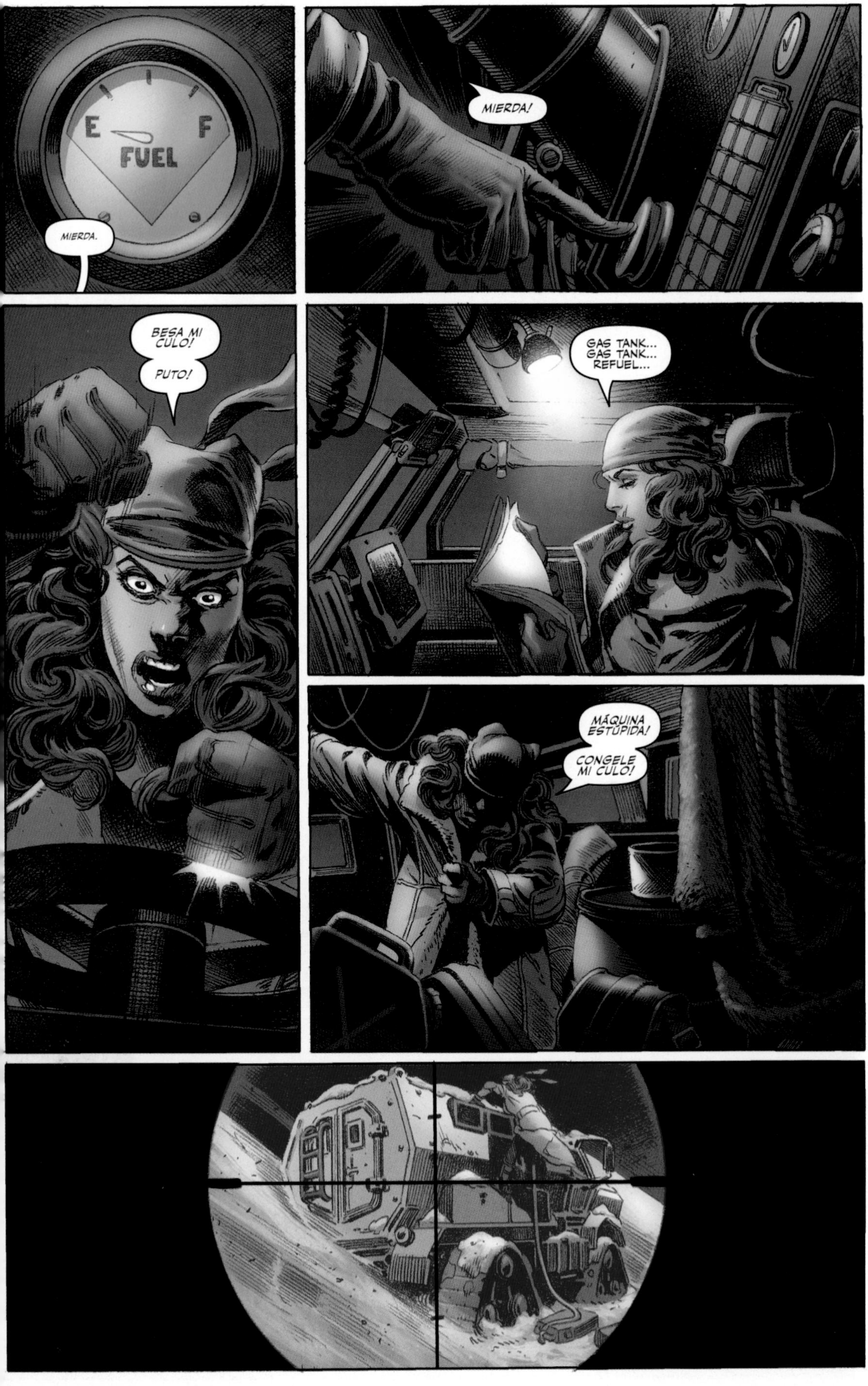

E
F
FUEL
MIERDA.
MIERDA!
BESA MI CULO!
PUTO!
GAS TANK... GAS TANK... REFUEL...
MÁQUINA ESTÚPIDA!
CONGELE MI CULO!

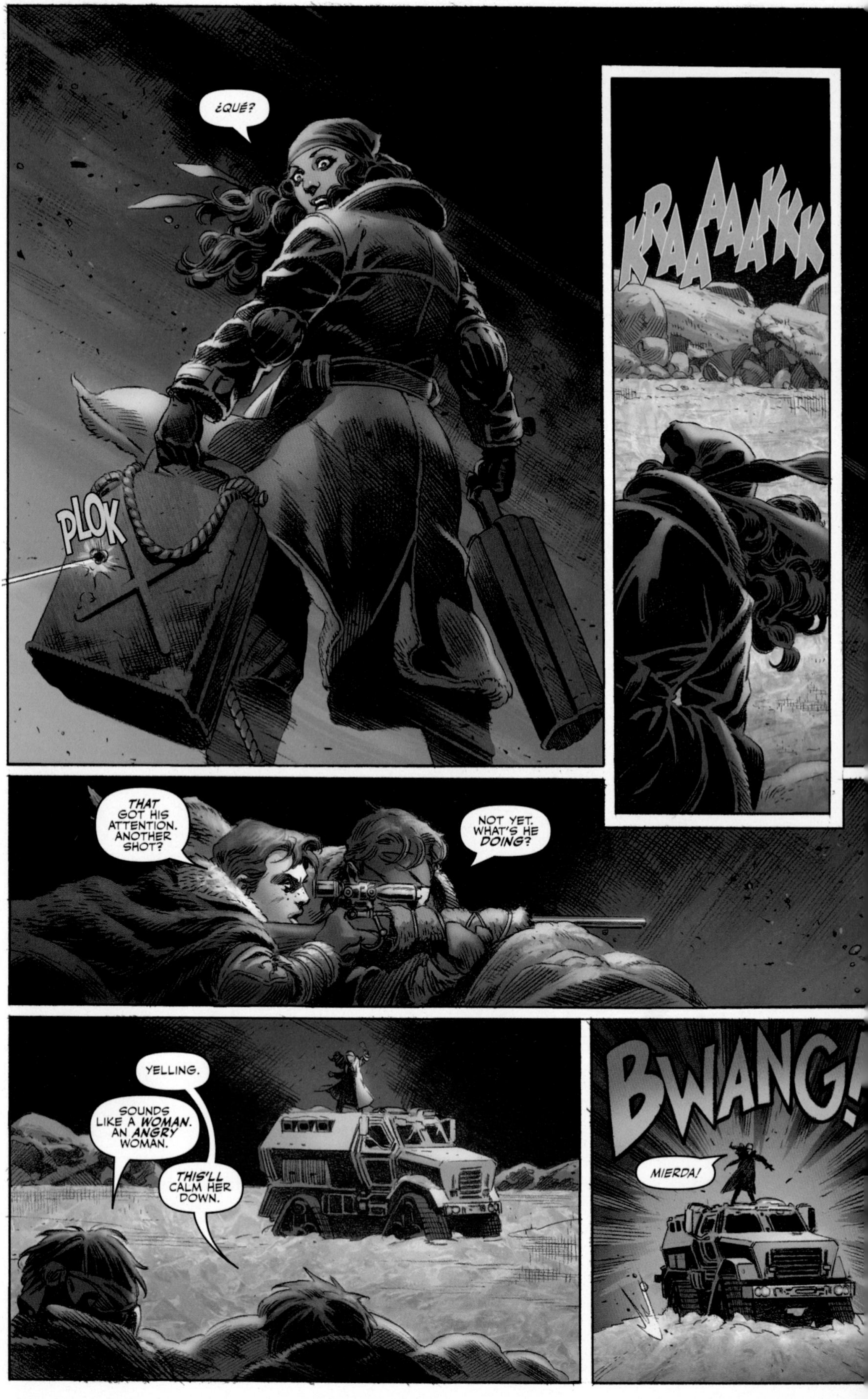
¿QUÉ?
PLOK
KRAAAAAAKKK
THAT GOT HIS ATTENTION. ANOTHER SHOT?
NOT YET. WHAT'S HE DOING?
YELLING.
SOUNDS LIKE A WOMAN. AN ANGRY WOMAN.
THIS'LL CALM HER DOWN.
BWANG!
MIERDA!

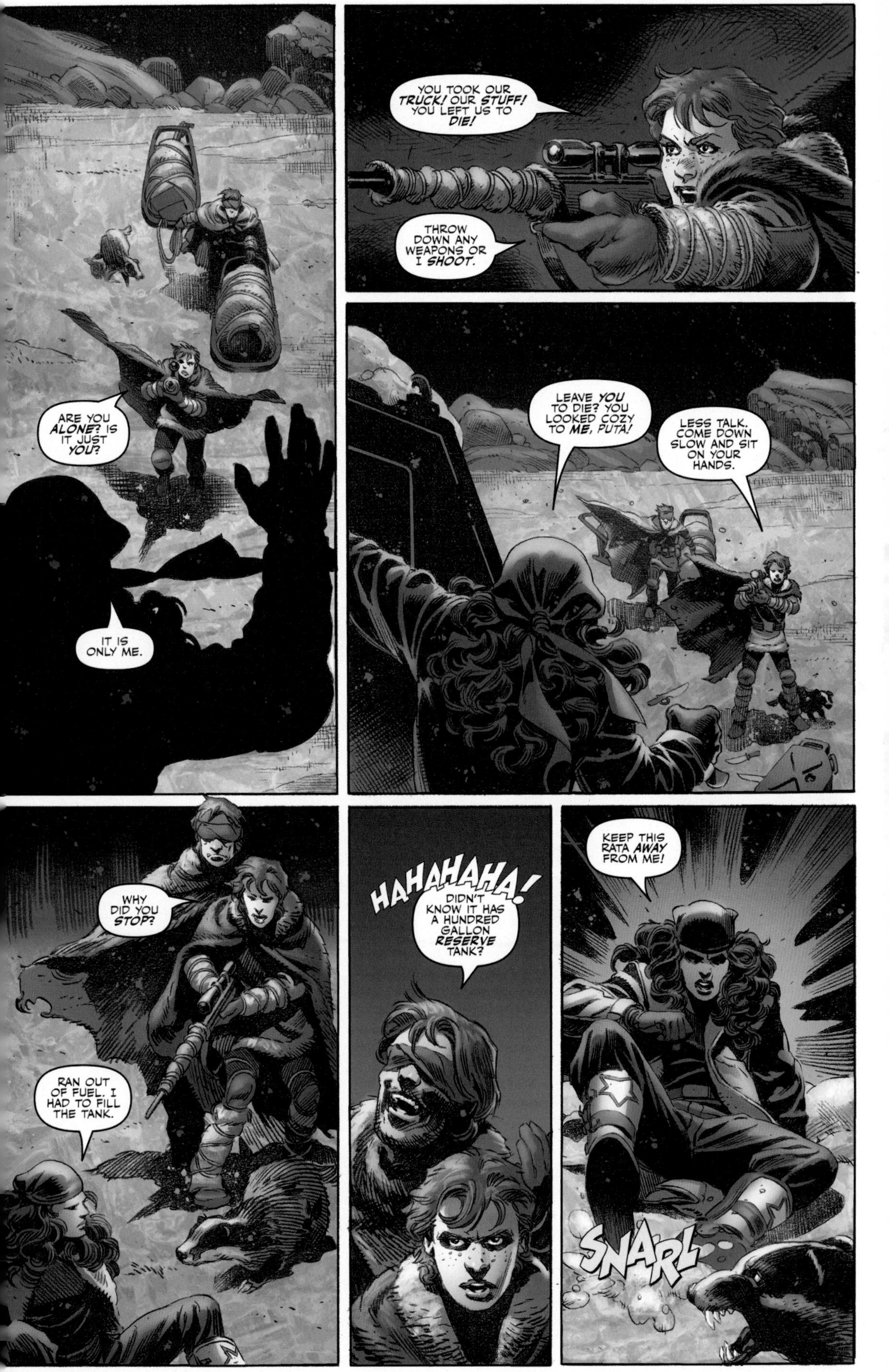
ARE YOU ALONE? IS IT JUST YOU?
IT IS ONLY ME.
YOU TOOK OUR TRUCK! OUR STUFF! YOU LEFT US TO DIE!
THROW DOWN ANY WEAPONS OR I SHOOT.
LEAVE YOU TO DIE? YOU LOOKED COZY TO ME, PUTA!
LESS TALK. COME DOWN SLOW AND SIT ON YOUR HANDS.
WHY DID YOU STOP?
RAN OUT OF FUEL. I HAD TO FILL THE TANK.
HAHAHAHA!
DIDN'T KNOW IT HAS A HUNDRED GALLON RESERVE TANK?
KEEP THIS RATA AWAY FROM ME!
SNARL

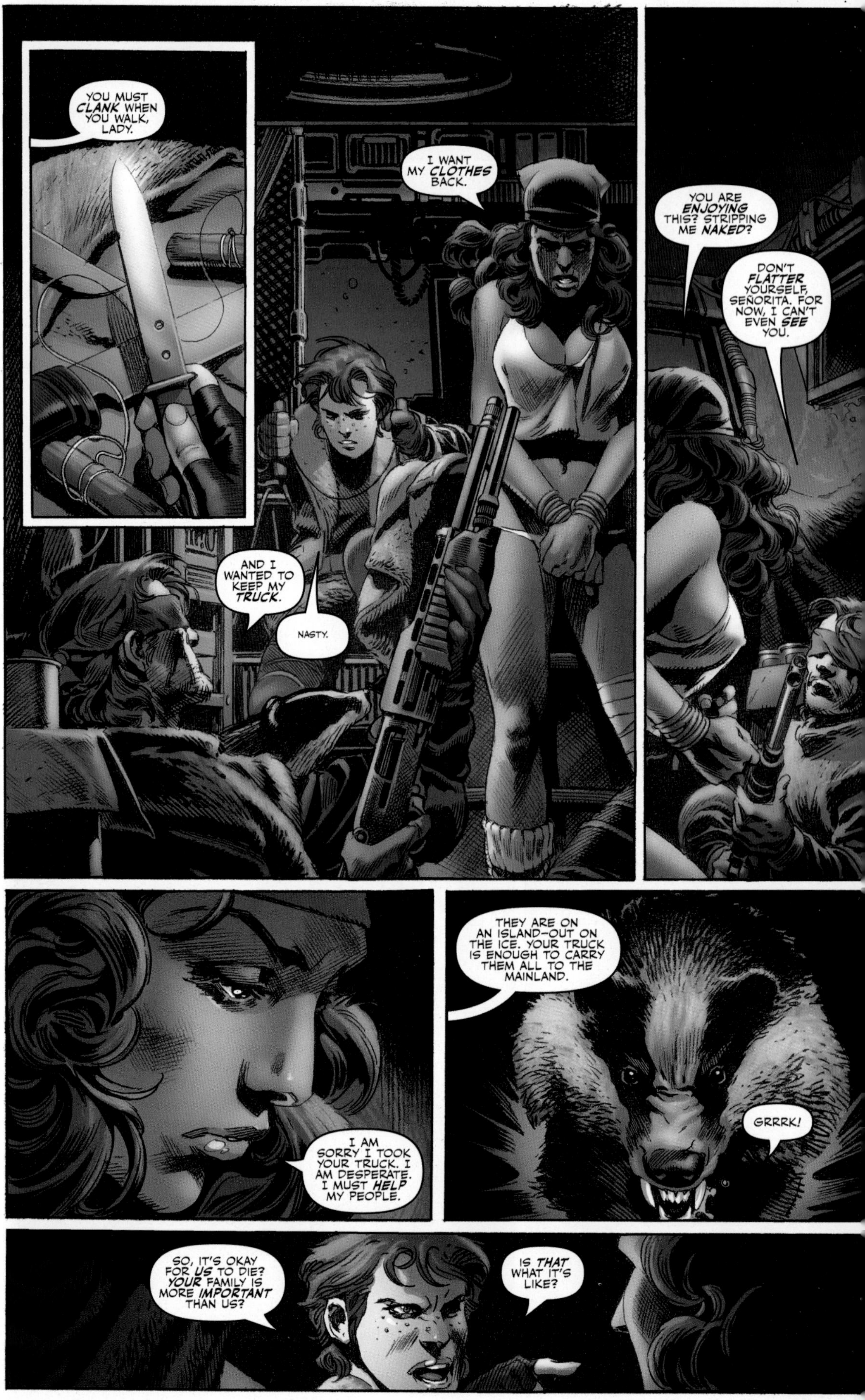
YOU MUST CLANK WHEN YOU WALK, LADY.
I WANT MY CLOTHES BACK.
AND I WANTED TO KEEP MY TRUCK.
NASTY.
YOU ARE ENJOYING THIS? STRIPPING ME NAKED?
DON'T FLATTER YOURSELF, SEÑORITA. FOR NOW, I CAN'T EVEN SEE YOU.
I AM SORRY I TOOK YOUR TRUCK. I AM DESPERATE. I MUST HELP MY PEOPLE.
THEY ARE ON AN ISLAND--OUT ON THE ICE. YOUR TRUCK IS ENOUGH TO CARRY THEM ALL TO THE MAINLAND.
GRRRK!
SO, IT'S OKAY FOR US TO DIE? YOUR FAMILY IS MORE IMPORTANT THAN US?
IS THAT WHAT IT'S LIKE?

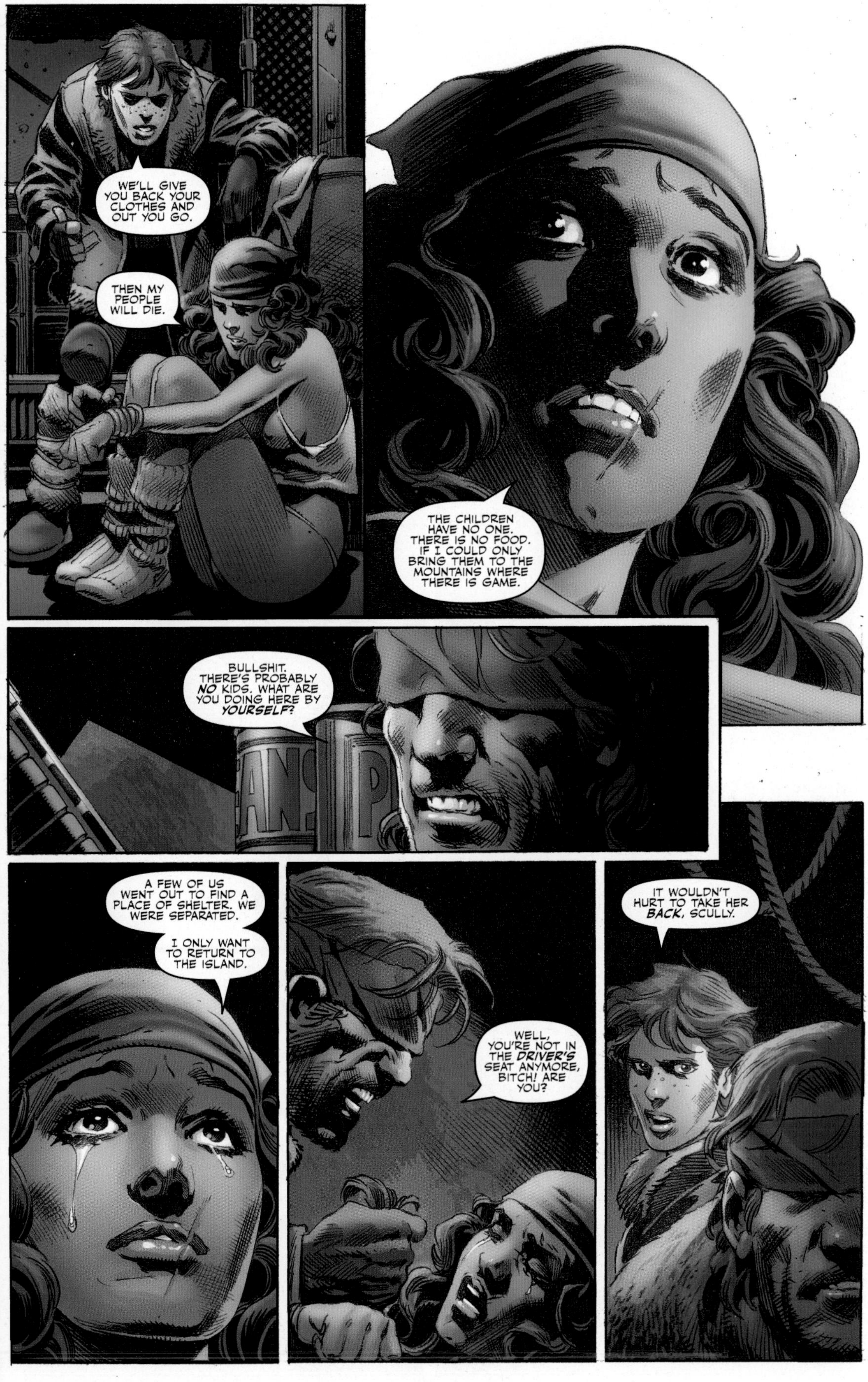

WE'LL GIVE YOU BACK YOUR CLOTHES AND OUT YOU GO.
THEN MY PEOPLE WILL DIE.
THE CHILDREN HAVE NO ONE. THERE IS NO FOOD. IF I COULD ONLY BRING THEM TO THE MOUNTAINS WHERE THERE IS GAME.
BULLSHIT. THERE'S PROBABLY NO KIDS. WHAT ARE YOU DOING HERE BY YOURSELF?
A FEW OF US WENT OUT TO FIND A PLACE OF SHELTER. WE WERE SEPARATED.
I ONLY WANT TO RETURN TO THE ISLAND.
WELL, YOU'RE NOT IN THE DRIVER'S SEAT ANYMORE, BITCH! ARE YOU?
IT WOULDN'T HURT TO TAKE HER BACK, SCULLY.

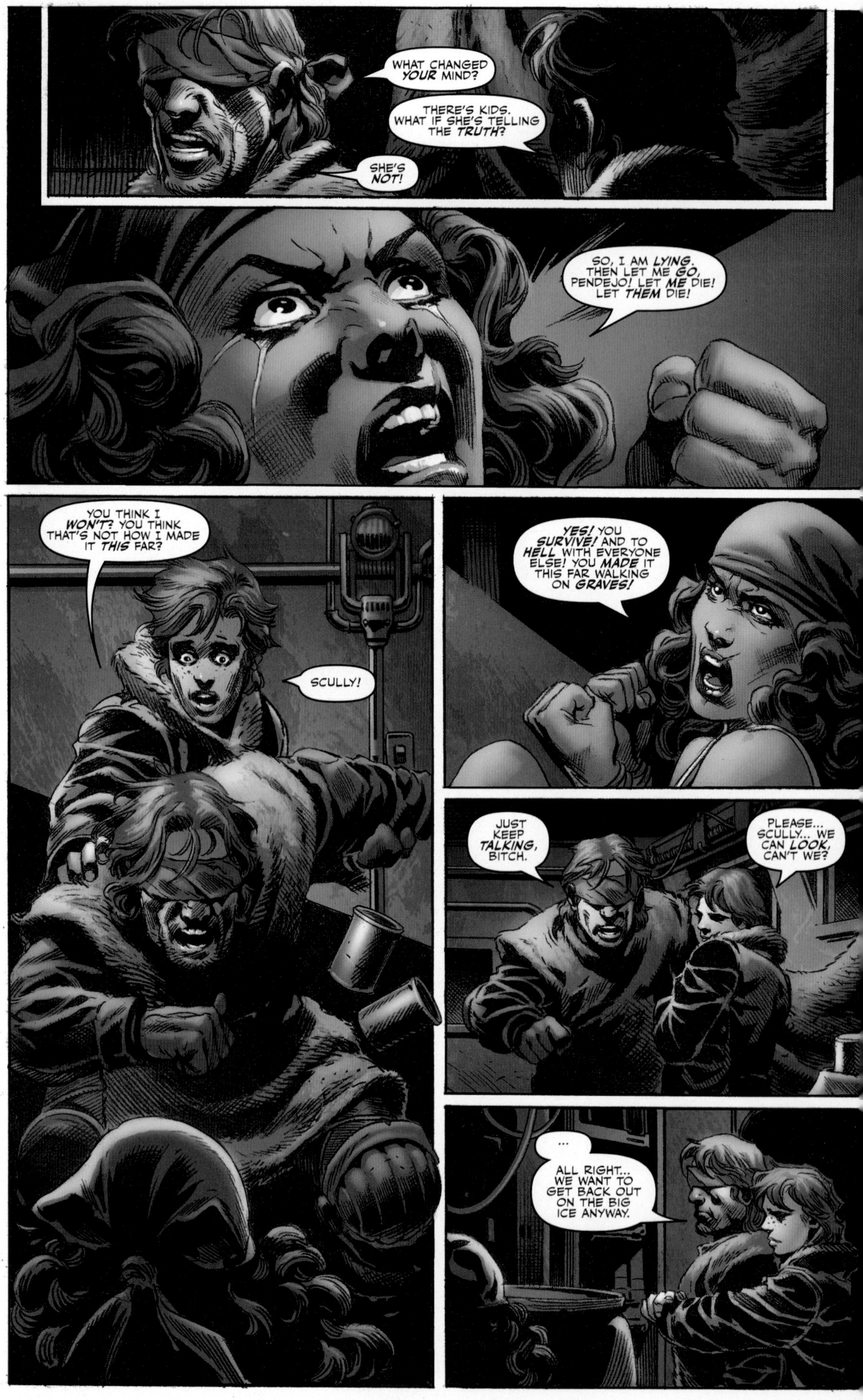
WHAT CHANGED *YOUR* MIND?
THERE'S KIDS. WHAT IF SHE'S TELLING THE *TRUTH*?
SHE'S *NOT*!
SO, I AM *LYING*. THEN LET ME *GO*, PENDEJO! LET *ME* DIE! LET *THEM* DIE!
YOU THINK I *WON'T*? YOU THINK THAT'S NOT HOW I MADE IT *THIS* FAR?
SCULLY!
YES! YOU *SURVIVE!* AND TO *HELL* WITH EVERYONE ELSE! YOU *MADE* IT THIS FAR WALKING ON *GRAVES!*
JUST KEEP *TALKING*, BITCH.
PLEASE... SCULLY... WE CAN *LOOK*, CAN'T WE?
...
ALL RIGHT... WE WANT TO GET BACK OUT ON THE BIG ICE ANYWAY.

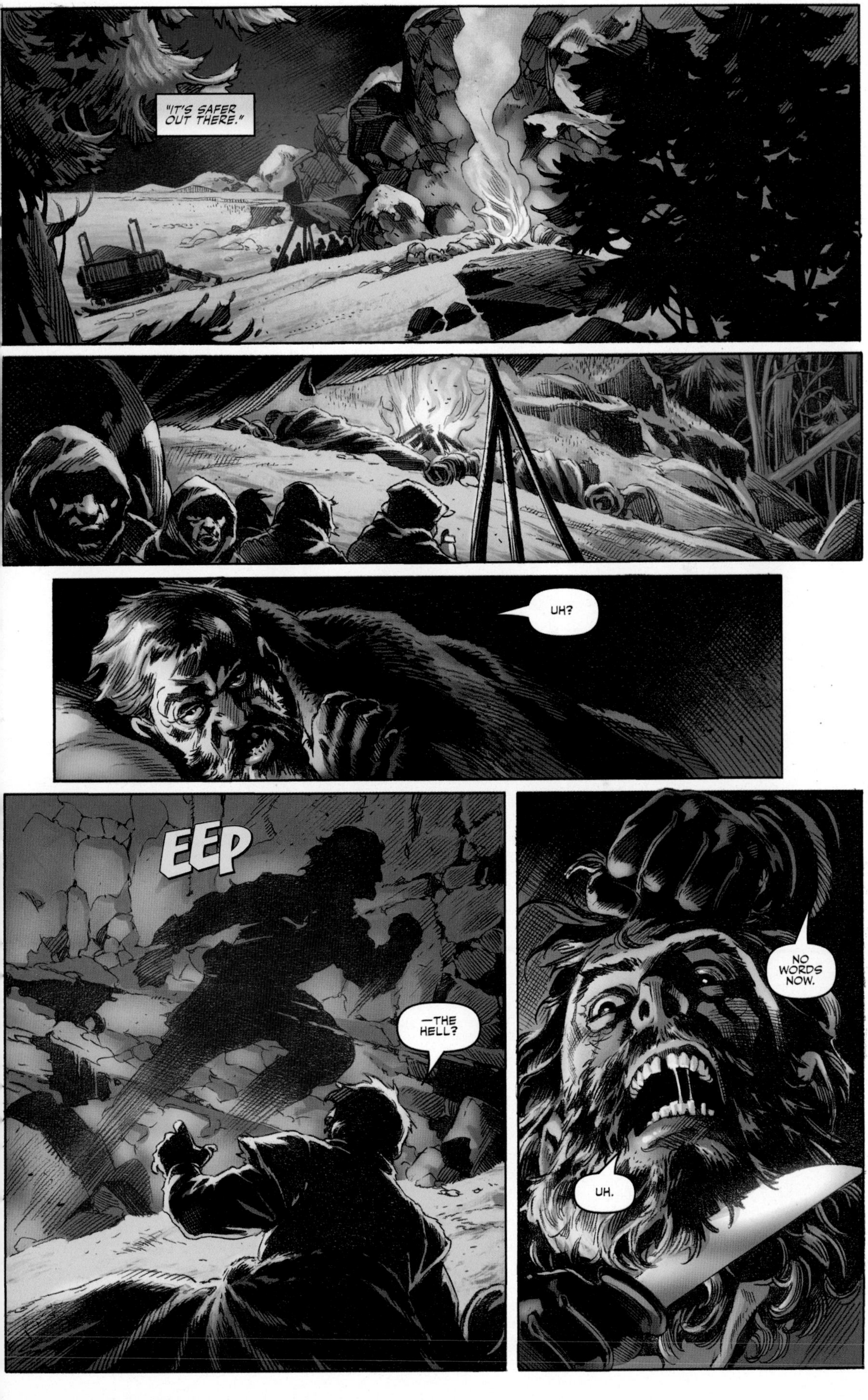

"IT'S SAFER OUT THERE."
UH?
EEP
—THE HELL?
NO WORDS NOW.
UH.

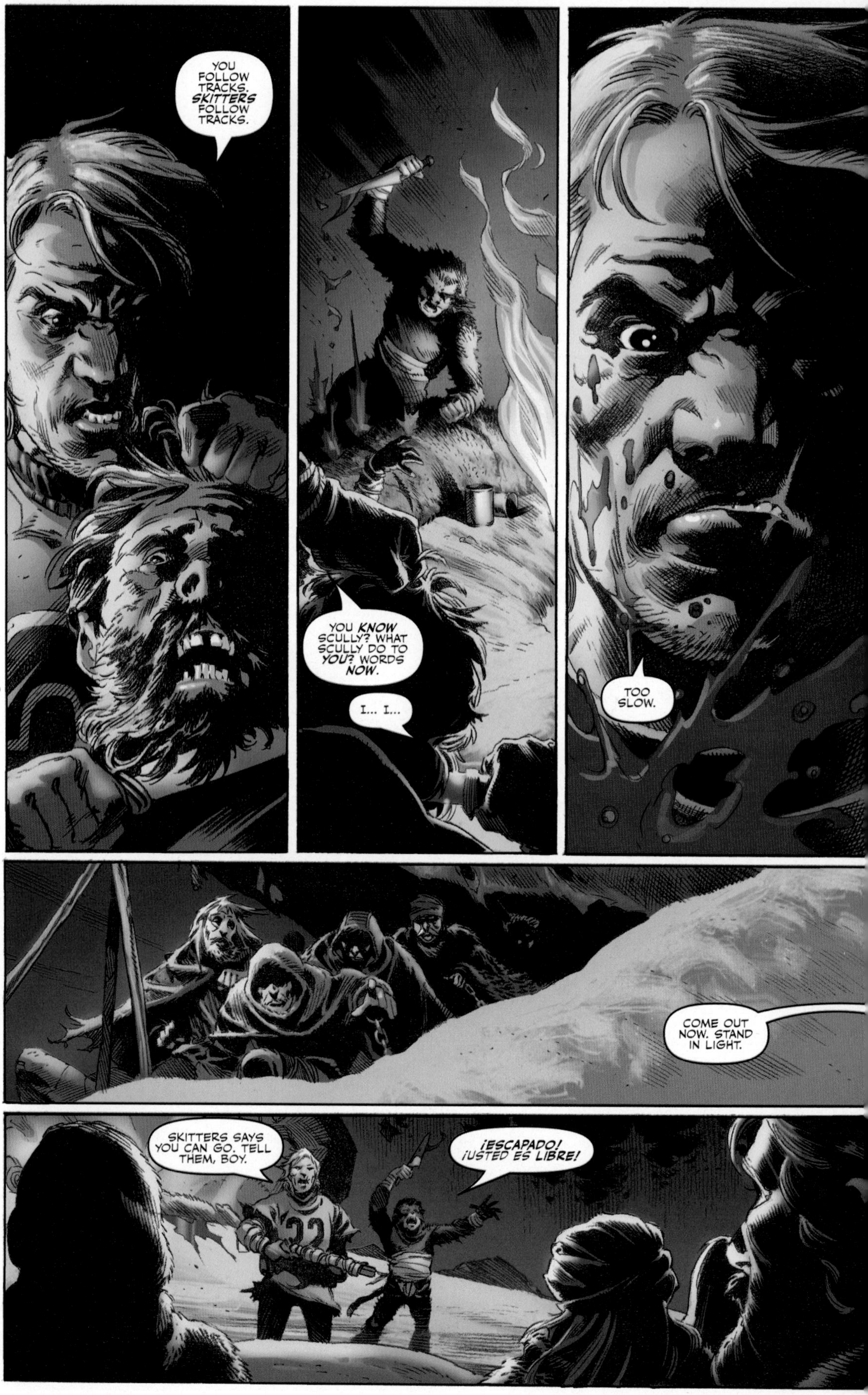
YOU FOLLOW TRACKS. SKITTERS FOLLOW TRACKS.
YOU KNOW SCULLY? WHAT SCULLY DO TO YOU? WORDS NOW.
I... I...
TOO SLOW.
COME OUT NOW. STAND IN LIGHT.
SKITTERS SAYS YOU CAN GO. TELL THEM, BOY.
¡ESCAPADO! ¡USTED ES LIBRE!

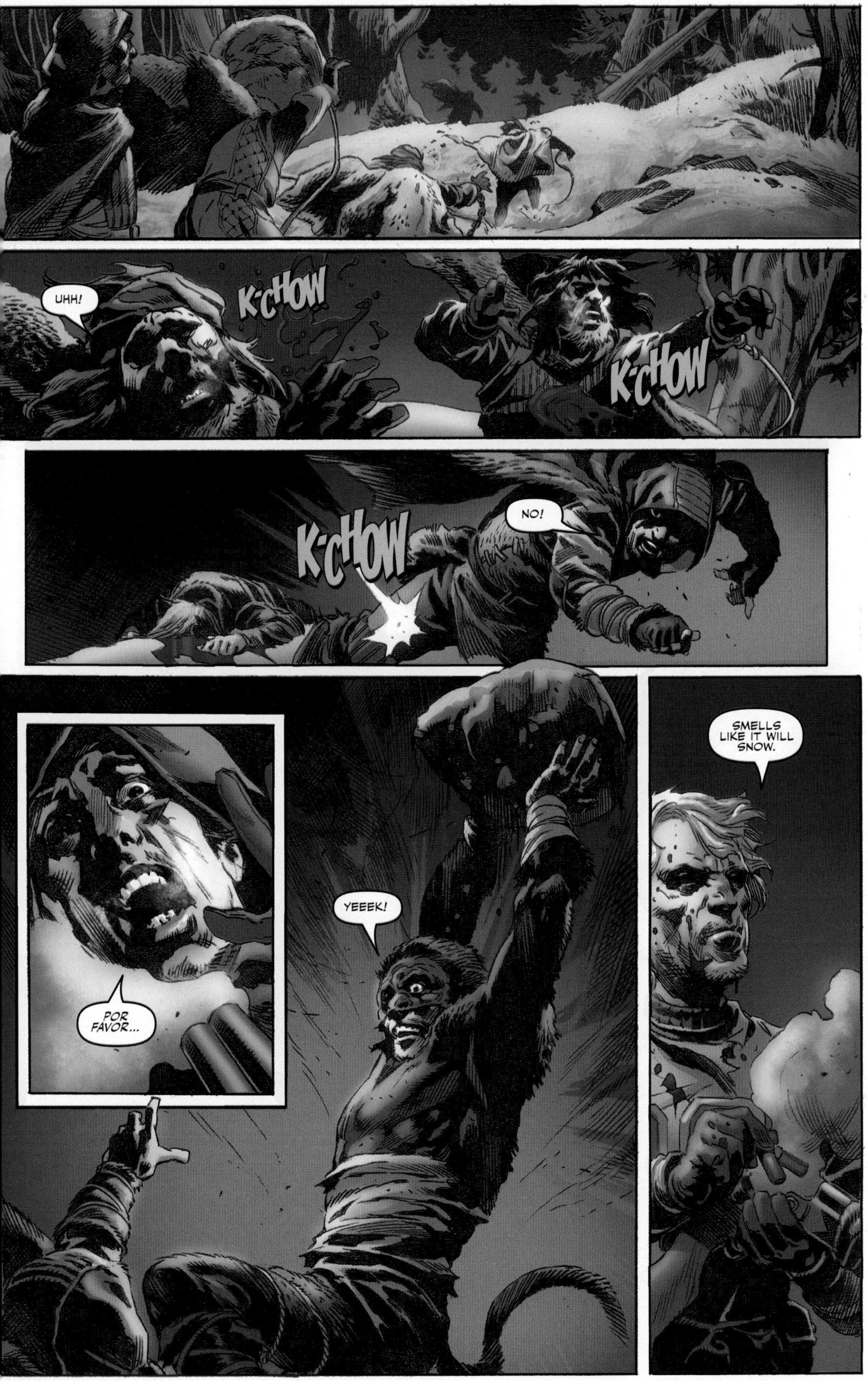
UHH!
K-CHOW
K-CHOW
K-CHOW
NO!
POR FAVOR...
YEEEK!
SMELLS LIKE IT WILL SNOW.

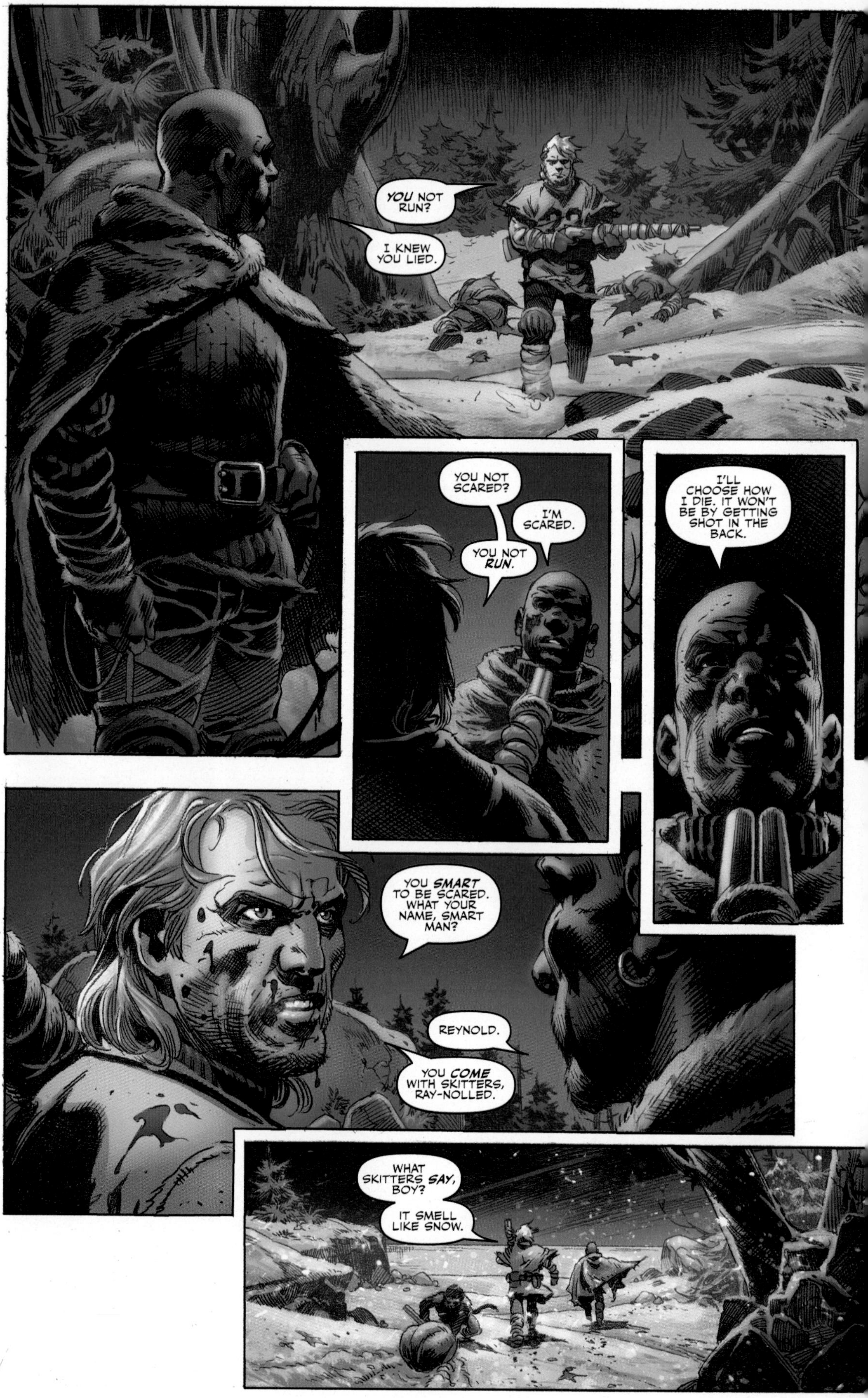
YOU NOT RUN?
I KNEW YOU LIED.
YOU NOT SCARED?
I'M SCARED.
YOU NOT RUN.
I'LL CHOOSE HOW I DIE. IT WON'T BE BY GETTING SHOT IN THE BACK.
YOU SMART TO BE SCARED. WHAT YOUR NAME, SMART MAN?
REYNOLD.
YOU COME WITH SKITTERS, RAY-NOLLED.
WHAT SKITTERS SAY, BOY?
IT SMELL LIKE SNOW.

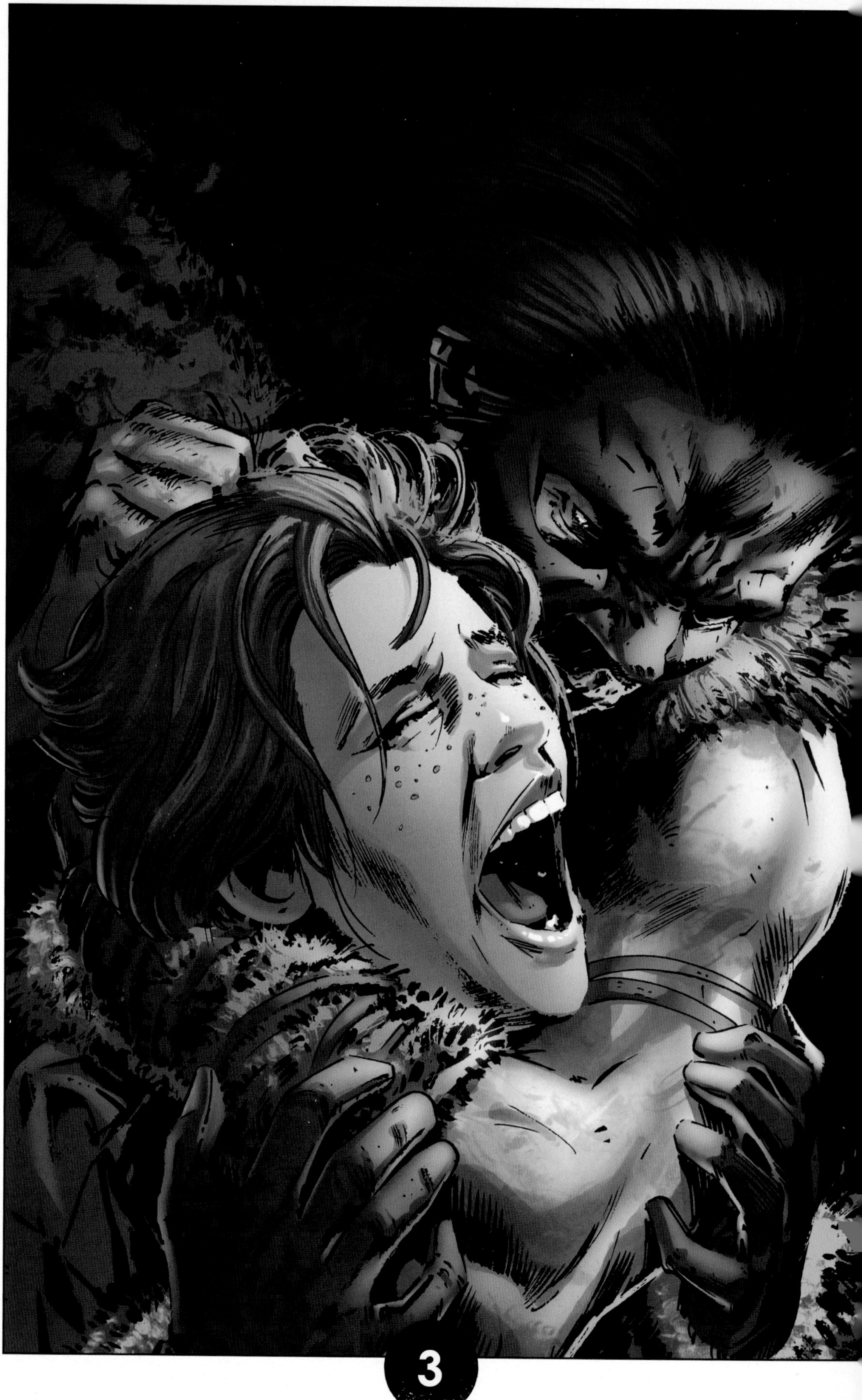

3

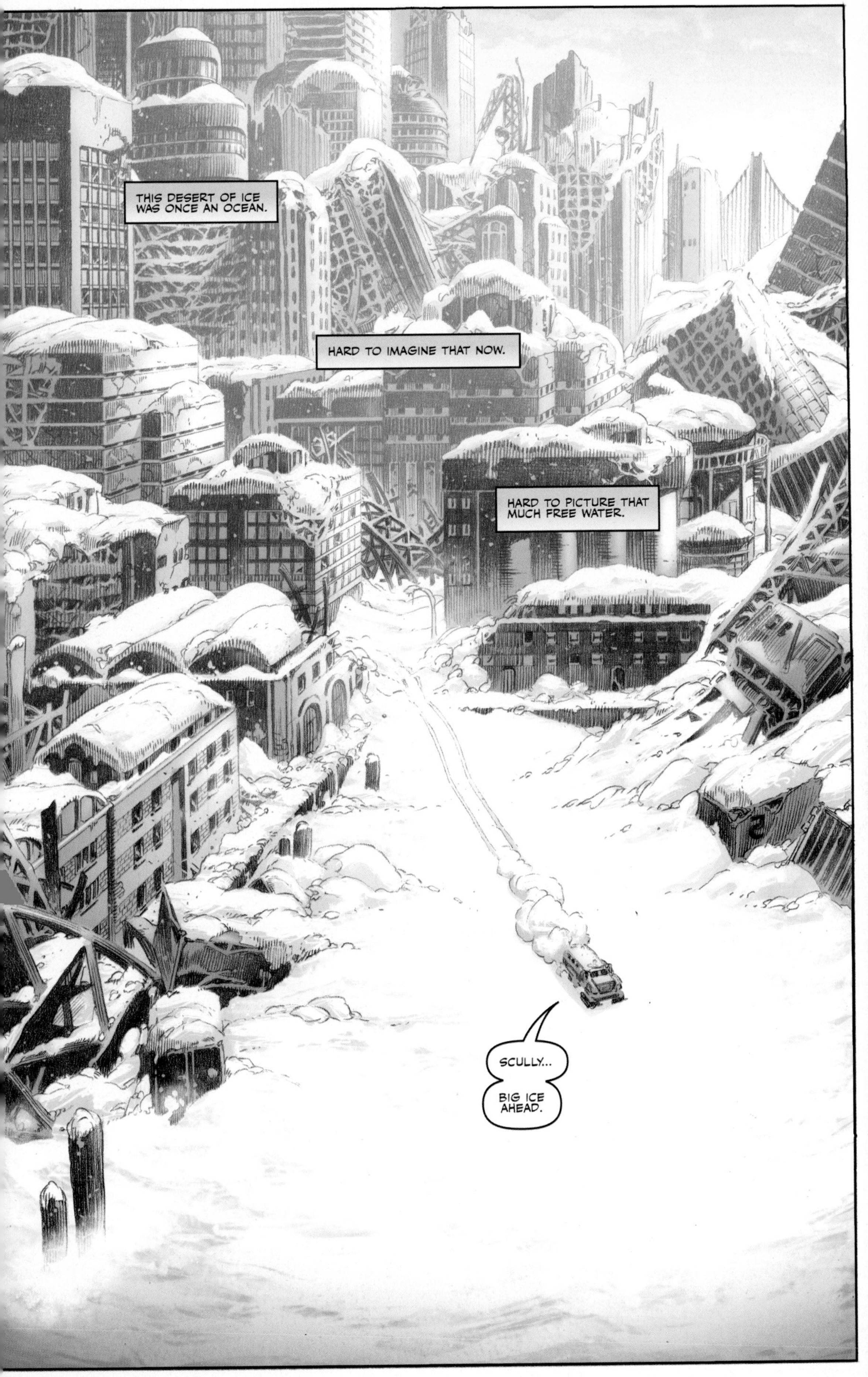

THIS DESERT OF ICE WAS ONCE AN OCEAN.
HARD TO IMAGINE THAT NOW.
HARD TO PICTURE THAT MUCH FREE WATER.
SCULLY...
BIG ICE AHEAD.

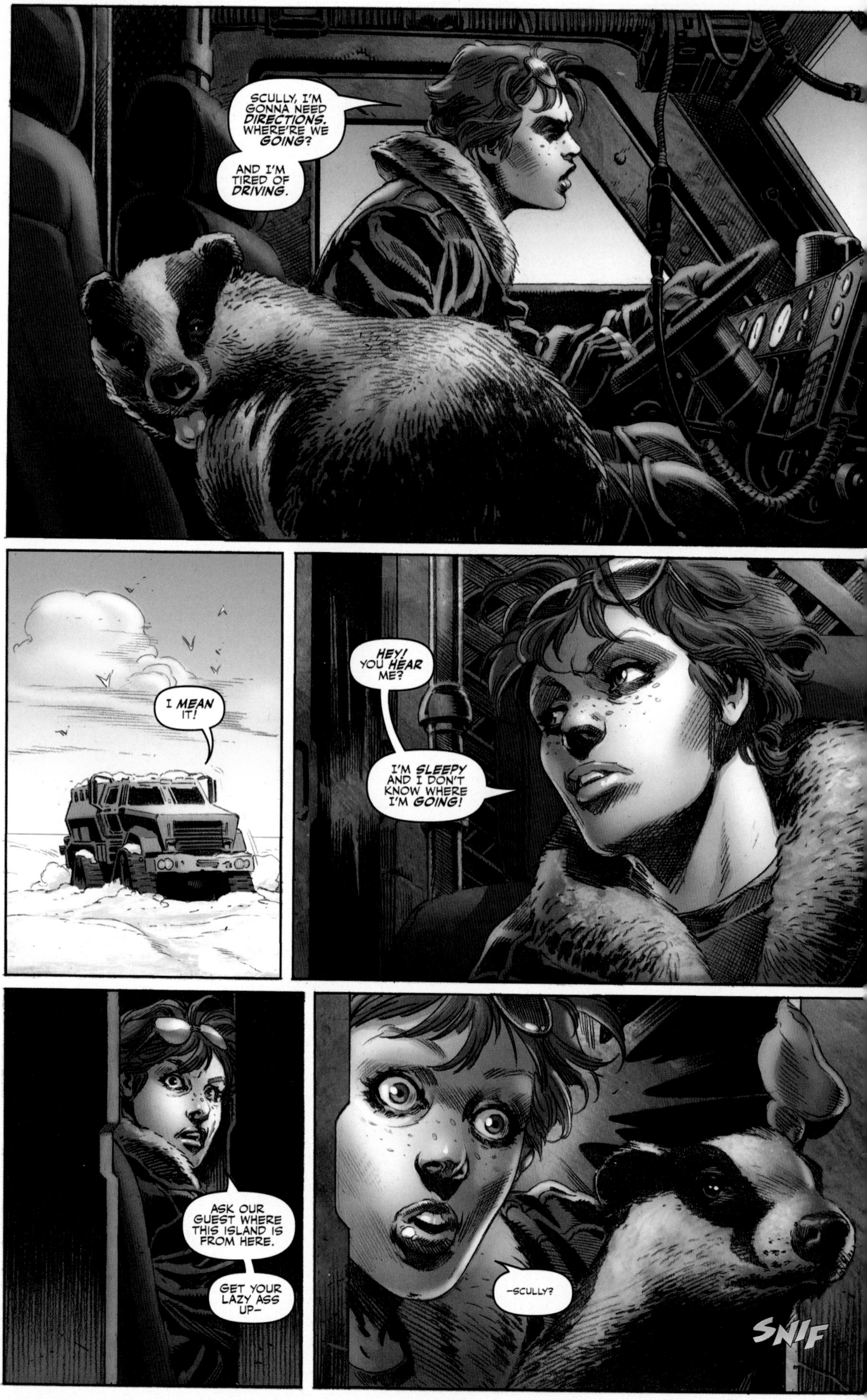
SCULLY, I'M GONNA NEED DIRECTIONS. WHERE'RE WE GOING?
AND I'M TIRED OF DRIVING.
I MEAN IT!
HEY! YOU HEAR ME?
I'M SLEEPY AND I DON'T KNOW WHERE I'M GOING!
ASK OUR GUEST WHERE THIS ISLAND IS FROM HERE.
GET YOUR LAZY ASS UP–
–SCULLY?
SNIF

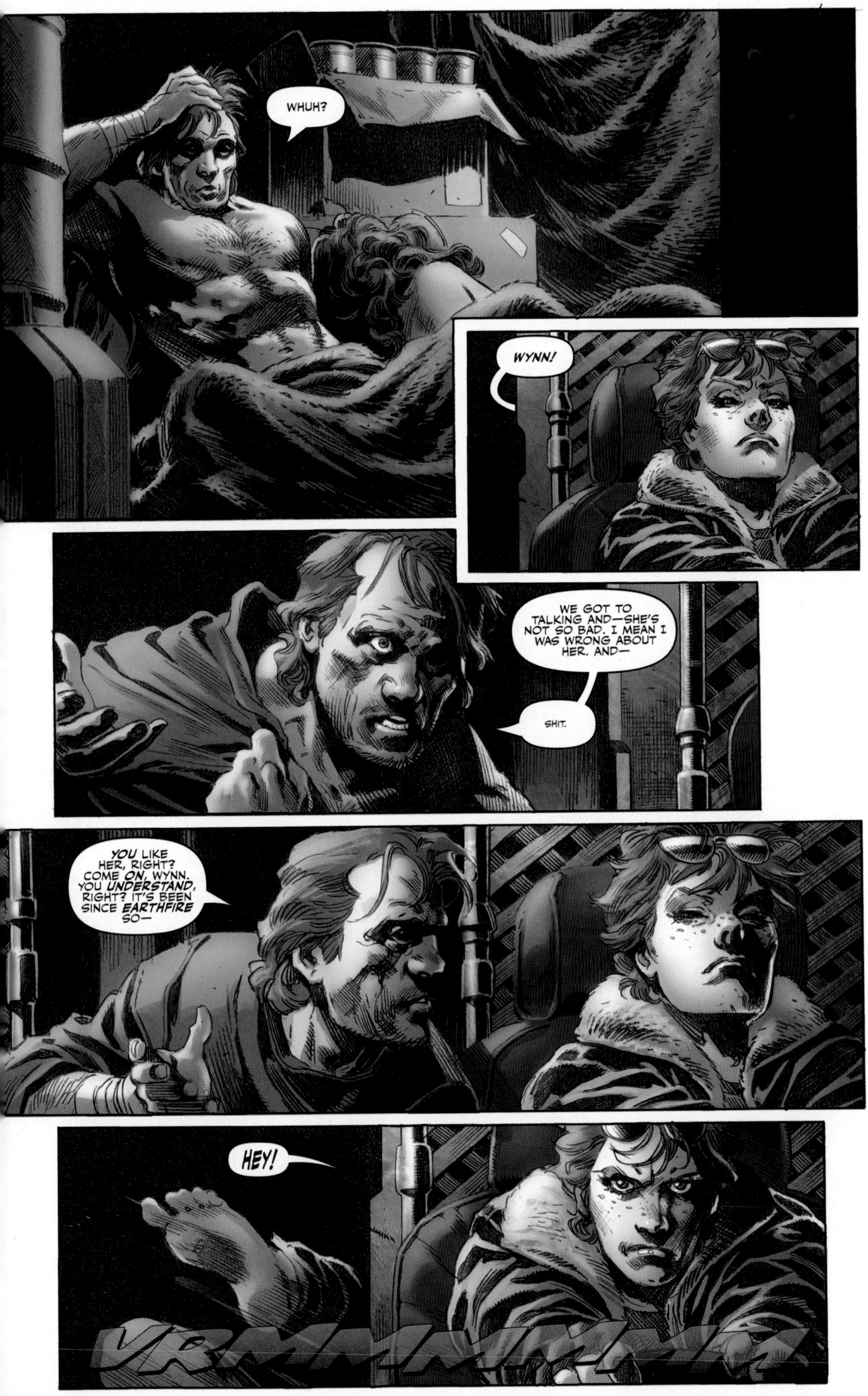
WHUH?
WYNN!
WE GOT TO TALKING AND—SHE'S NOT SO BAD. I MEAN I WAS WRONG ABOUT HER. AND—
SHIT.
YOU LIKE HER, RIGHT? COME ON, WYNN. YOU UNDERSTAND, RIGHT? IT'S BEEN SINCE EARTHFIRE SO—
HEY!
VRMMMMMM

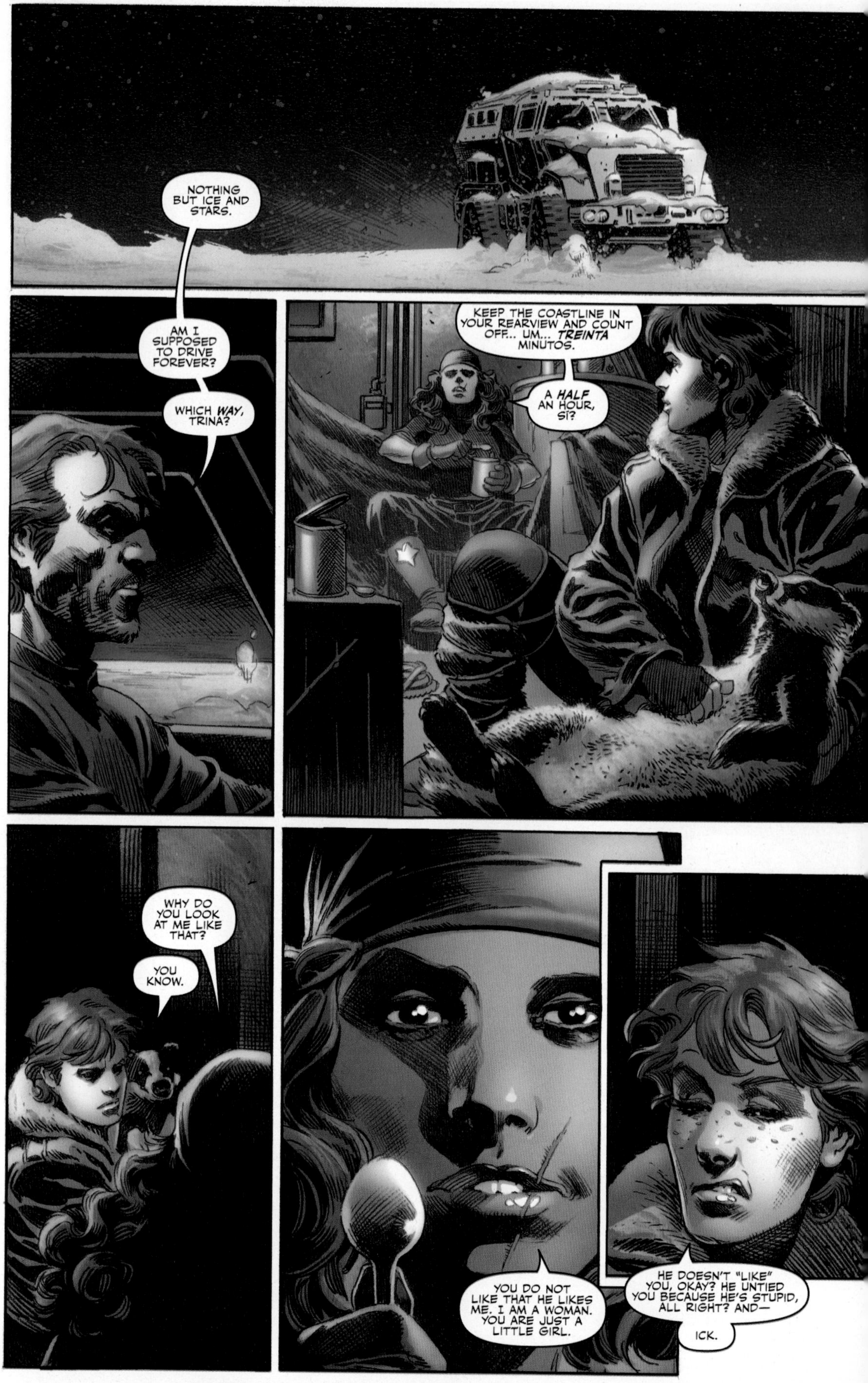

NOTHING BUT ICE AND STARS.
AM I SUPPOSED TO DRIVE FOREVER?
WHICH *WAY*, TRINA?
KEEP THE COASTLINE IN YOUR REARVIEW AND COUNT OFF... UM... *TREINTA* MINUTOS.
A *HALF* AN HOUR, SÍ?
WHY DO YOU LOOK AT ME LIKE THAT?
YOU KNOW.
YOU DO NOT LIKE THAT HE LIKES ME. I AM A WOMAN. YOU ARE JUST A LITTLE GIRL.
HE DOESN'T "LIKE" YOU, OKAY? HE UNTIED YOU BECAUSE HE'S STUPID, ALL RIGHT? AND—
ICK.

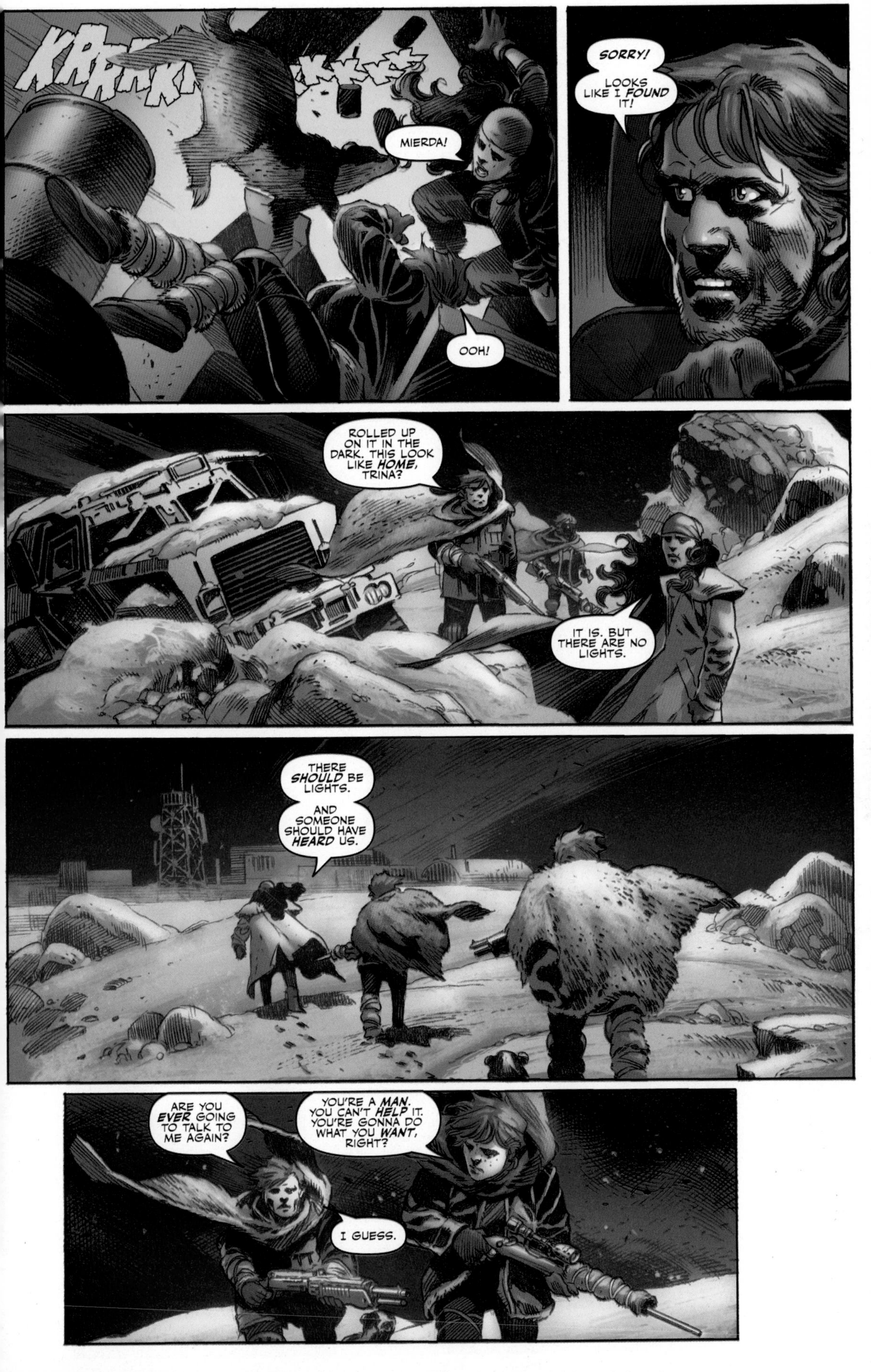
KRRRKKKKKKKK
MIERDA!
OOH!
SORRY!
LOOKS LIKE I FOUND IT!
ROLLED UP ON IT IN THE DARK. THIS LOOK LIKE HOME, TRINA?
IT IS. BUT THERE ARE NO LIGHTS.
THERE SHOULD BE LIGHTS.
AND SOMEONE SHOULD HAVE HEARD US.
ARE YOU EVER GOING TO TALK TO ME AGAIN?
YOU'RE A MAN. YOU CAN'T HELP IT. YOU'RE GONNA DO WHAT YOU WANT, RIGHT?
I GUESS.

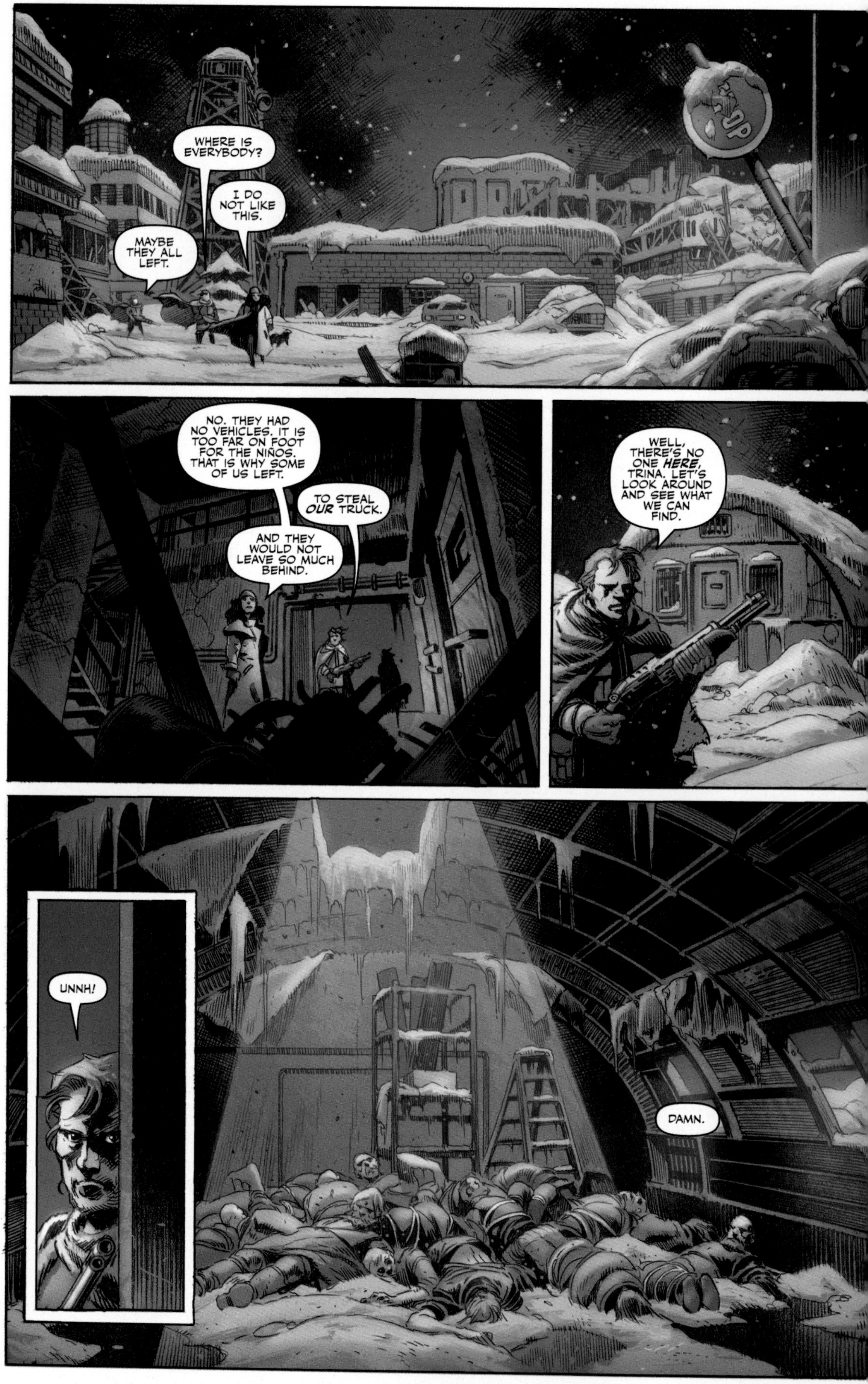
WHERE IS EVERYBODY?
I DO NOT LIKE THIS.
MAYBE THEY ALL LEFT.
NO. THEY HAD NO VEHICLES. IT IS TOO FAR ON FOOT FOR THE NIÑOS. THAT IS WHY SOME OF US LEFT.
TO STEAL OUR TRUCK.
AND THEY WOULD NOT LEAVE SO MUCH BEHIND.
WELL, THERE'S NO ONE HERE, TRINA. LET'S LOOK AROUND AND SEE WHAT WE CAN FIND.
UNNH!
DAMN.

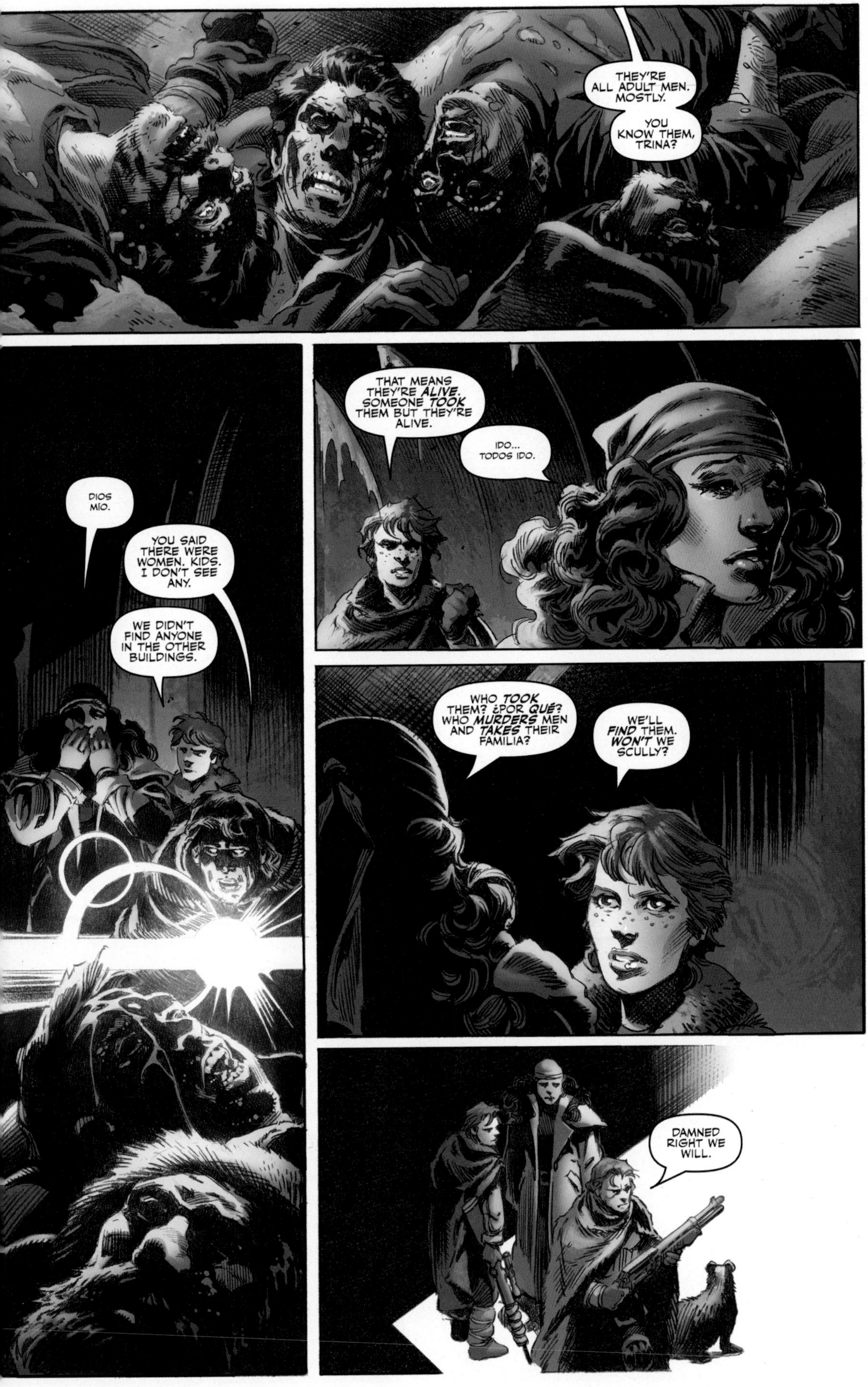
THEY'RE ALL ADULT MEN. MOSTLY.
YOU KNOW THEM, TRINA?
DIOS MÍO.
YOU SAID THERE WERE WOMEN. KIDS. I DON'T SEE ANY.
WE DIDN'T FIND ANYONE IN THE OTHER BUILDINGS.
THAT MEANS THEY'RE ALIVE. SOMEONE TOOK THEM BUT THEY'RE ALIVE.
IDO... TODOS IDO.
WHO TOOK THEM? ¿POR QUÉ? WHO MURDERS MEN AND TAKES THEIR FAMILIA?
WE'LL FIND THEM. WON'T WE SCULLY?
DAMNED RIGHT WE WILL.

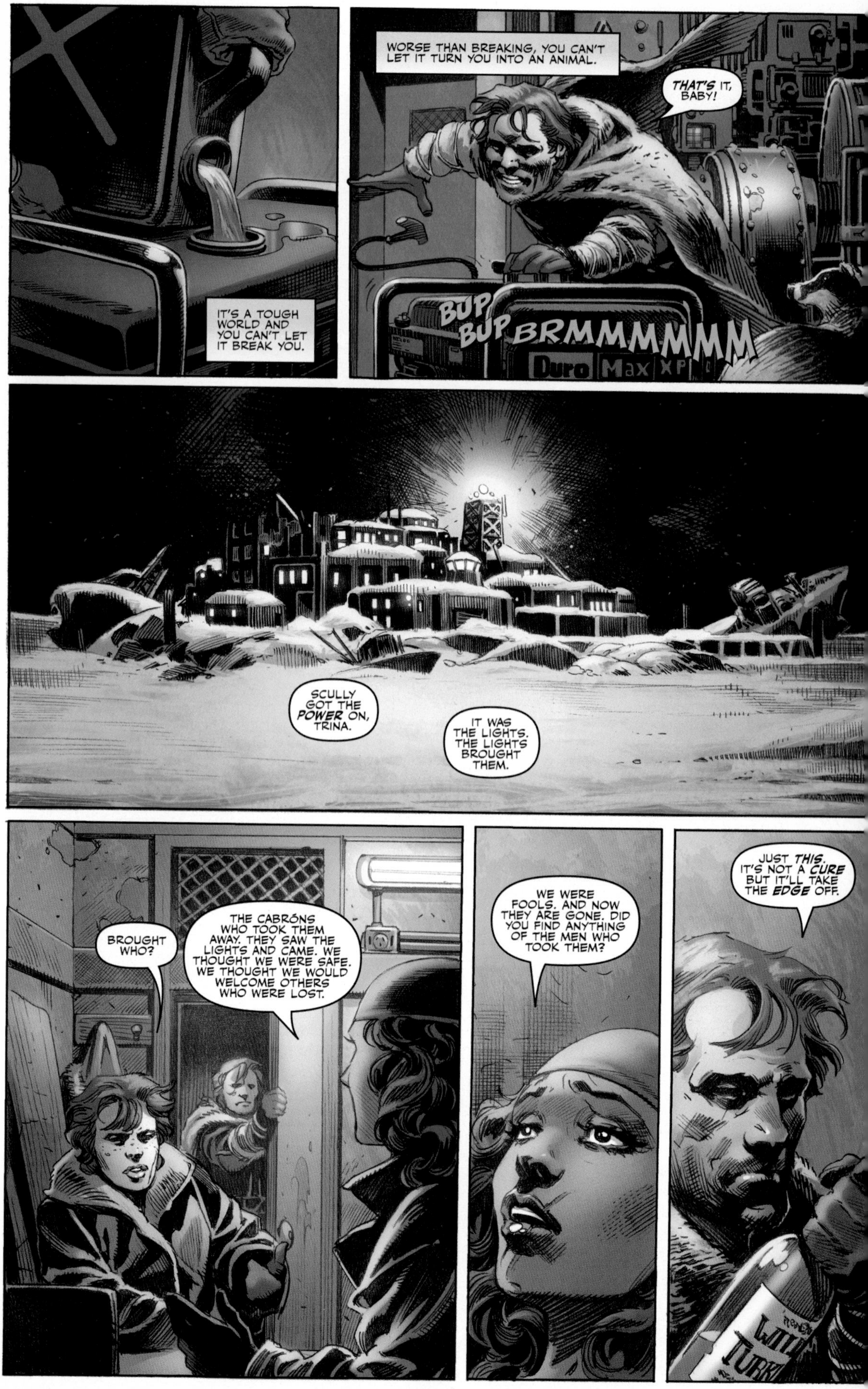
IT'S A TOUGH WORLD AND YOU CAN'T LET IT BREAK YOU.
WORSE THAN BREAKING, YOU CAN'T LET IT TURN YOU INTO AN ANIMAL.
THAT'S IT, BABY!
BUP BUP BRMMMMMMM
Duro Max XP
SCULLY GOT THE *POWER* ON, TRINA.
IT WAS THE LIGHTS. THE LIGHTS BROUGHT THEM.
BROUGHT WHO?
THE CABRÓNS WHO TOOK THEM AWAY. THEY SAW THE LIGHTS AND CAME. WE THOUGHT WE WERE SAFE. WE THOUGHT WE WOULD WELCOME OTHERS WHO WERE LOST.
WE WERE FOOLS. AND NOW THEY ARE GONE. DID YOU FIND ANYTHING OF THE MEN WHO TOOK THEM?
JUST *THIS*. IT'S NOT A *CURE* BUT IT'LL TAKE THE *EDGE* OFF.

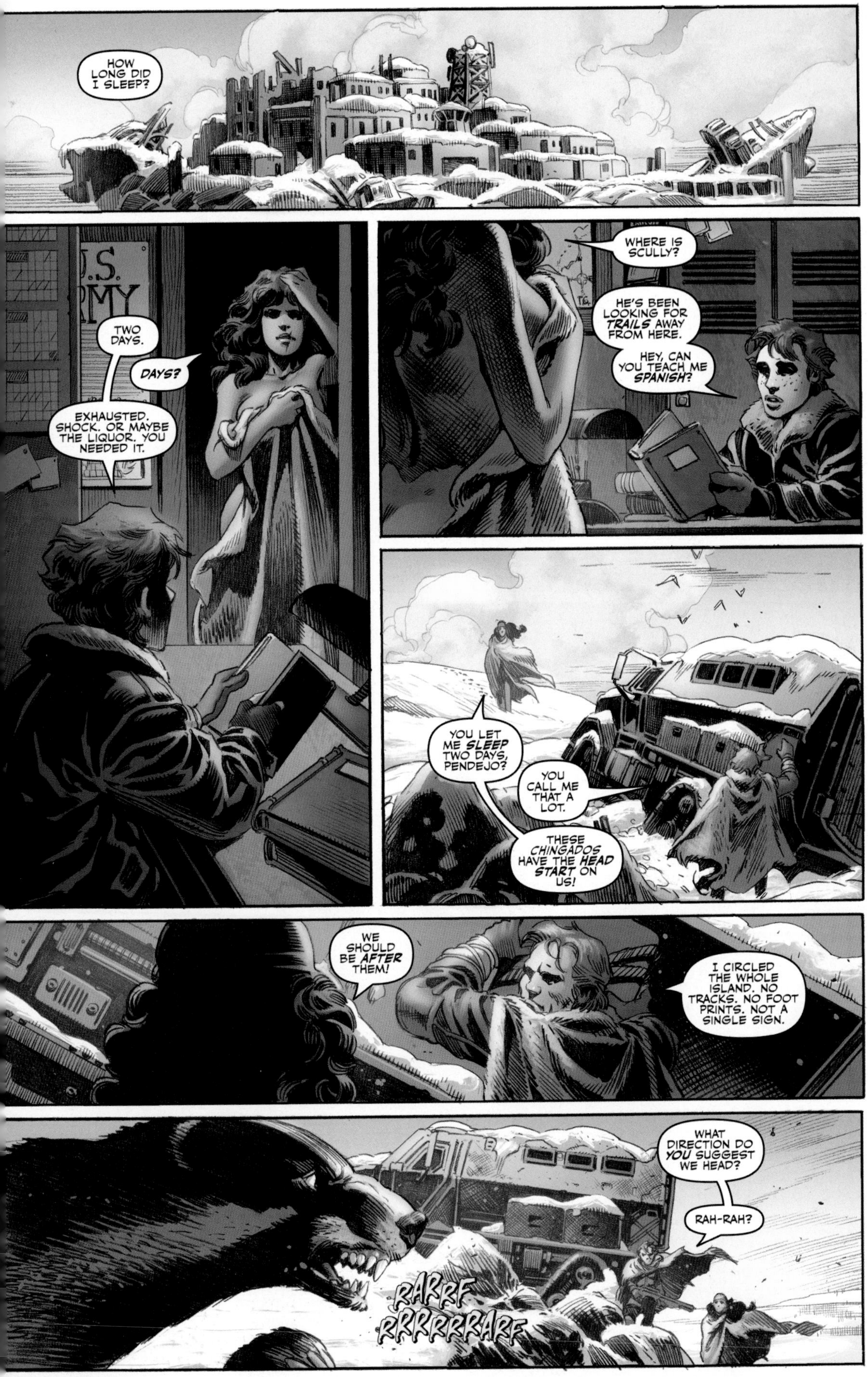
HOW LONG DID I SLEEP?
TWO DAYS.
DAYS?
EXHAUSTED. SHOCK. OR MAYBE THE LIQUOR. YOU NEEDED IT.
WHERE IS SCULLY?
HE'S BEEN LOOKING FOR TRAILS AWAY FROM HERE.
HEY, CAN YOU TEACH ME SPANISH?
YOU LET ME SLEEP TWO DAYS, PENDEJO?
YOU CALL ME THAT A LOT.
THESE CHINGADOS HAVE THE HEAD START ON US!
WE SHOULD BE AFTER THEM!
I CIRCLED THE WHOLE ISLAND. NO TRACKS. NO FOOT PRINTS. NOT A SINGLE SIGN.
WHAT DIRECTION DO YOU SUGGEST WE HEAD?
RAH-RAH?
RARRF RRRRRRARF

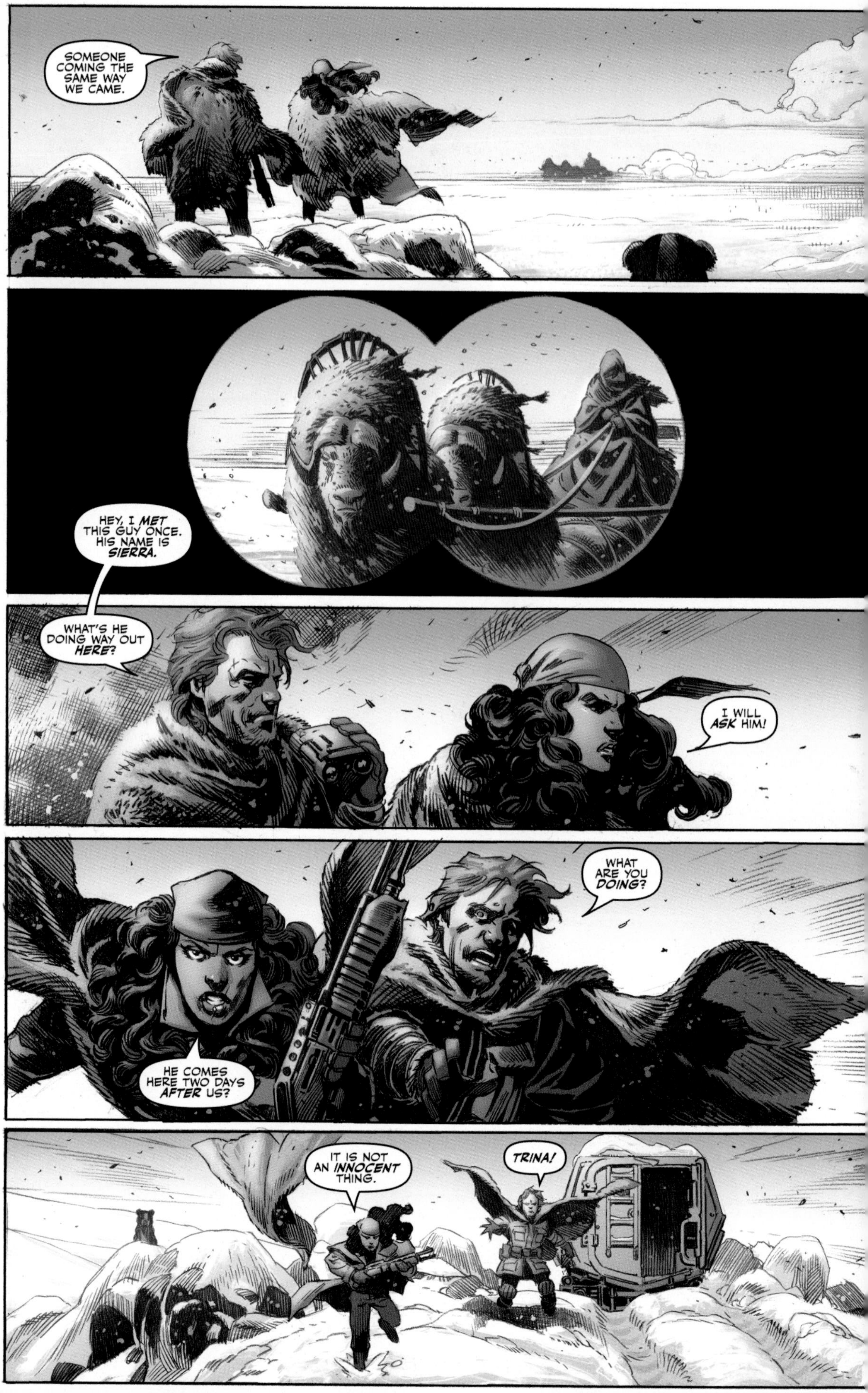

SOMEONE COMING THE SAME WAY WE CAME.
HEY, I MET THIS GUY ONCE. HIS NAME IS SIERRA.
WHAT'S HE DOING WAY OUT HERE?
I WILL ASK HIM!
WHAT ARE YOU DOING?
HE COMES HERE TWO DAYS AFTER US?
IT IS NOT AN INNOCENT THING.
TRINA!

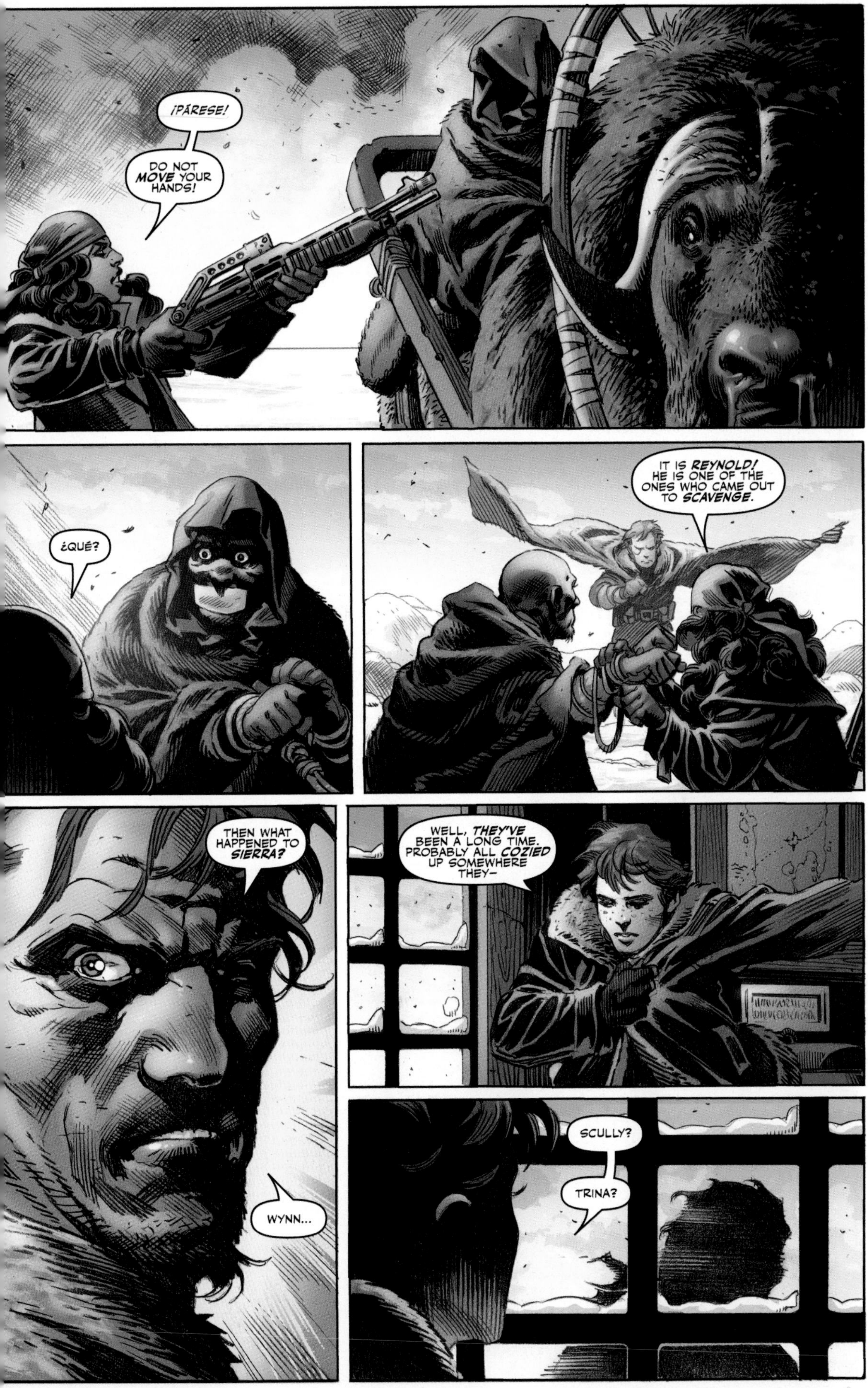

¡PÁRESE!
DO NOT MOVE YOUR HANDS!
¿QUÉ?
IT IS REYNOLD! HE IS ONE OF THE ONES WHO CAME OUT TO SCAVENGE.
THEN WHAT HAPPENED TO SIERRA?
WYNN...
WELL, THEY'VE BEEN A LONG TIME. PROBABLY ALL COZIED UP SOMEWHERE THEY–
SCULLY?
TRINA?

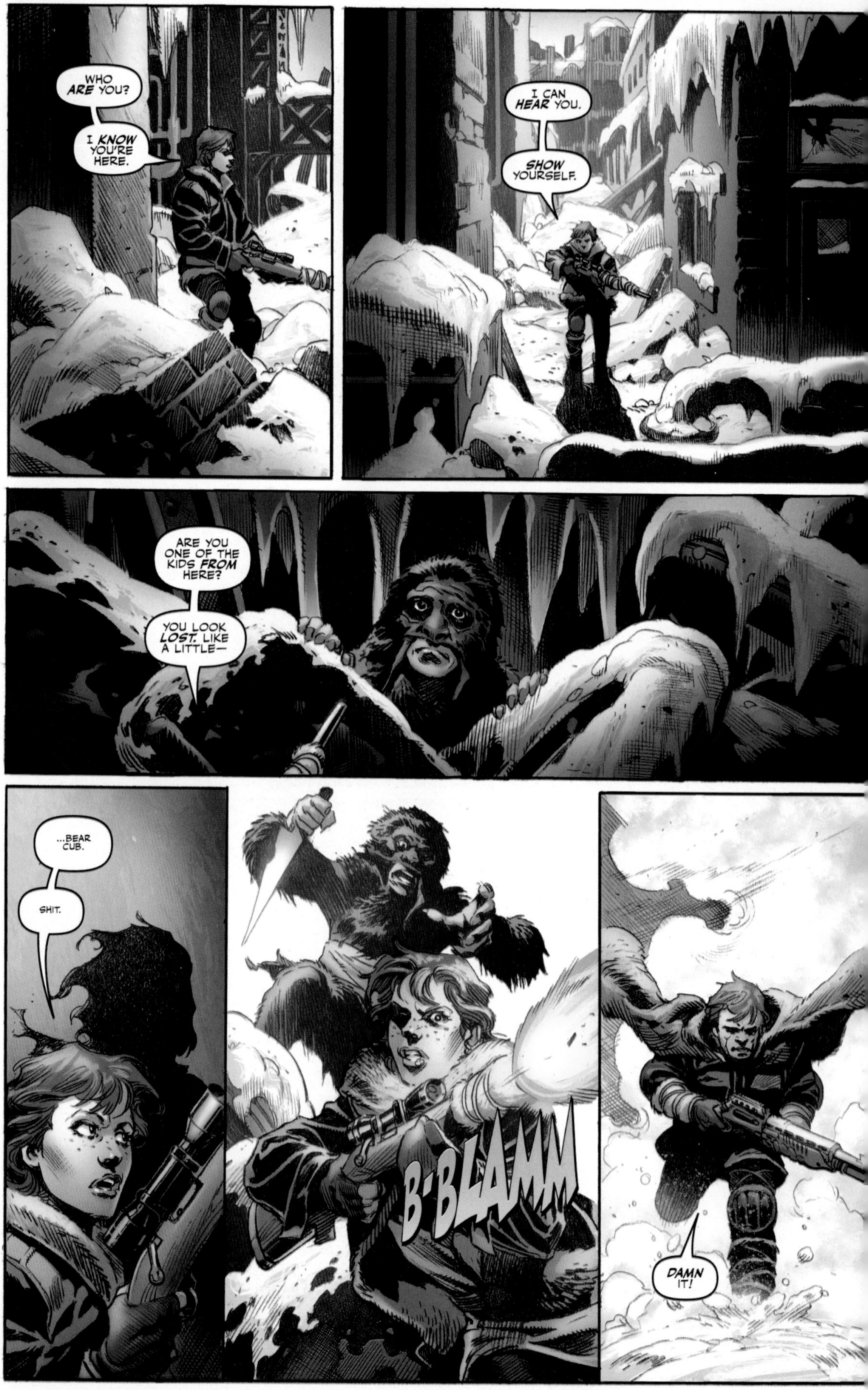
WHO ARE YOU?
I KNOW YOU'RE HERE.
I CAN HEAR YOU.
SHOW YOURSELF.
ARE YOU ONE OF THE KIDS FROM HERE?
YOU LOOK LOST. LIKE A LITTLE—
...BEAR CUB.
SHIT.
B-BLAMM
DAMN IT!

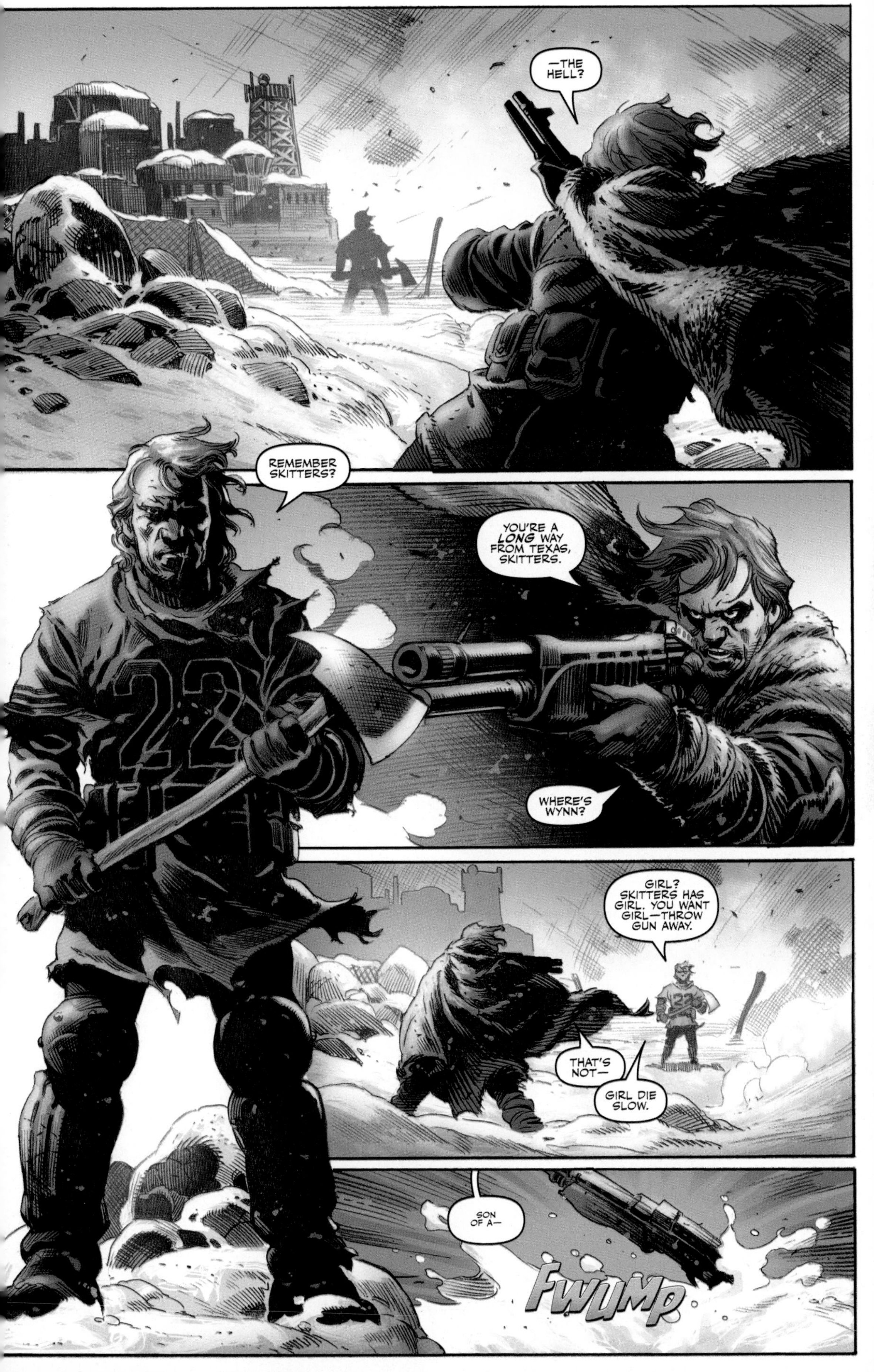
—THE HELL?
REMEMBER SKITTERS?
YOU'RE A LONG WAY FROM TEXAS, SKITTERS.
WHERE'S WYNN?
GIRL? SKITTERS HAS GIRL. YOU WANT GIRL—THROW GUN AWAY.
THAT'S NOT—
GIRL DIE SLOW.
SON OF A—
FWUMP

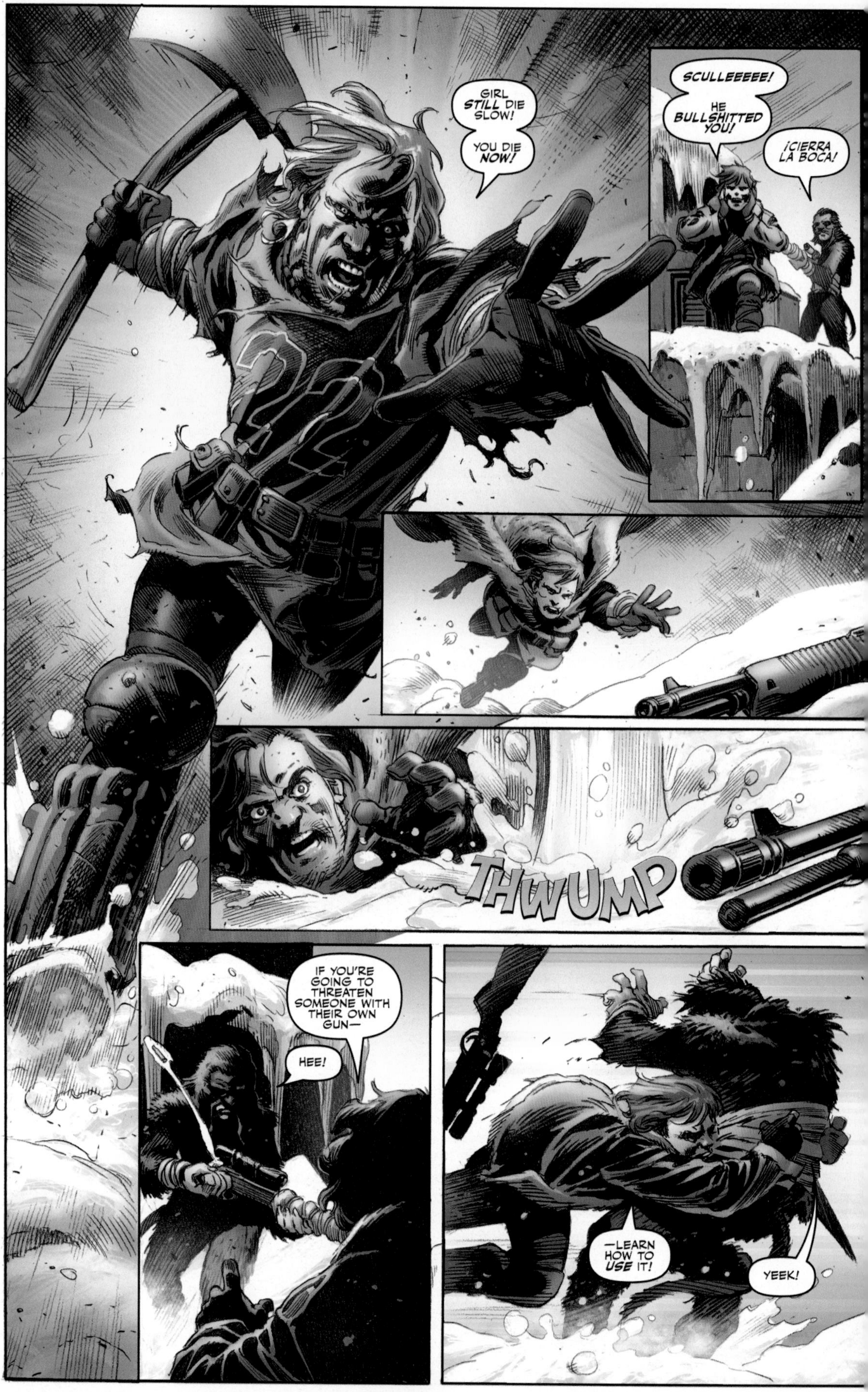
GIRL STILL DIE SLOW!
YOU DIE NOW!
SCULLEEEEE!
HE BULLSHITTED YOU!
¡CIERRA LA BOCA!
THWUMP
IF YOU'RE GOING TO THREATEN SOMEONE WITH THEIR OWN GUN—
HEE!
—LEARN HOW TO USE IT!
YEEK!

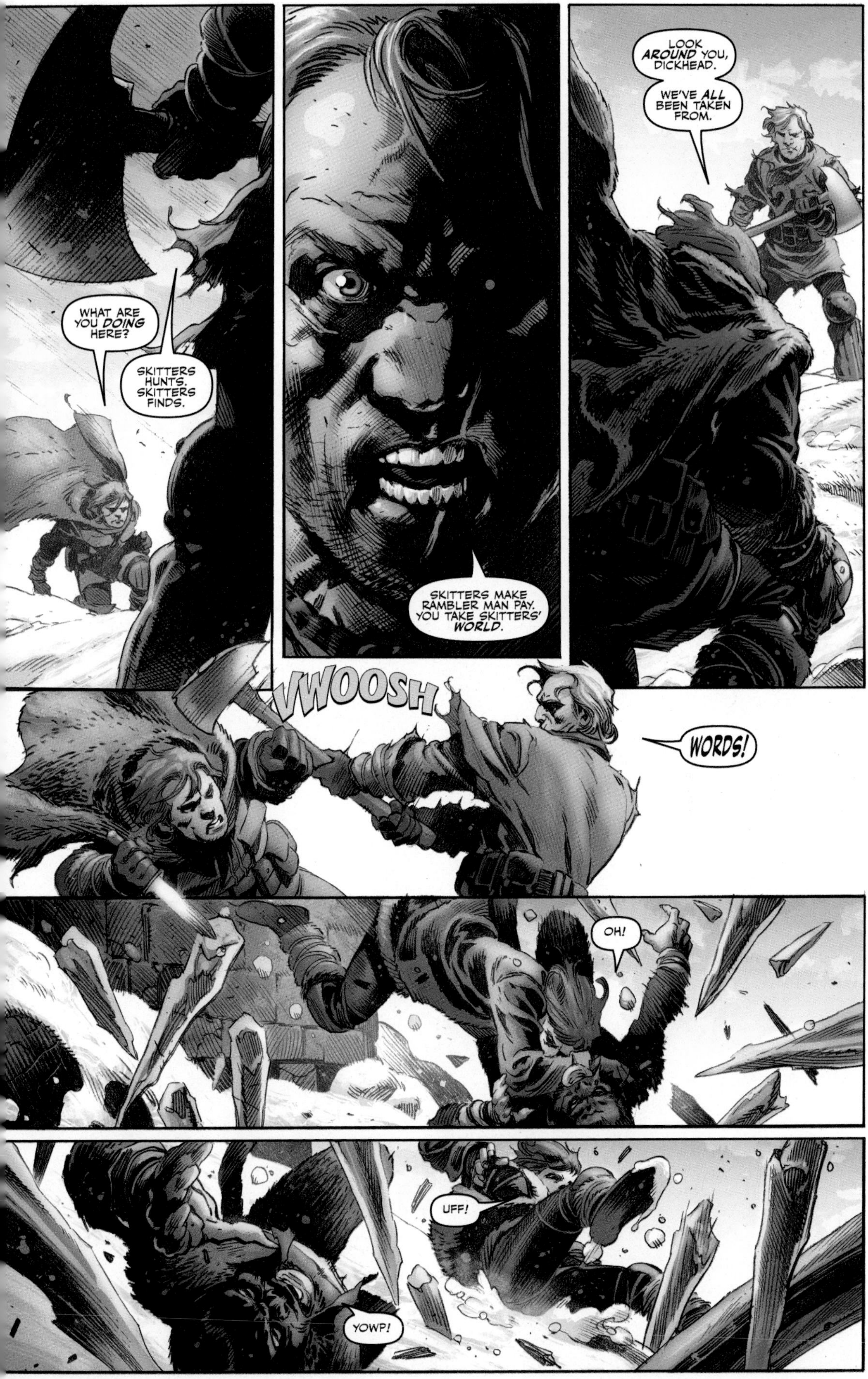
WHAT ARE YOU DOING HERE?
SKITTERS HUNTS. SKITTERS FINDS.
SKITTERS MAKE RAMBLER MAN PAY. YOU TAKE SKITTERS' WORLD.
LOOK AROUND YOU, DICKHEAD.
WE'VE ALL BEEN TAKEN FROM.
VWOOSH
WORDS!
OH!
UFF!
YOWP!

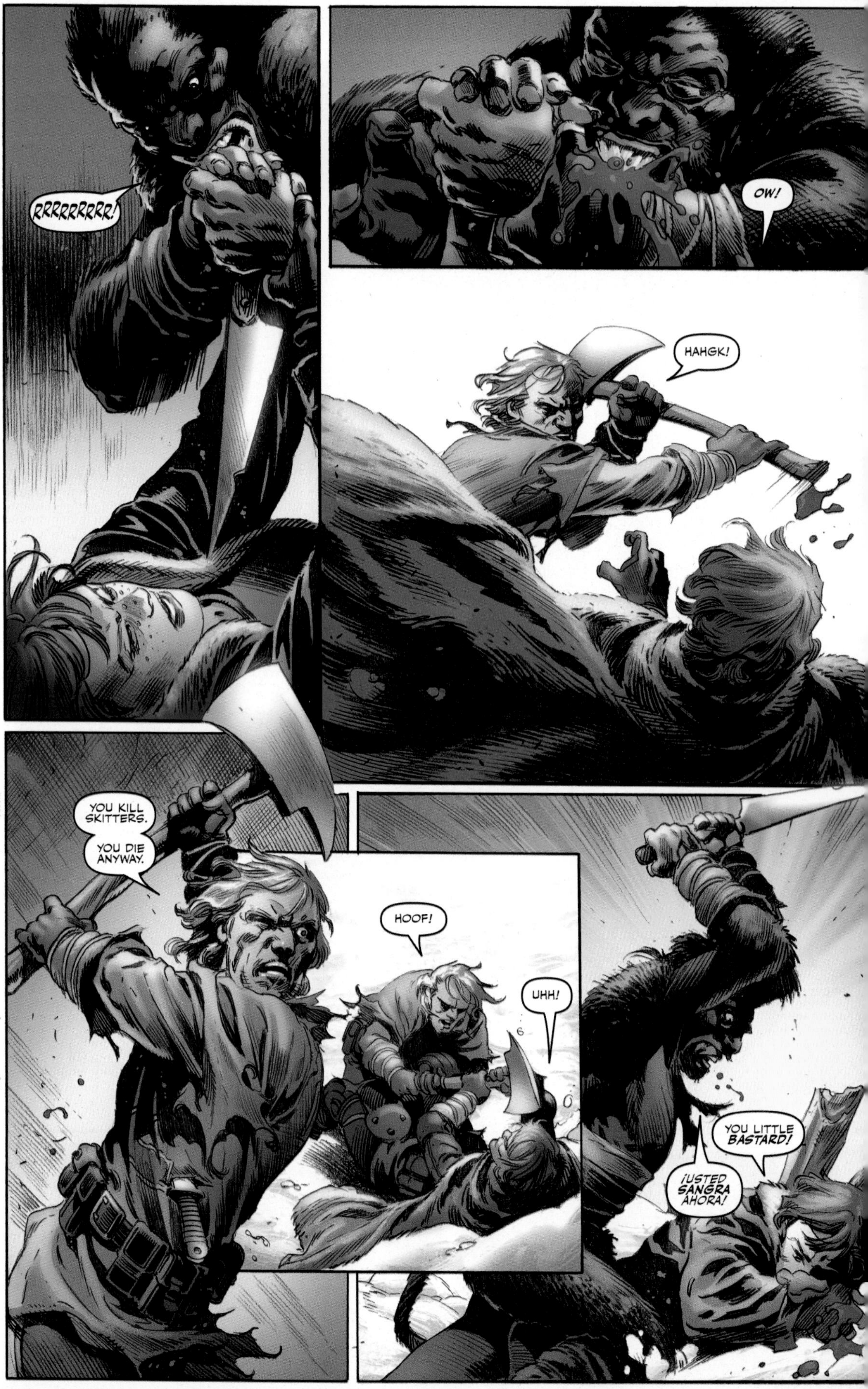
RRRRRRRRR!
OW!
HAHGK!
YOU KILL SKITTERS.
YOU DIE ANYWAY.
HOOF!
UHH!
YOU LITTLE BASTARD!
¡USTED SANGRA AHORA!

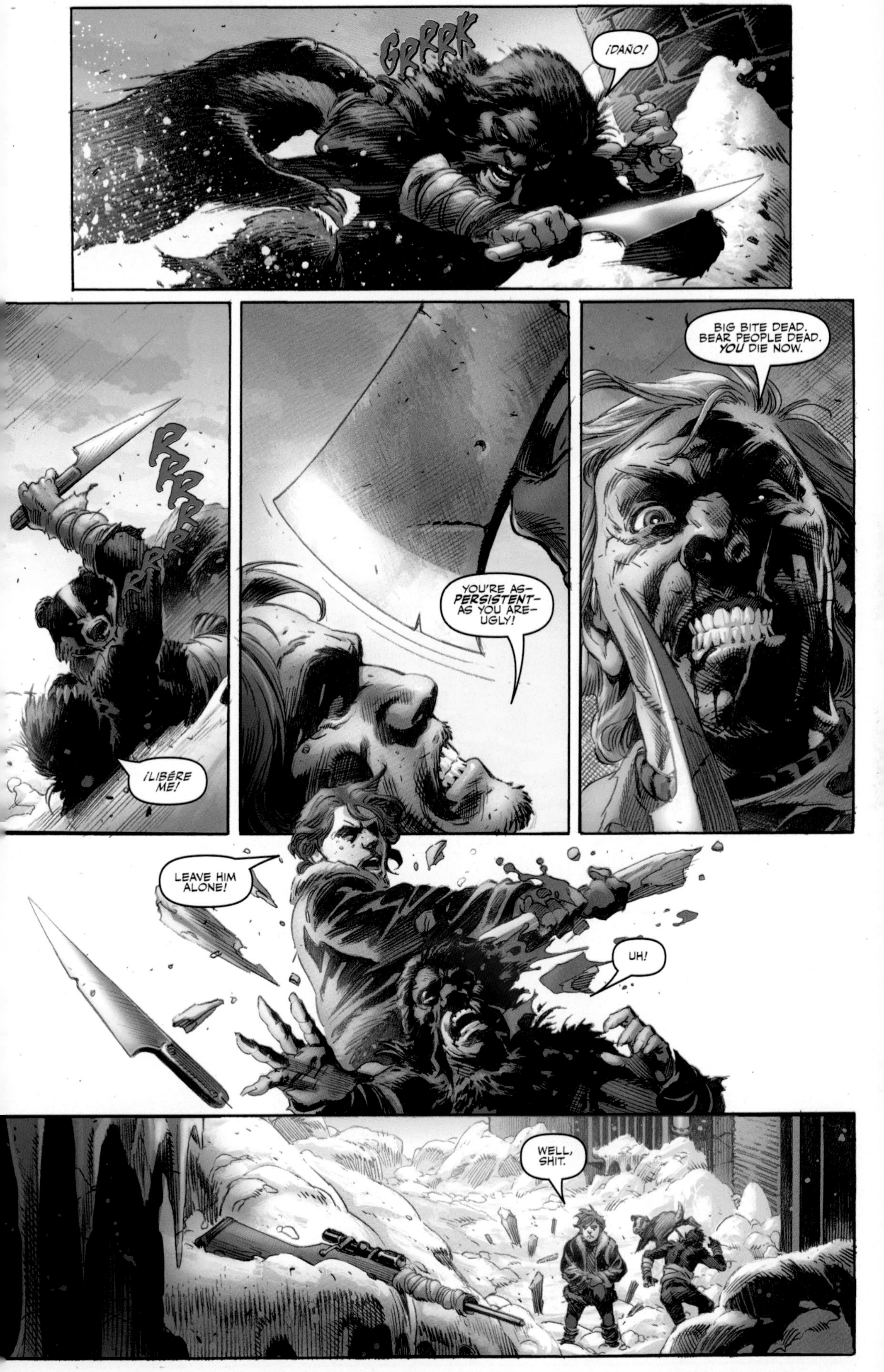
GRRRK
¡DAÑO!
RRRRRRR
¡LIBÉRE ME!
YOU'RE AS-PERSISTENT-AS YOU ARE-UGLY!
BIG BITE DEAD. BEAR PEOPLE DEAD. YOU DIE NOW.
LEAVE HIM ALONE!
UH!
WELL, SHIT.

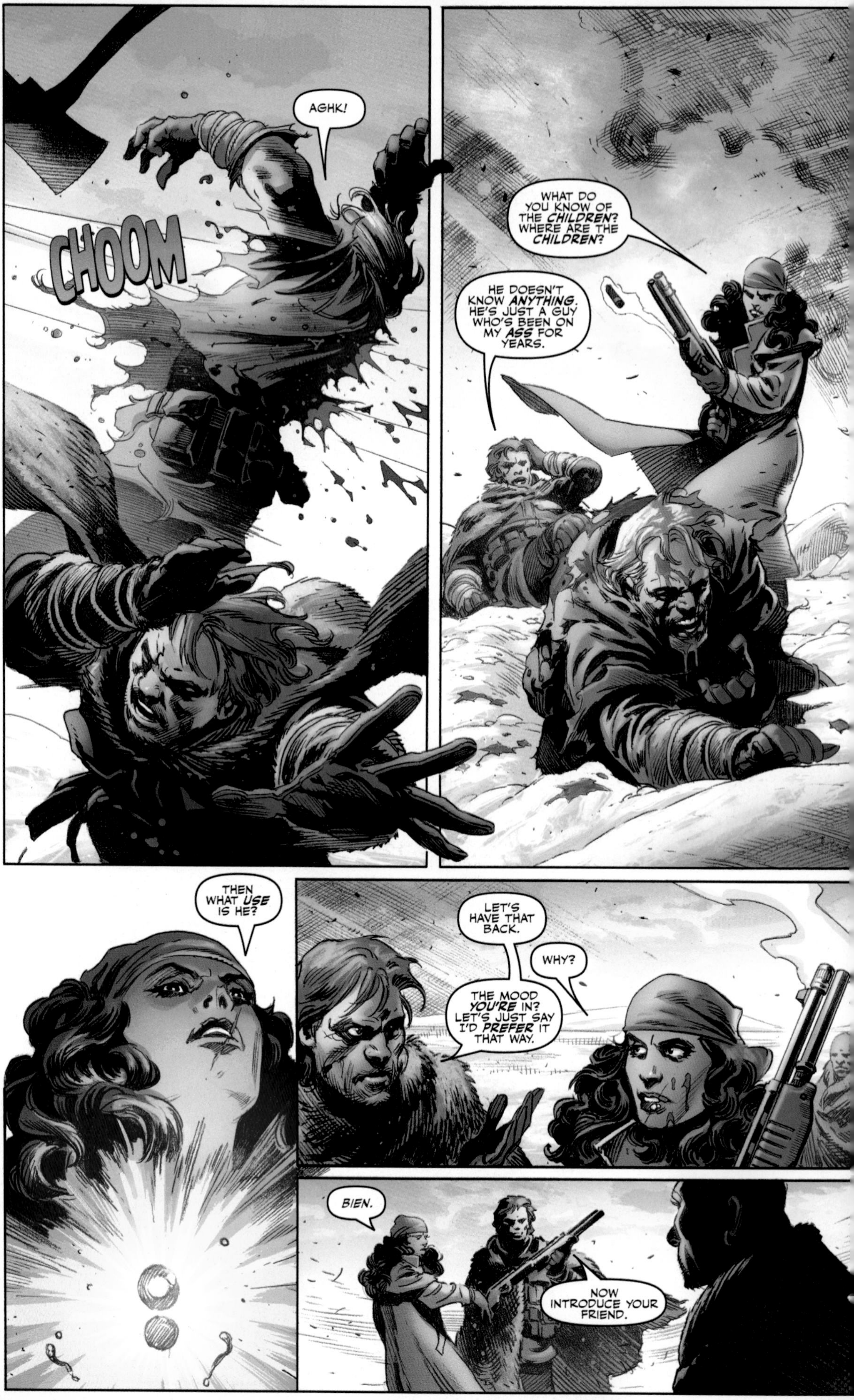
AGHK!
CHOOM
WHAT DO YOU KNOW OF THE *CHILDREN*? WHERE ARE THE *CHILDREN*?
HE DOESN'T KNOW *ANYTHING*. HE'S JUST A GUY WHO'S BEEN ON MY *ASS* FOR YEARS.
THEN WHAT *USE* IS HE?
LET'S HAVE THAT BACK.
WHY?
THE MOOD *YOU'RE* IN? LET'S JUST SAY I'D *PREFER* IT THAT WAY.
BIEN.
NOW INTRODUCE YOUR FRIEND.

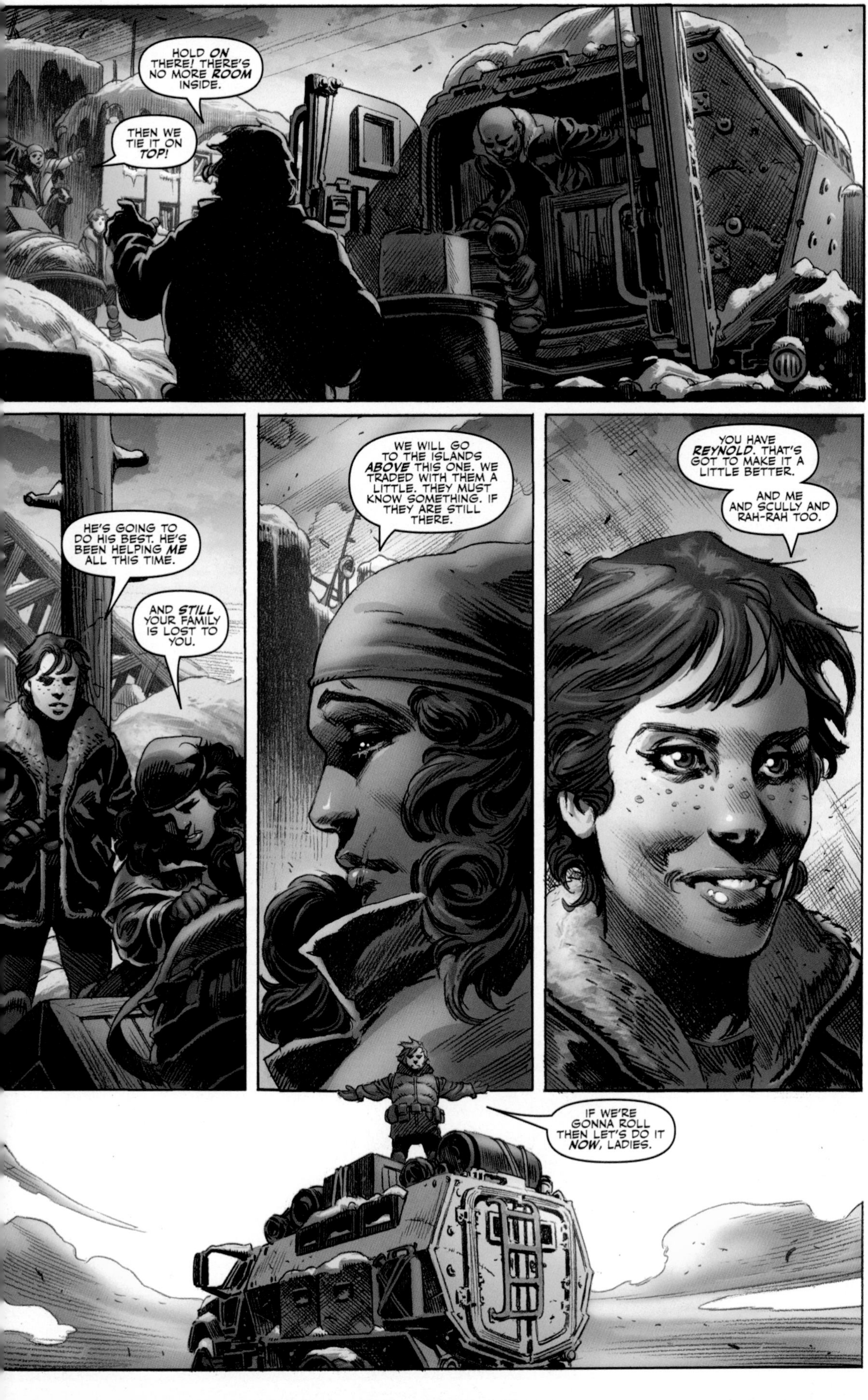
HOLD ON THERE! THERE'S NO MORE ROOM INSIDE.
THEN WE TIE IT ON TOP!
HE'S GOING TO DO HIS BEST. HE'S BEEN HELPING ME ALL THIS TIME.
AND STILL YOUR FAMILY IS LOST TO YOU.
WE WILL GO TO THE ISLANDS ABOVE THIS ONE. WE TRADED WITH THEM A LITTLE. THEY MUST KNOW SOMETHING. IF THEY ARE STILL THERE.
YOU HAVE REYNOLD. THAT'S GOT TO MAKE IT A LITTLE BETTER.
AND ME AND SCULLY AND RAH-RAH TOO.
IF WE'RE GONNA ROLL THEN LET'S DO IT NOW, LADIES.

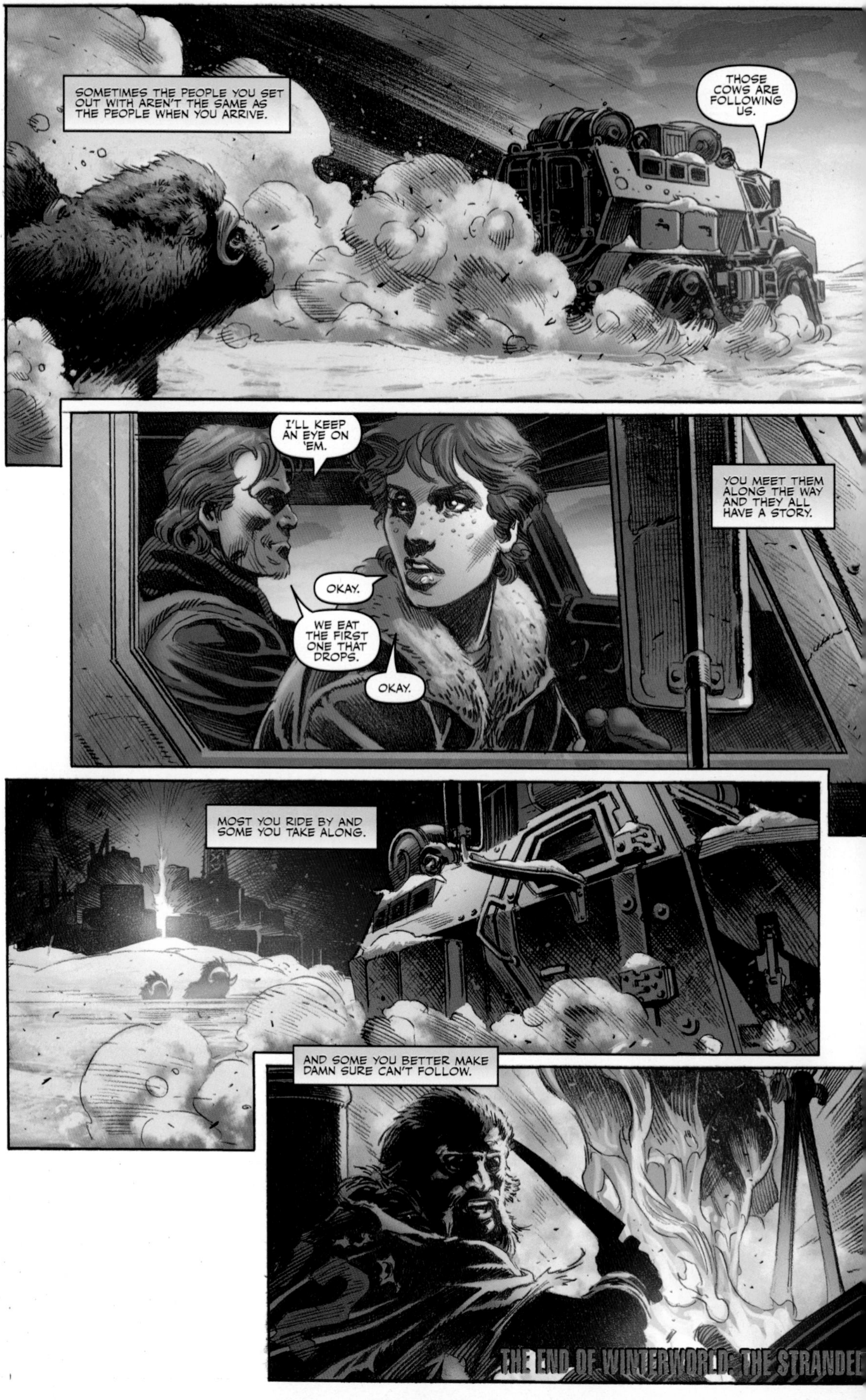
SOMETIMES THE PEOPLE YOU SET OUT WITH AREN'T THE SAME AS THE PEOPLE WHEN YOU ARRIVE.
THOSE COWS ARE FOLLOWING US.
I'LL KEEP AN EYE ON 'EM.
YOU MEET THEM ALONG THE WAY AND THEY ALL HAVE A STORY.
OKAY.
WE EAT THE FIRST ONE THAT DROPS.
OKAY.
MOST YOU RIDE BY AND SOME YOU TAKE ALONG.
AND SOME YOU BETTER MAKE DAMN SURE CAN'T FOLLOW.
THE END OF WINTERWORLD: THE STRANDED

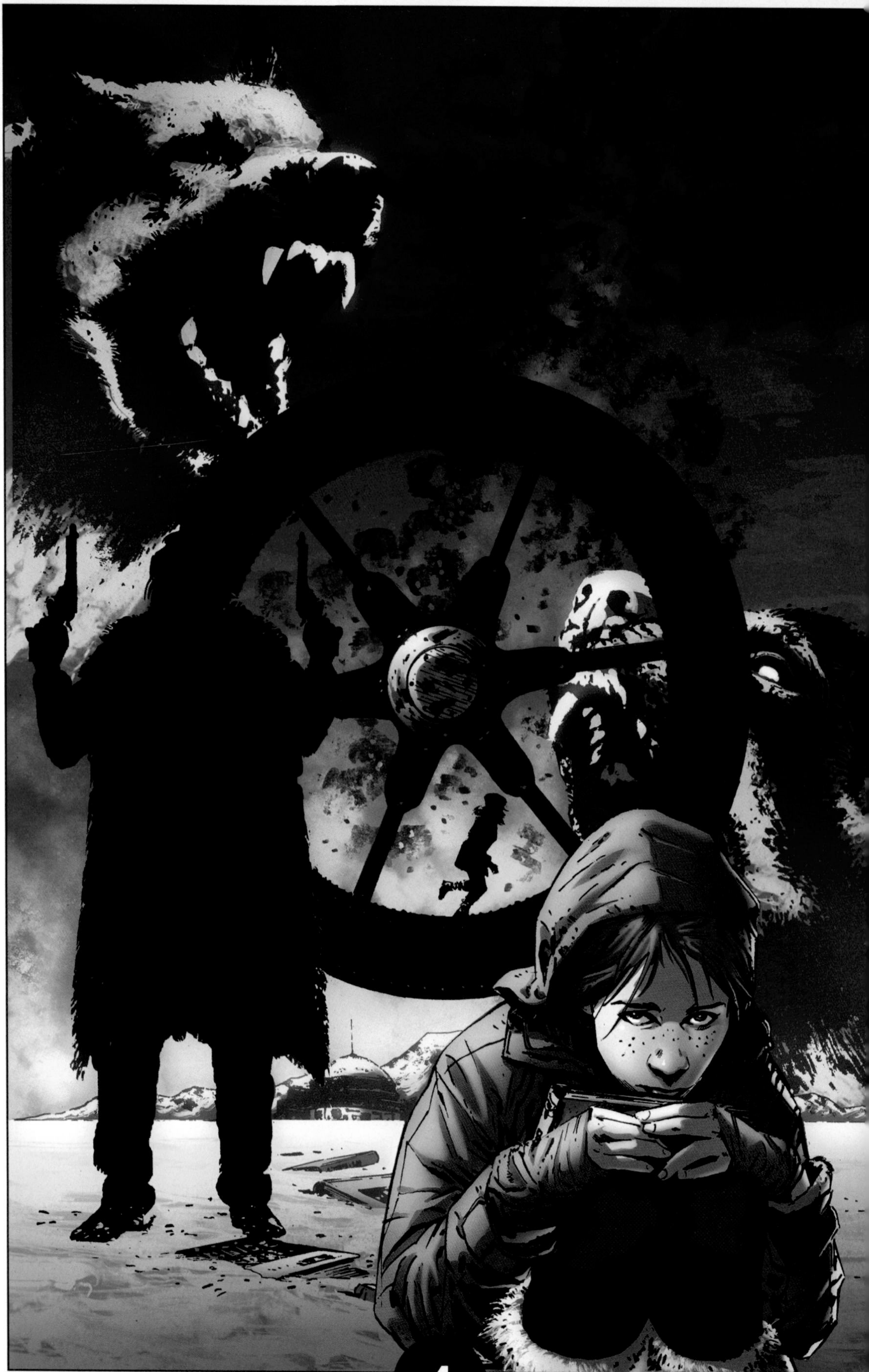

4

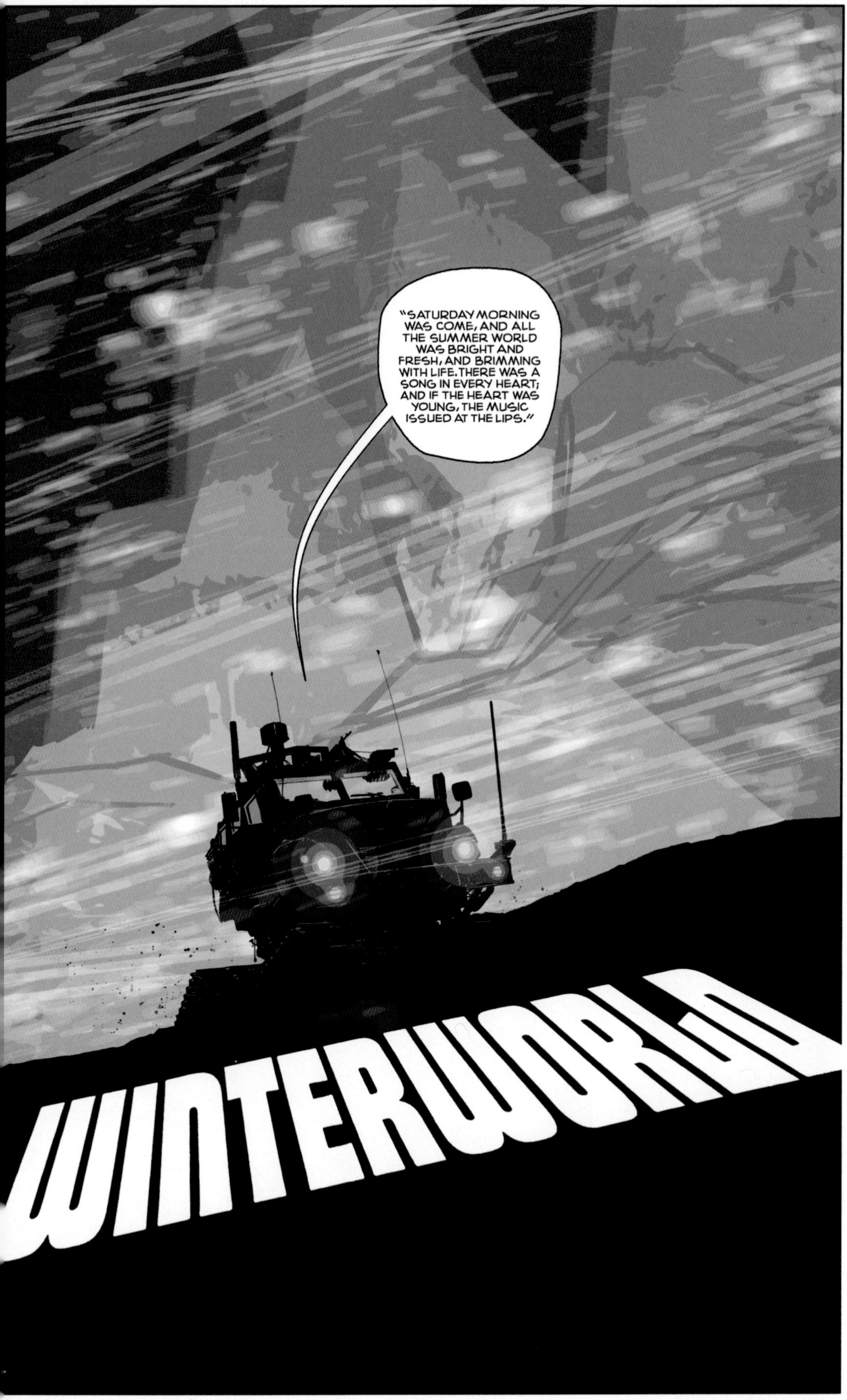
"SATURDAY MORNING WAS COME, AND ALL THE SUMMER WORLD WAS BRIGHT AND FRESH, AND BRIMMING WITH LIFE. THERE WAS A SONG IN EVERY HEART; AND IF THE HEART WAS YOUNG, THE MUSIC ISSUED AT THE LIPS."
WINTERWORLD

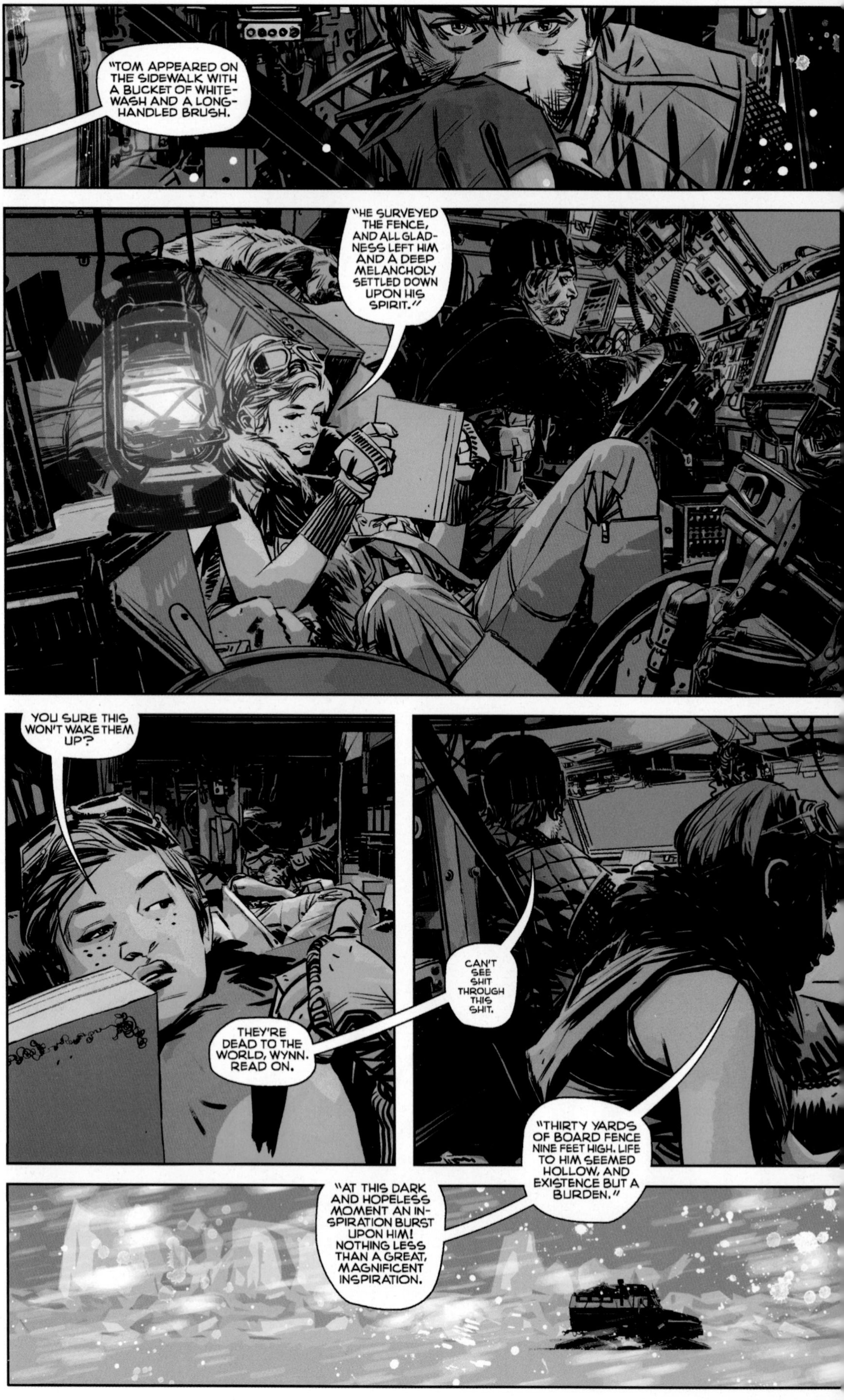
"TOM APPEARED ON THE SIDEWALK WITH A BUCKET OF WHITE-WASH AND A LONG-HANDLED BRUSH.
"HE SURVEYED THE FENCE, AND ALL GLADNESS LEFT HIM AND A DEEP MELANCHOLY SETTLED DOWN UPON HIS SPIRIT."
YOU SURE THIS WON'T WAKE THEM UP?
THEY'RE DEAD TO THE WORLD, WYNN. READ ON.
CAN'T SEE SHIT THROUGH THIS SHIT.
"THIRTY YARDS OF BOARD FENCE NINE FEET HIGH. LIFE TO HIM SEEMED HOLLOW, AND EXISTENCE BUT A BURDEN."
"AT THIS DARK AND HOPELESS MOMENT AN IN-SPIRATION BURST UPON HIM! NOTHING LESS THAN A GREAT, MAGNIFICENT INSPIRATION.

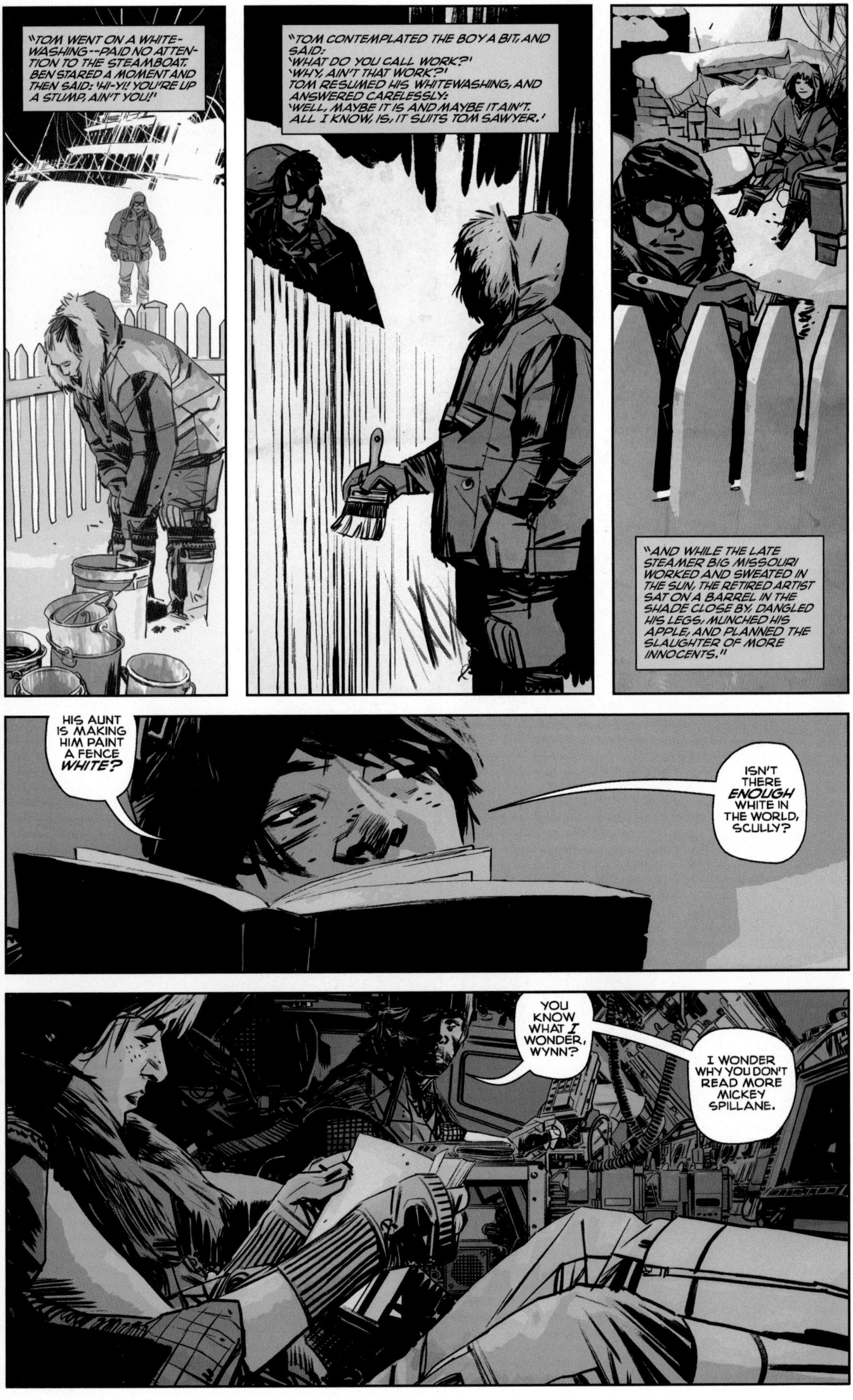
"TOM WENT ON A WHITE-WASHING--PAID NO ATTENTION TO THE STEAMBOAT. BEN STARED A MOMENT AND THEN SAID: 'HI-YI! YOU'RE UP A STUMP, AIN'T YOU!'
"TOM CONTEMPLATED THE BOY A BIT, AND SAID: 'WHAT DO YOU CALL WORK?' 'WHY, AIN'T THAT WORK?' TOM RESUMED HIS WHITEWASHING, AND ANSWERED CARELESSLY: 'WELL, MAYBE IT IS AND MAYBE IT AIN'T. ALL I KNOW, IS, IT SUITS TOM SAWYER.'
"AND WHILE THE LATE STEAMER BIG MISSOURI WORKED AND SWEATED IN THE SUN, THE RETIRED ARTIST SAT ON A BARREL IN THE SHADE CLOSE BY, DANGLED HIS LEGS, MUNCHED HIS APPLE, AND PLANNED THE SLAUGHTER OF MORE INNOCENTS."
HIS AUNT IS MAKING HIM PAINT A FENCE WHITE?
ISN'T THERE ENOUGH WHITE IN THE WORLD, SCULLY?
YOU KNOW WHAT I WONDER, WYNN?
I WONDER WHY YOU DON'T READ MORE MICKEY SPILLANE.

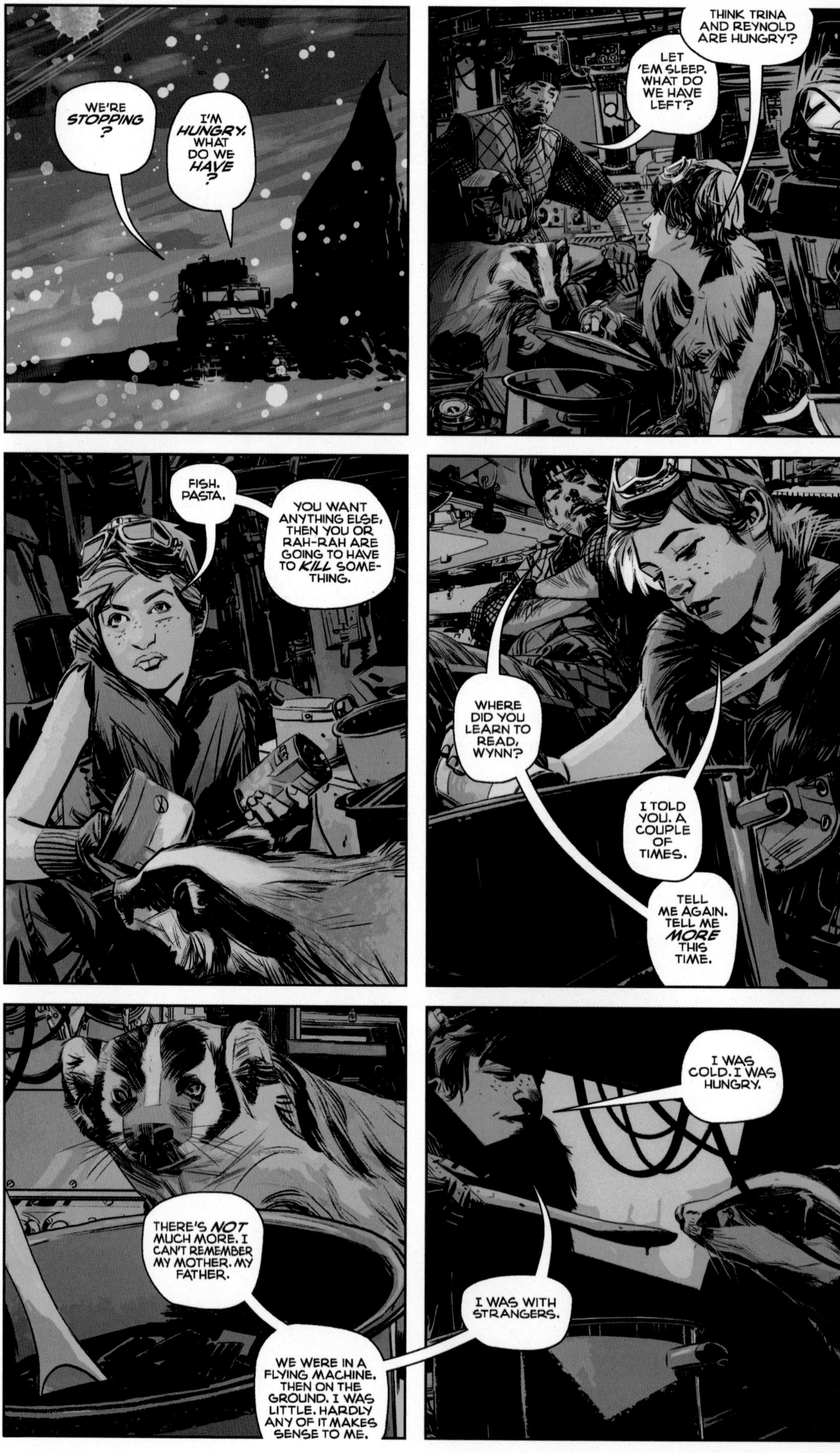
WE'RE STOPPING?
I'M HUNGRY. WHAT DO WE HAVE?
THINK TRINA AND REYNOLD ARE HUNGRY?
LET 'EM SLEEP. WHAT DO WE HAVE LEFT?
FISH. PASTA.
YOU WANT ANYTHING ELSE, THEN YOU OR RAH-RAH ARE GOING TO HAVE TO KILL SOMETHING.
WHERE DID YOU LEARN TO READ, WYNN?
I TOLD YOU. A COUPLE OF TIMES.
TELL ME AGAIN. TELL ME MORE THIS TIME.
THERE'S NOT MUCH MORE. I CAN'T REMEMBER MY MOTHER. MY FATHER.
WE WERE IN A FLYING MACHINE. THEN ON THE GROUND. I WAS LITTLE. HARDLY ANY OF IT MAKES SENSE TO ME.
I WAS WITH STRANGERS.
I WAS COLD. I WAS HUNGRY.

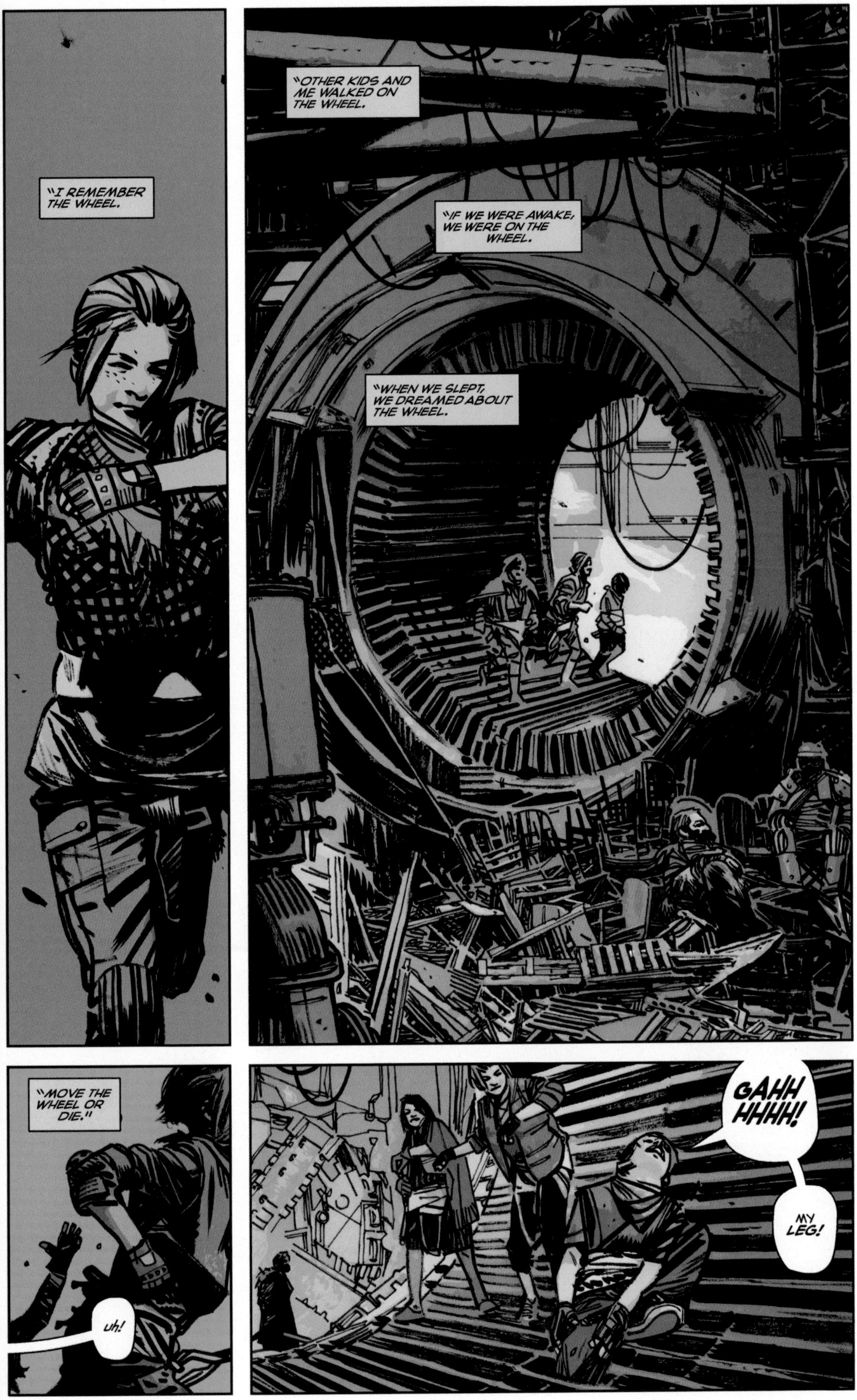
"I REMEMBER THE WHEEL.
"OTHER KIDS AND ME WALKED ON THE WHEEL.
"IF WE WERE AWAKE, WE WERE ON THE WHEEL.
"WHEN WE SLEPT, WE DREAMED ABOUT THE WHEEL.
"MOVE THE WHEEL OR DIE."
uh!
GAHH HHHH!
MY LEG!

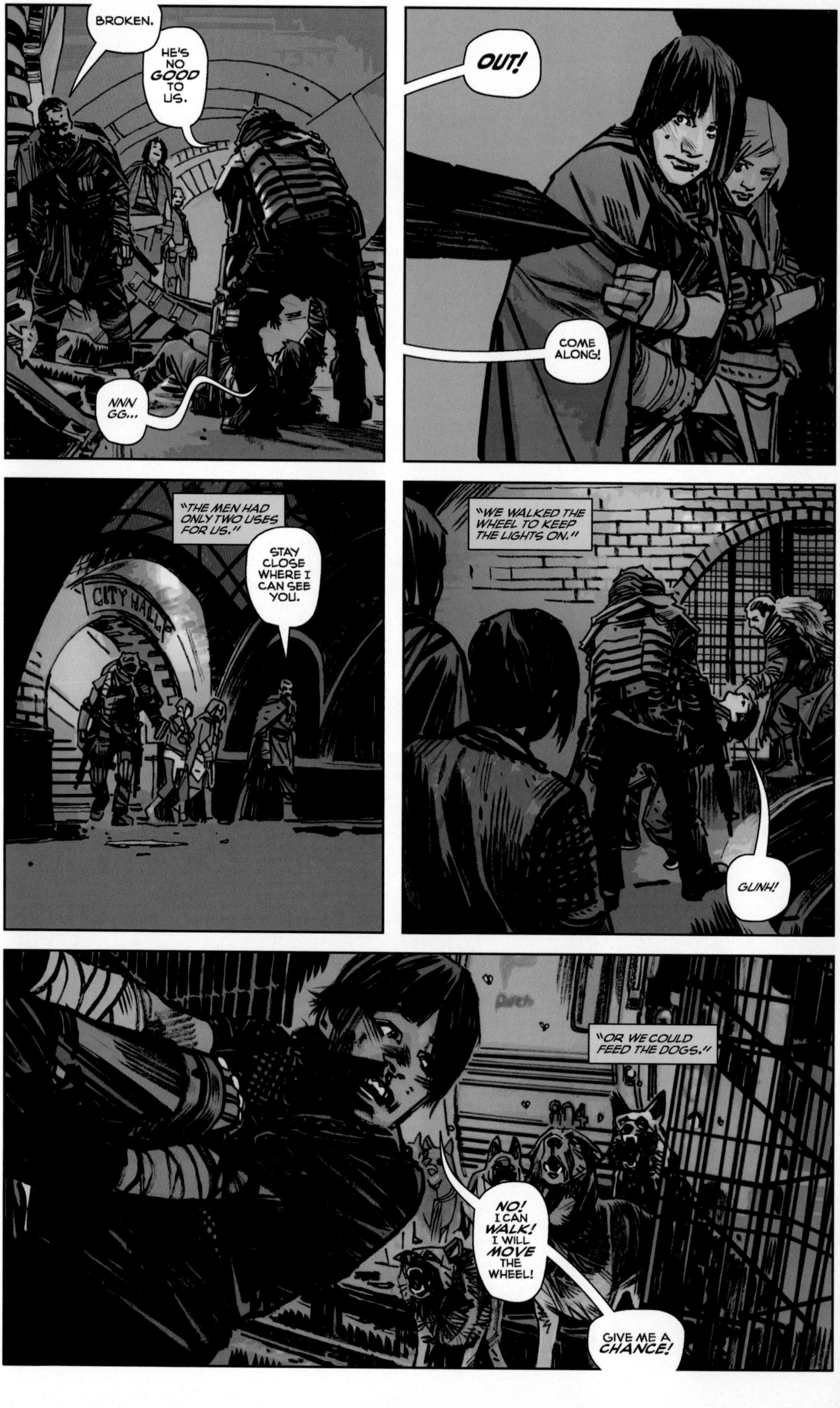
BROKEN.
HE'S NO GOOD TO US.
NNN GG...
OUT!
COME ALONG!
"THE MEN HAD ONLY TWO USES FOR US."
STAY CLOSE WHERE I CAN SEE YOU.
CITY HALL
"WE WALKED THE WHEEL TO KEEP THE LIGHTS ON."
GUNH!
"OR WE COULD FEED THE DOGS."
NO! I CAN WALK! I WILL MOVE THE WHEEL!
GIVE ME A CHANCE!

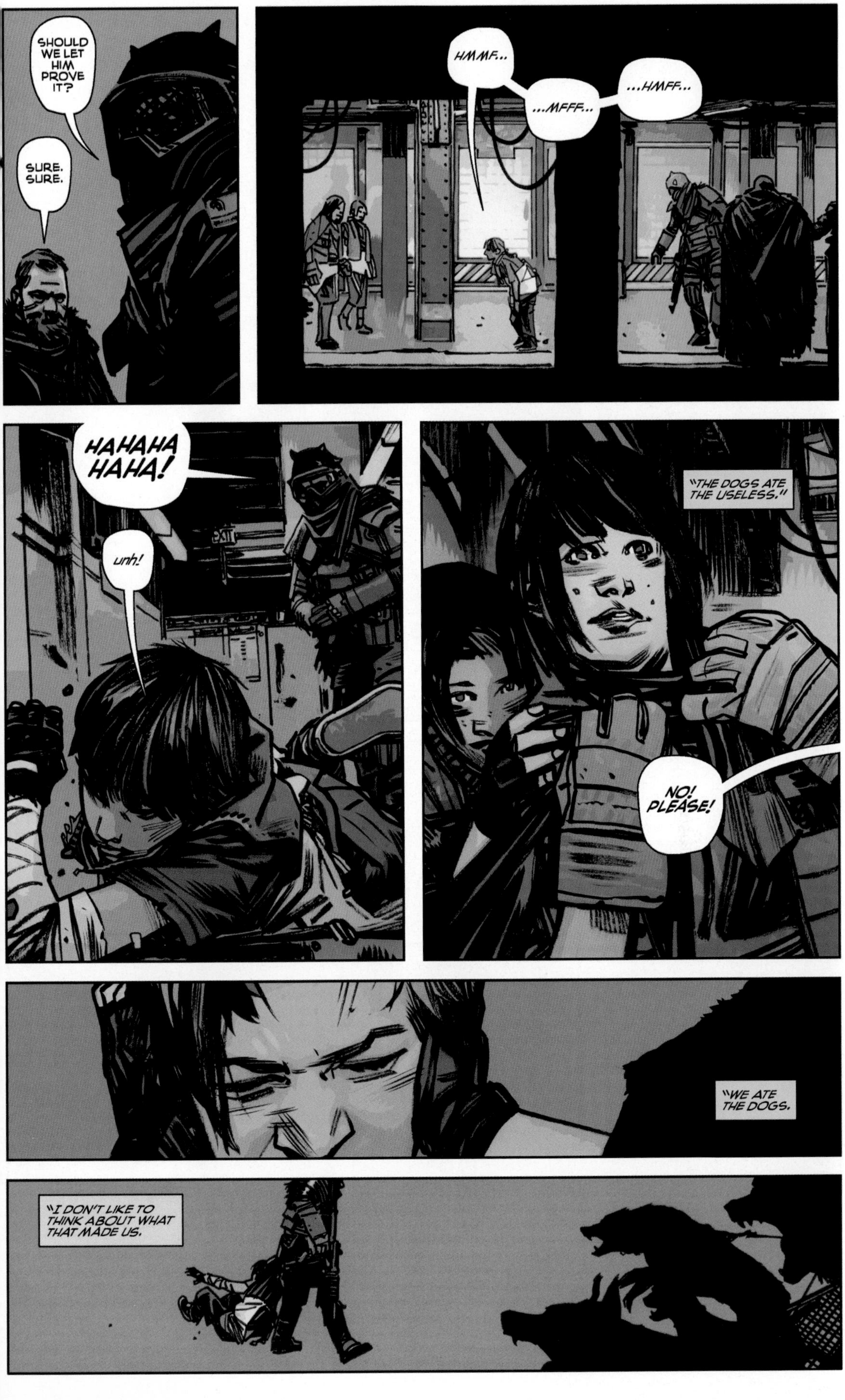
SHOULD WE LET HIM PROVE IT?
SURE. SURE.
HMMF...
...MFFF...
...HMFF...
HAHAHA HAHA!
unh!
"THE DOGS ATE THE USELESS."
NO! PLEASE!
"WE ATE THE DOGS.
"I DON'T LIKE TO THINK ABOUT WHAT THAT MADE US.

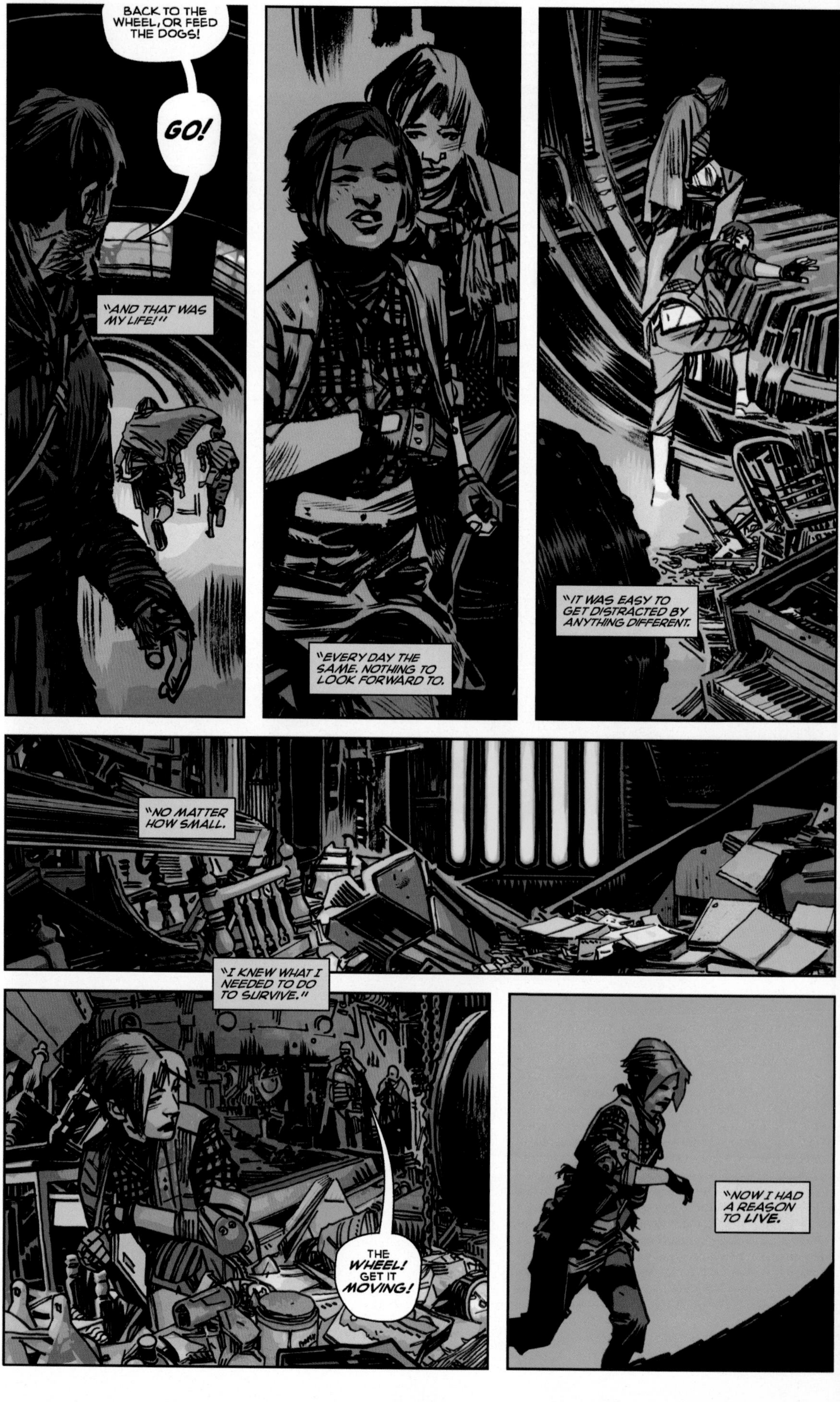
BACK TO THE WHEEL, OR FEED THE DOGS!
GO!
"AND THAT WAS MY LIFE!"
"EVERY DAY THE SAME. NOTHING TO LOOK FORWARD TO.
"IT WAS EASY TO GET DISTRACTED BY ANYTHING DIFFERENT.
"NO MATTER HOW SMALL.
"I KNEW WHAT I NEEDED TO DO TO SURVIVE."
THE WHEEL! GET IT MOVING!
"NOW I HAD A REASON TO LIVE.

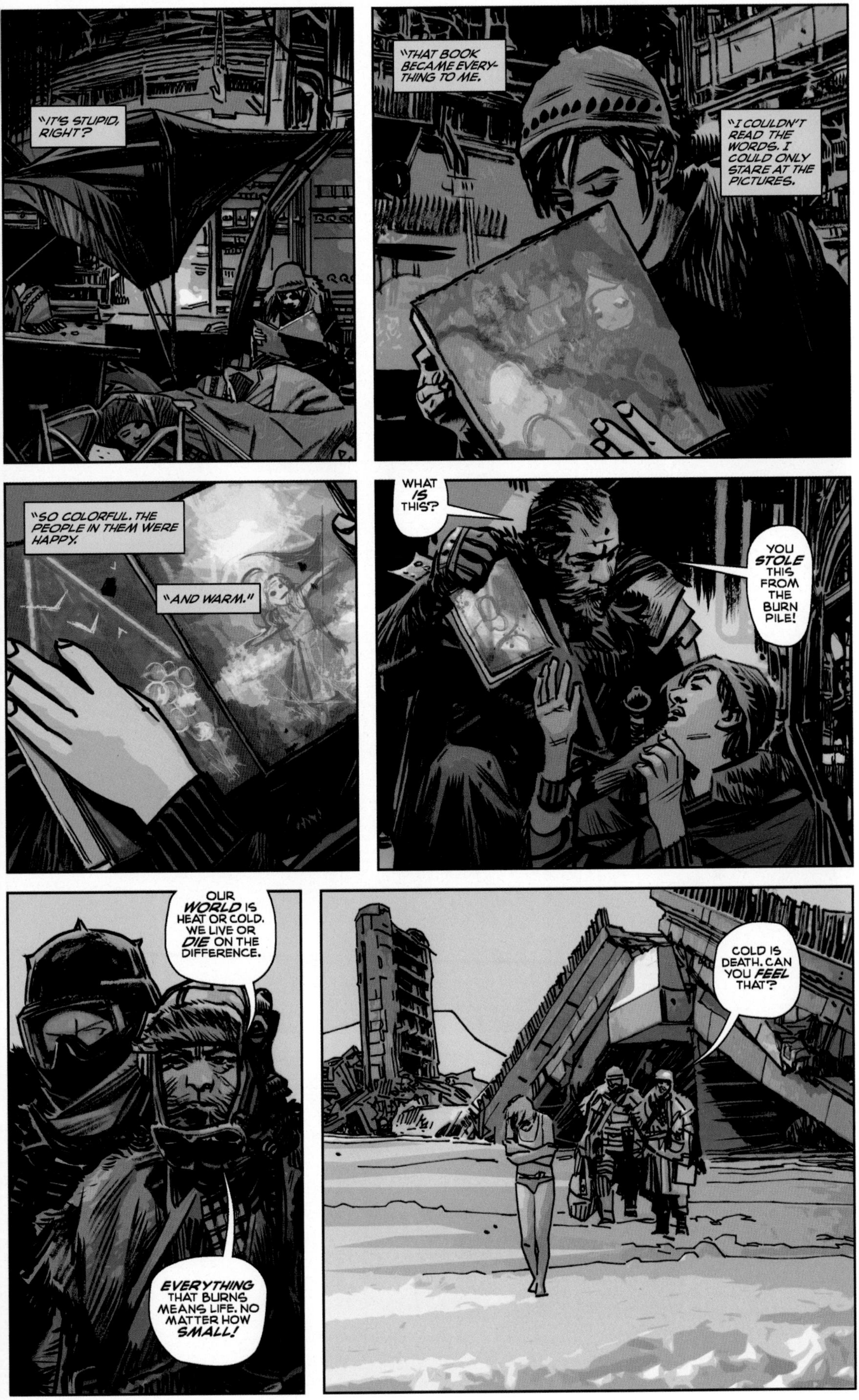
"IT'S STUPID, RIGHT?
"THAT BOOK BECAME EVERYTHING TO ME.
"I COULDN'T READ THE WORDS. I COULD ONLY STARE AT THE PICTURES.
"SO COLORFUL. THE PEOPLE IN THEM WERE HAPPY.
"AND WARM."
WHAT IS THIS?
YOU STOLE THIS FROM THE BURN PILE!
OUR WORLD IS HEAT OR COLD. WE LIVE OR DIE ON THE DIFFERENCE.
EVERYTHING THAT BURNS MEANS LIFE. NO MATTER HOW SMALL!
COLD IS DEATH. CAN YOU FEEL THAT?

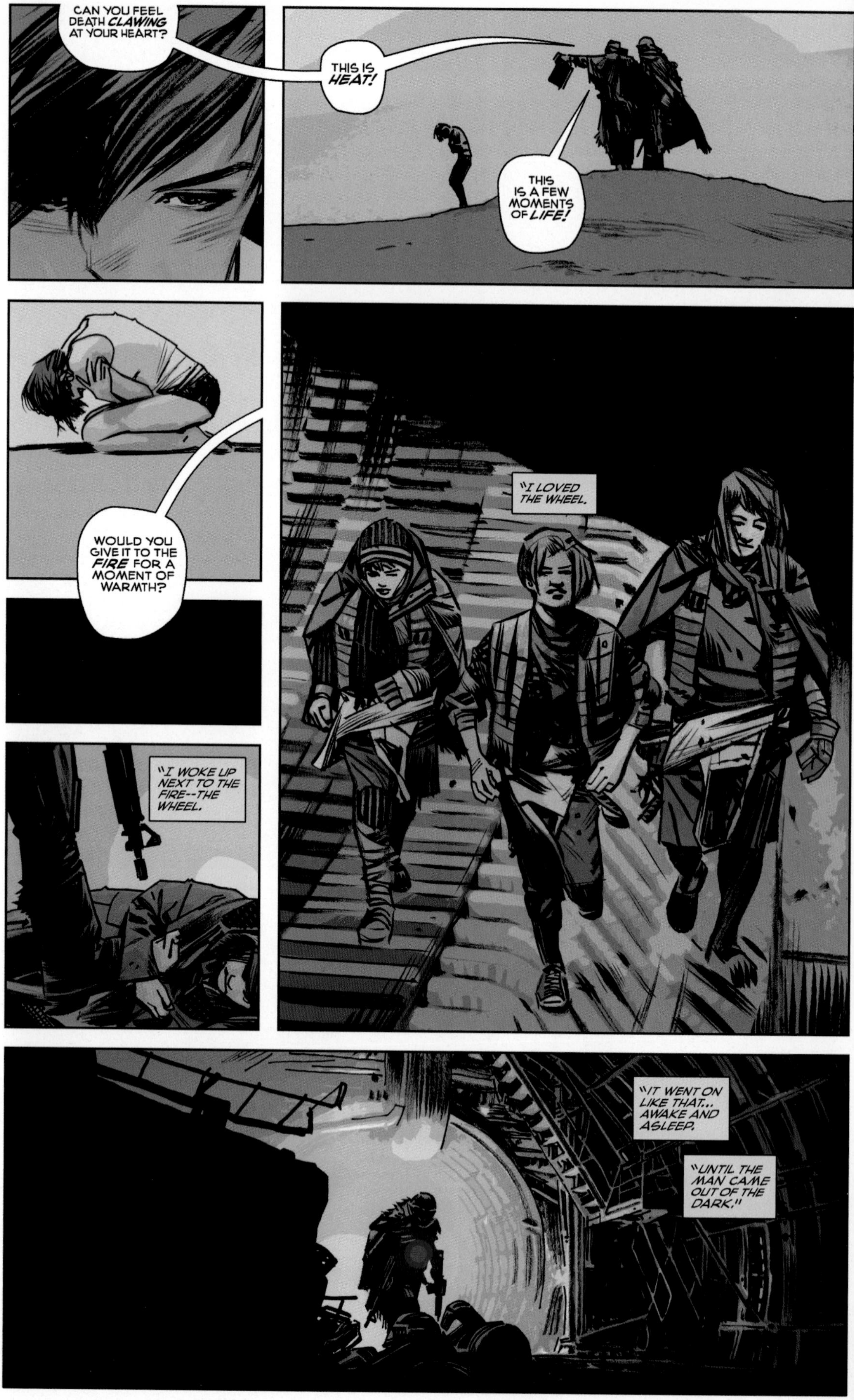

CAN YOU FEEL DEATH CLAWING AT YOUR HEART?
THIS IS HEAT!
THIS IS A FEW MOMENTS OF LIFE!
WOULD YOU GIVE IT TO THE FIRE FOR A MOMENT OF WARMTH?
"I LOVED THE WHEEL.
"I WOKE UP NEXT TO THE FIRE--THE WHEEL.
"IT WENT ON LIKE THAT... AWAKE AND ASLEEP.
"UNTIL THE MAN CAME OUT OF THE DARK."

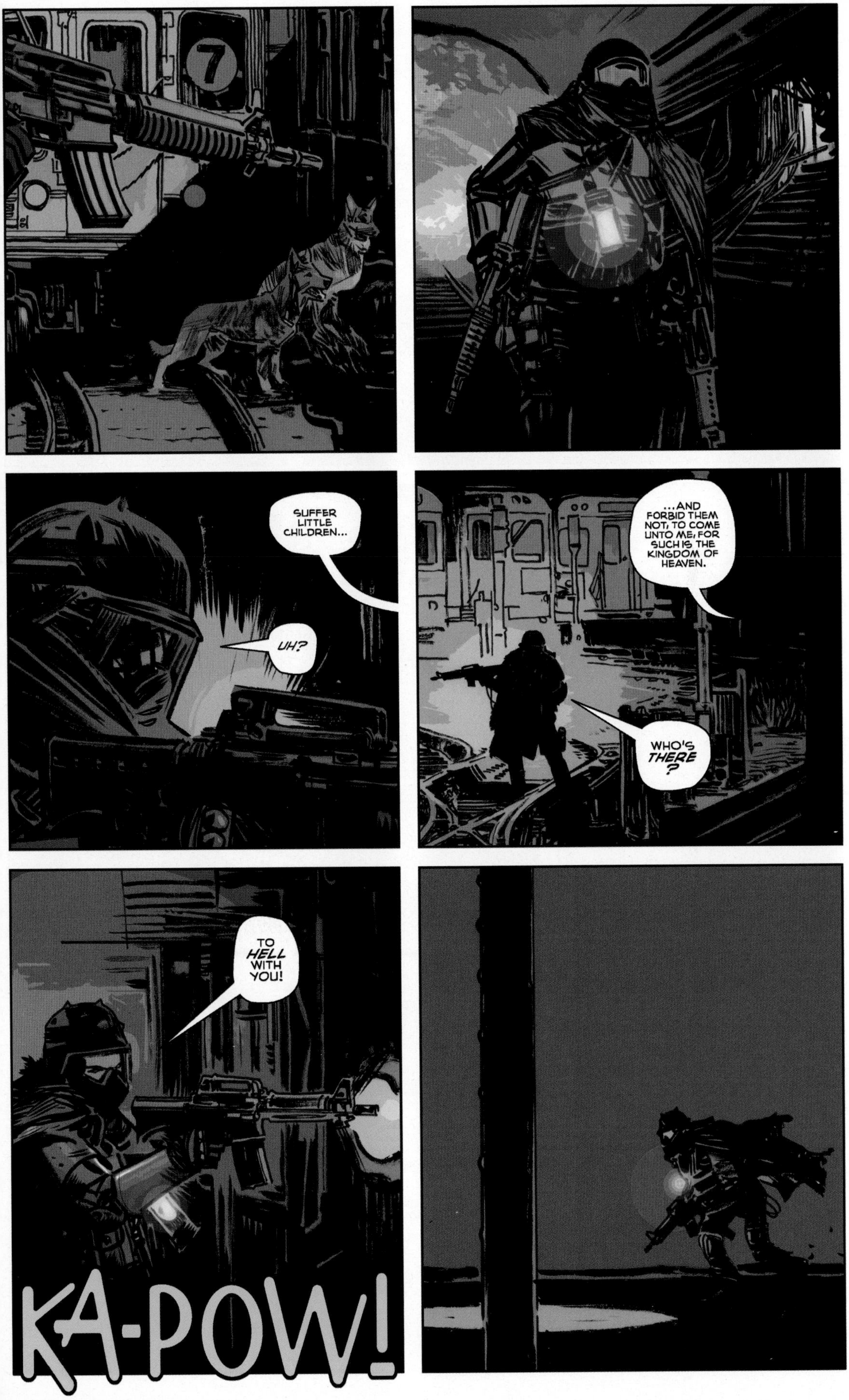
SUFFER LITTLE CHILDREN...
UH?
...AND FORBID THEM NOT, TO COME UNTO ME, FOR SUCH IS THE KINGDOM OF HEAVEN.
WHO'S THERE?
TO HELL WITH YOU!
KA-POW!

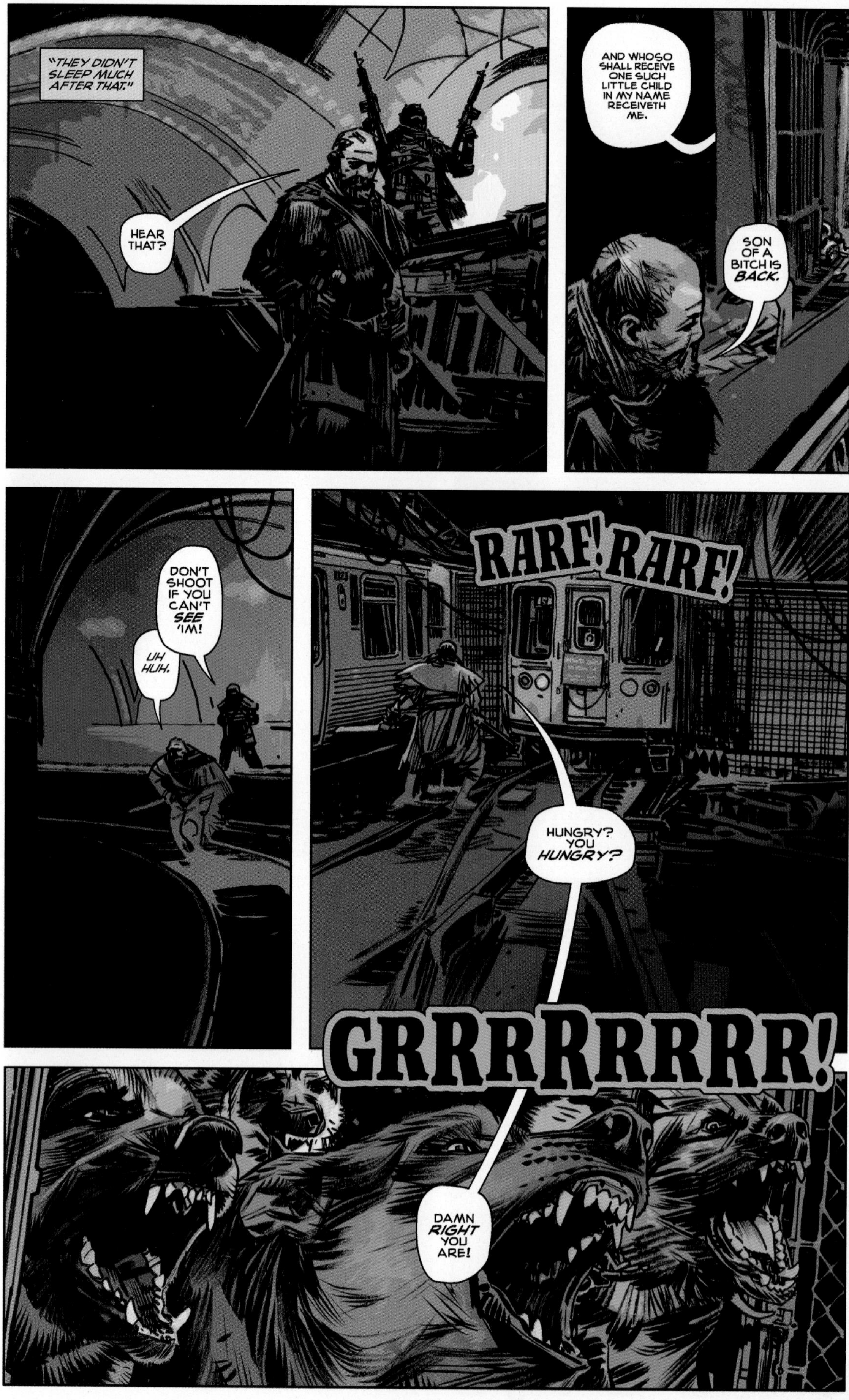
"THEY DIDN'T SLEEP MUCH AFTER THAT."
HEAR THAT?
AND WHOSO SHALL RECEIVE ONE SUCH LITTLE CHILD IN MY NAME RECEIVETH ME.
SON OF A BITCH IS BACK.
DON'T SHOOT IF YOU CAN'T SEE 'IM!
UH HUH.
RARF! RARF!
HUNGRY? YOU HUNGRY?
GRRRRRRRR!
DAMN RIGHT YOU ARE!

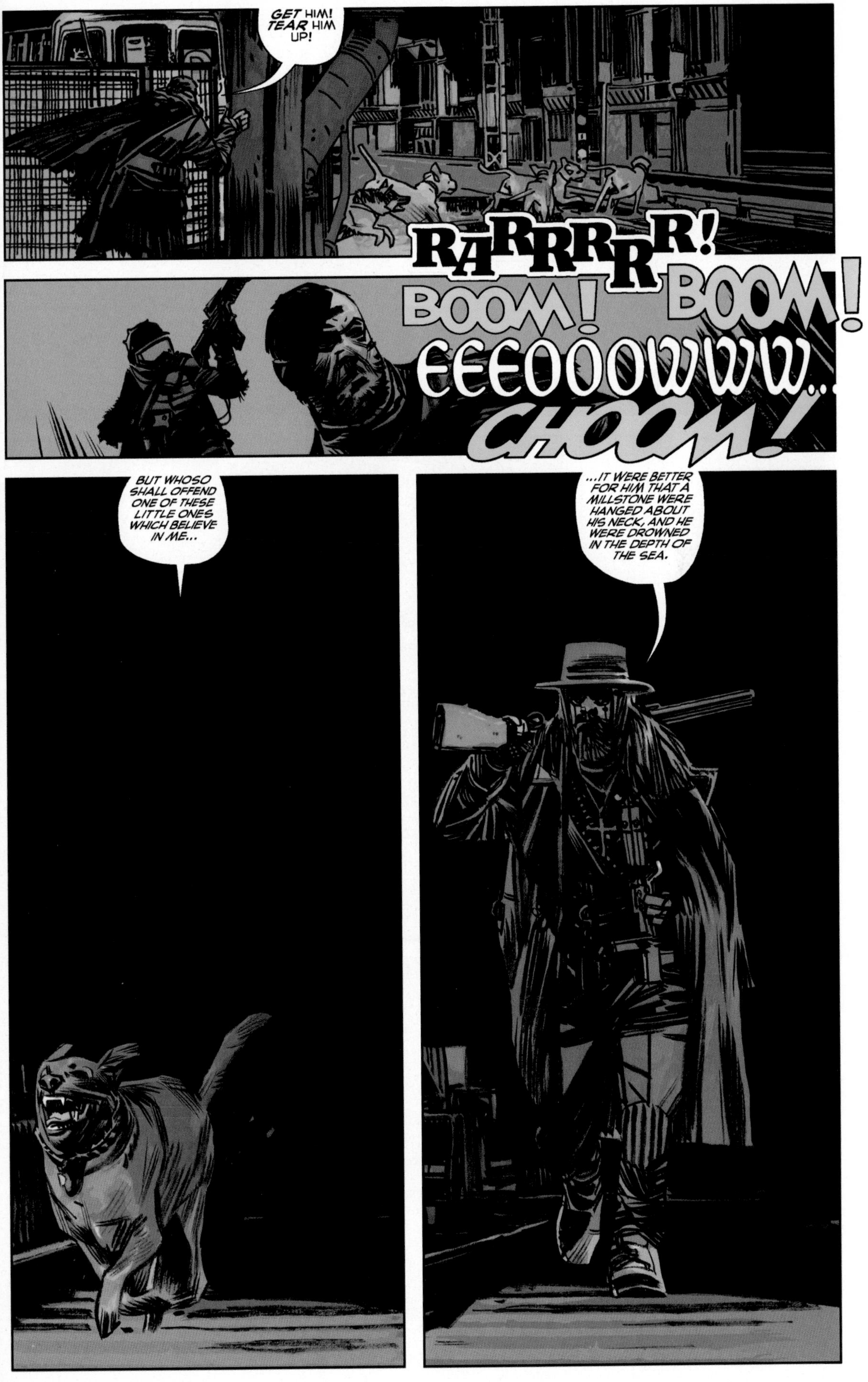
GET HIM! TEAR HIM UP!
RARRRRR!
BOOM! BOOM!
EEEOOOWWW...
CHOOM!
BUT WHOSO SHALL OFFEND ONE OF THESE LITTLE ONES WHICH BELIEVE IN ME...
...IT WERE BETTER FOR HIM THAT A MILLSTONE WERE HANGED ABOUT HIS NECK, AND HE WERE DROWNED IN THE DEPTH OF THE SEA.

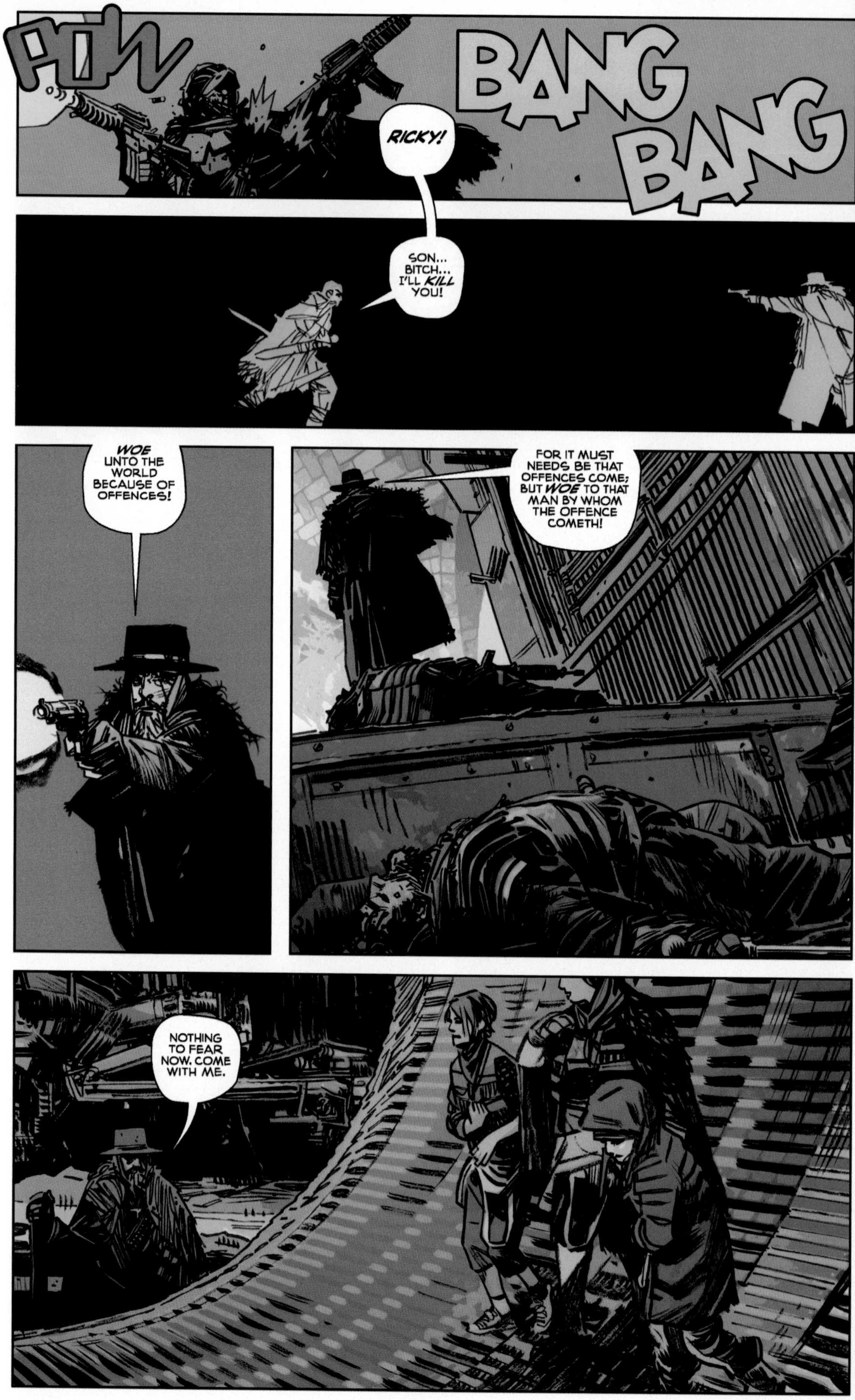
PTOW
BANG
BANG
RICKY!
SON... BITCH... I'LL KILL YOU!
WOE UNTO THE WORLD BECAUSE OF OFFENCES!
FOR IT MUST NEEDS BE THAT OFFENCES COME; BUT WOE TO THAT MAN BY WHOM THE OFFENCE COMETH!
NOTHING TO FEAR NOW. COME WITH ME.

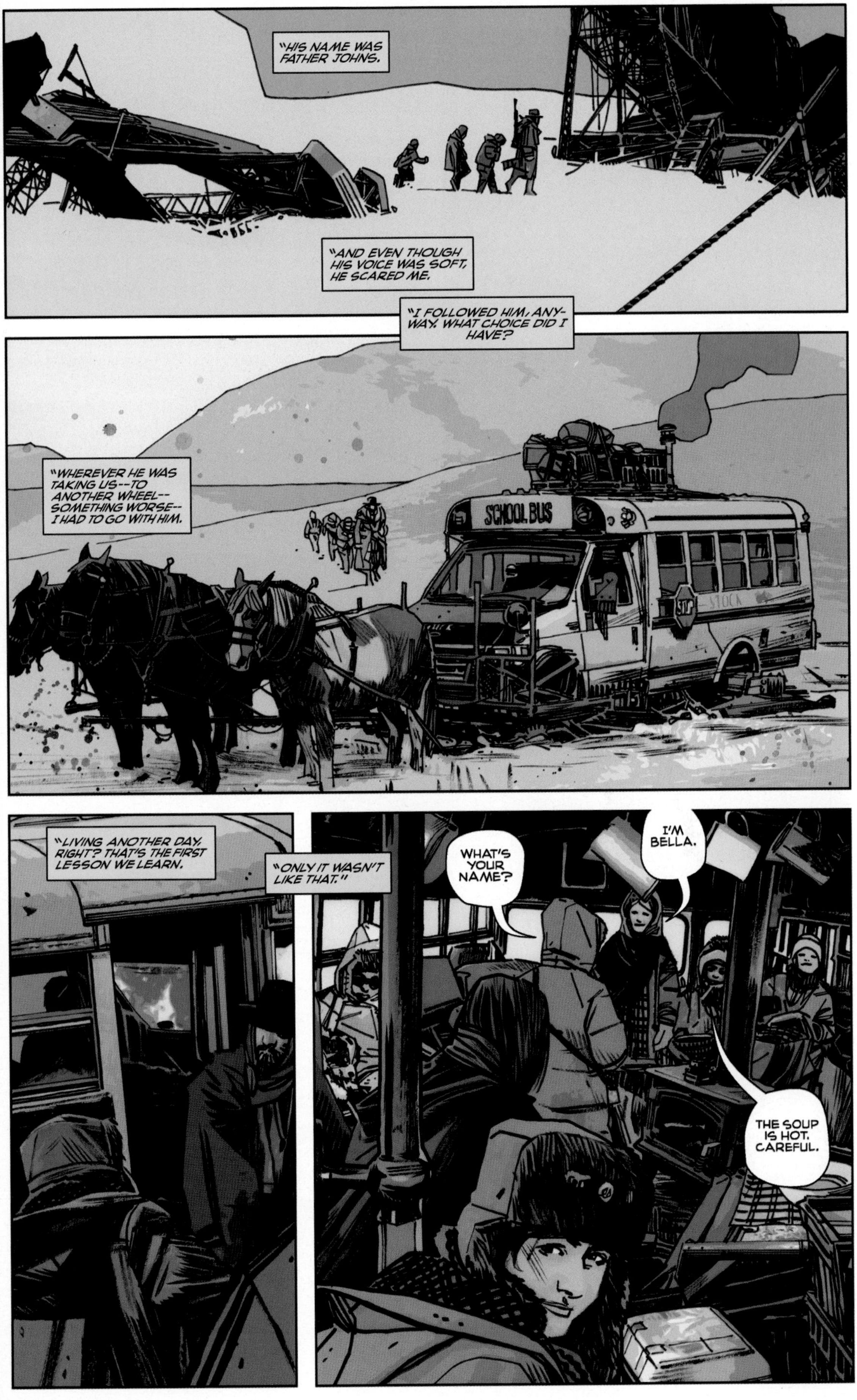
"HIS NAME WAS FATHER JOHNS.
"AND EVEN THOUGH HIS VOICE WAS SOFT, HE SCARED ME.
"I FOLLOWED HIM, ANYWAY. WHAT CHOICE DID I HAVE?
"WHEREVER HE WAS TAKING US--TO ANOTHER WHEEL--SOMETHING WORSE--I HAD TO GO WITH HIM.
SCHOOL BUS
"LIVING ANOTHER DAY. RIGHT? THAT'S THE FIRST LESSON WE LEARN.
"ONLY IT WASN'T LIKE THAT."
WHAT'S YOUR NAME?
I'M BELLA.
THE SOUP IS HOT. CAREFUL.

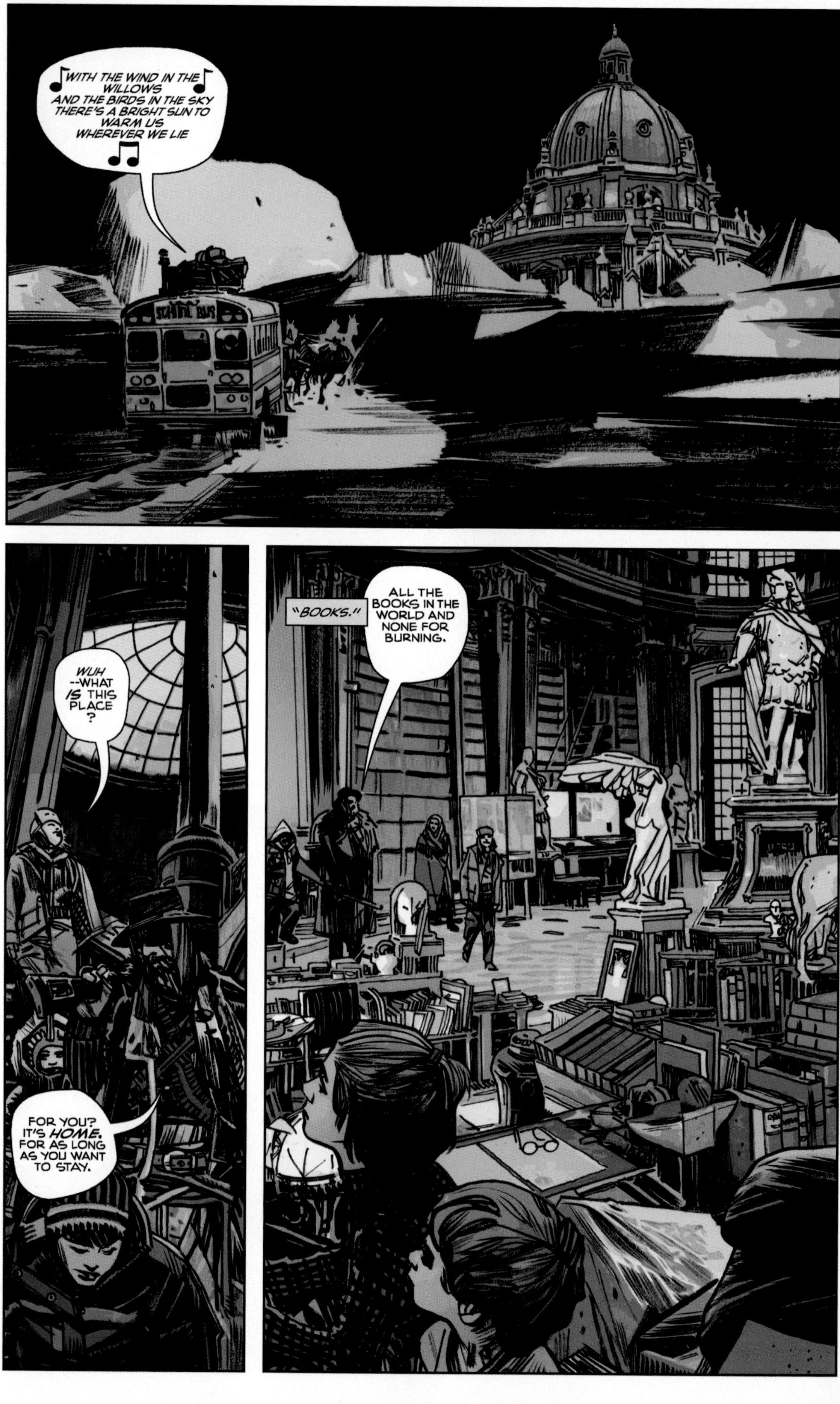
WITH THE WIND IN THE WILLOWS AND THE BIRDS IN THE SKY THERE'S A BRIGHT SUN TO WARM US WHEREVER WE LIE
WUH --WHAT *IS* THIS PLACE ?
FOR YOU? IT'S ***HOME.*** FOR AS LONG AS YOU WANT TO STAY.
"BOOKS."
ALL THE BOOKS IN THE WORLD AND NONE FOR BURNING.

"THE OLDER KIDS TAUGHT ME TO READ.

"THERE WAS WORK, TOO, BUT WE ALL SHARED IN IT.

"AND FOOD. WE ATE AT LEAST ONCE A DAY.

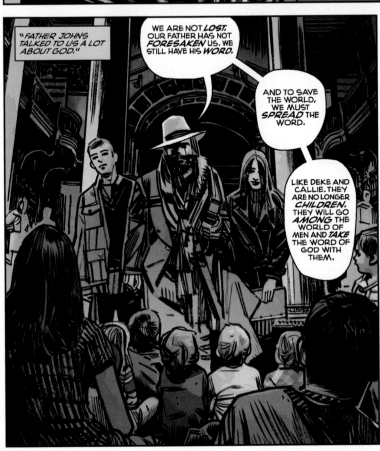

"FATHER JOHN'S TALKED TO US A LOT ABOUT GOD."

WE ARE NOT *LOST*. OUR FATHER HAS NOT *FORESAKEN* US. WE STILL HAVE HIS *WORD*.

AND TO SAVE THE WORLD, WE MUST *SPREAD* THE WORD.

LIKE DEKE AND CALLIE. THEY ARE NO LONGER *CHILDREN*. THEY WILL GO *AMONG* THE WORLD OF MEN AND *TAKE* THE WORD OF GOD WITH THEM.

AS WILL YOU *ALL* WHEN *YOUR* DAY COMES.

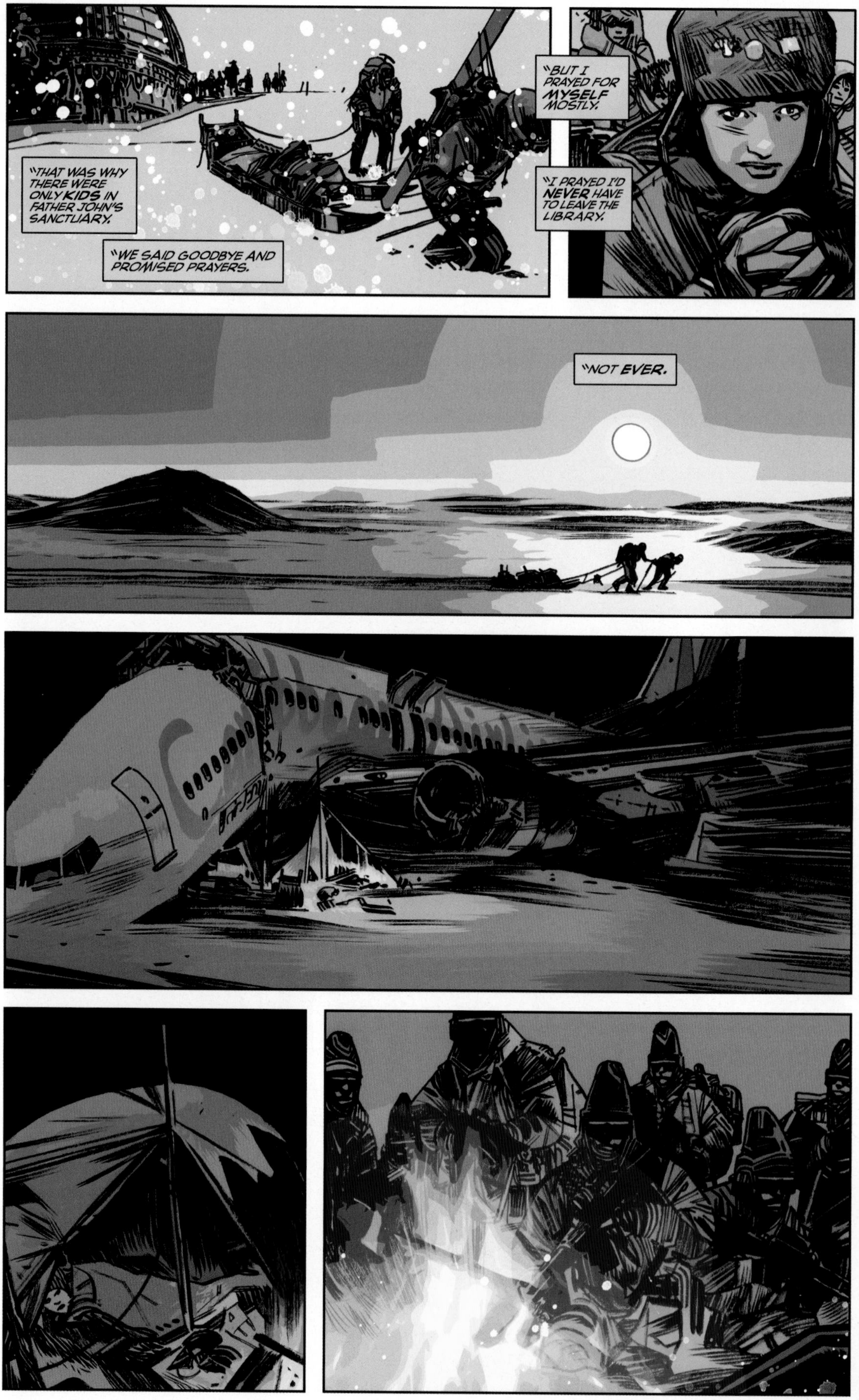
"THAT WAS WHY THERE WERE ONLY KIDS IN FATHER JOHN'S SANCTUARY.
"WE SAID GOODBYE AND PROMISED PRAYERS.
"BUT I PRAYED FOR MYSELF MOSTLY.
"I PRAYED I'D NEVER HAVE TO LEAVE THE LIBRARY.
"NOT EVER.

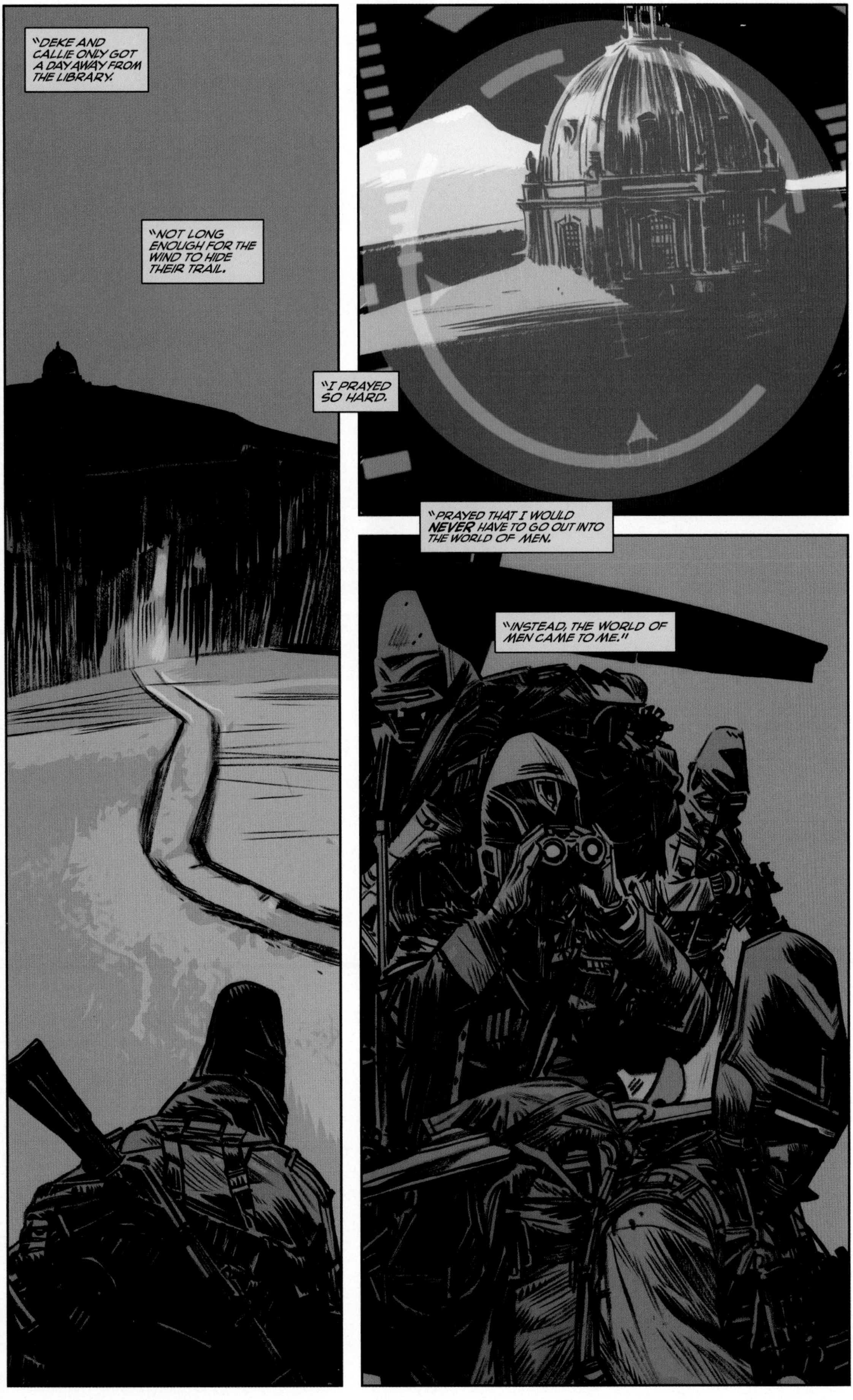
"DEKE AND CALLIE ONLY GOT A DAY AWAY FROM THE LIBRARY.
"NOT LONG ENOUGH FOR THE WIND TO HIDE THEIR TRAIL.
"I PRAYED SO HARD.
"PRAYED THAT I WOULD NEVER HAVE TO GO OUT INTO THE WORLD OF MEN.
"INSTEAD, THE WORLD OF MEN CAME TO ME."

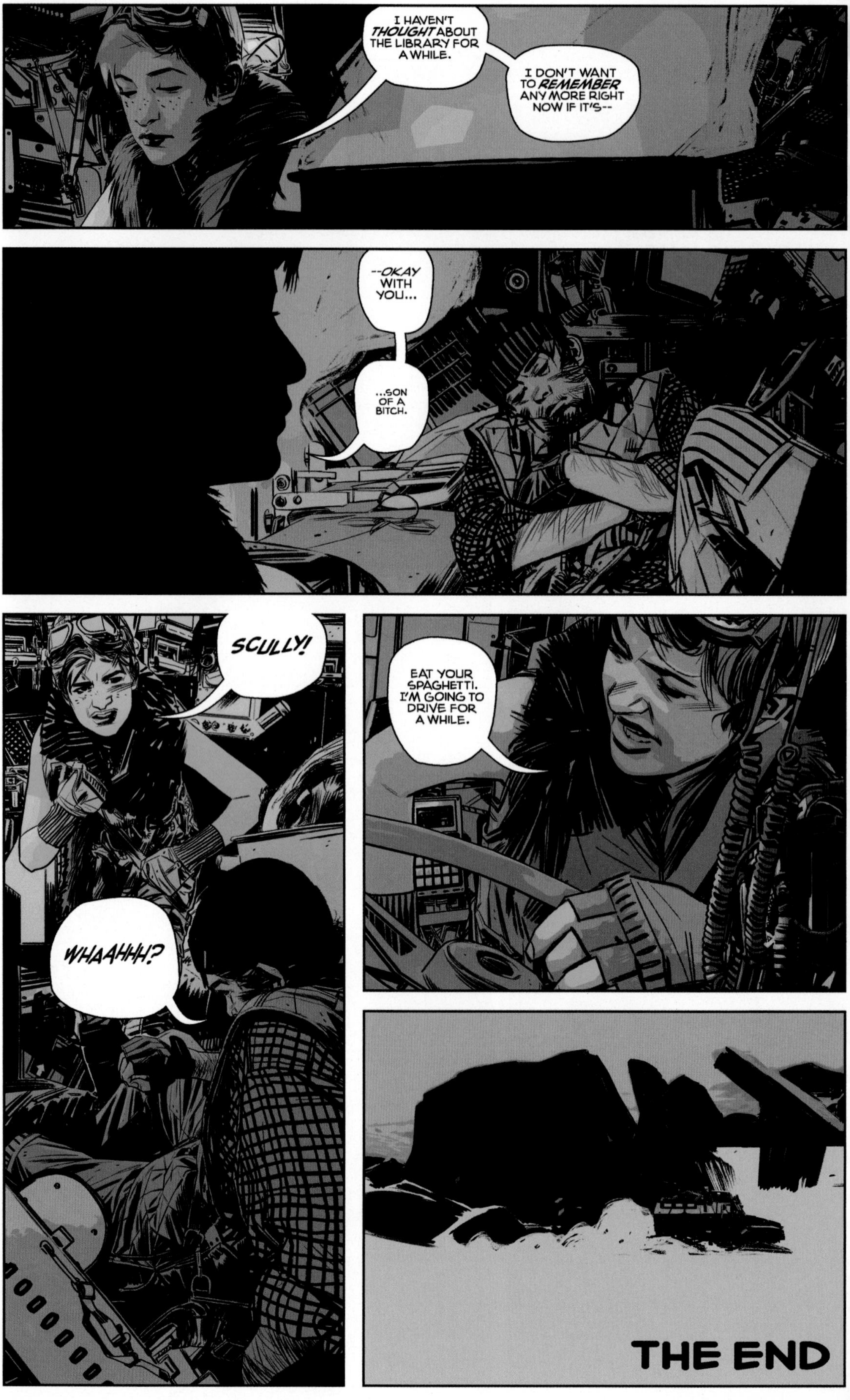
I HAVEN'T *THOUGHT* ABOUT THE LIBRARY FOR A WHILE.
I DON'T WANT TO *REMEMBER* ANY MORE RIGHT NOW IF IT'S--
--*OKAY* WITH YOU...
...SON OF A BITCH.
SCULLY!
WHAAHHH?
EAT YOUR SPAGHETTI. I'M GOING TO DRIVE FOR A WHILE.
THE END

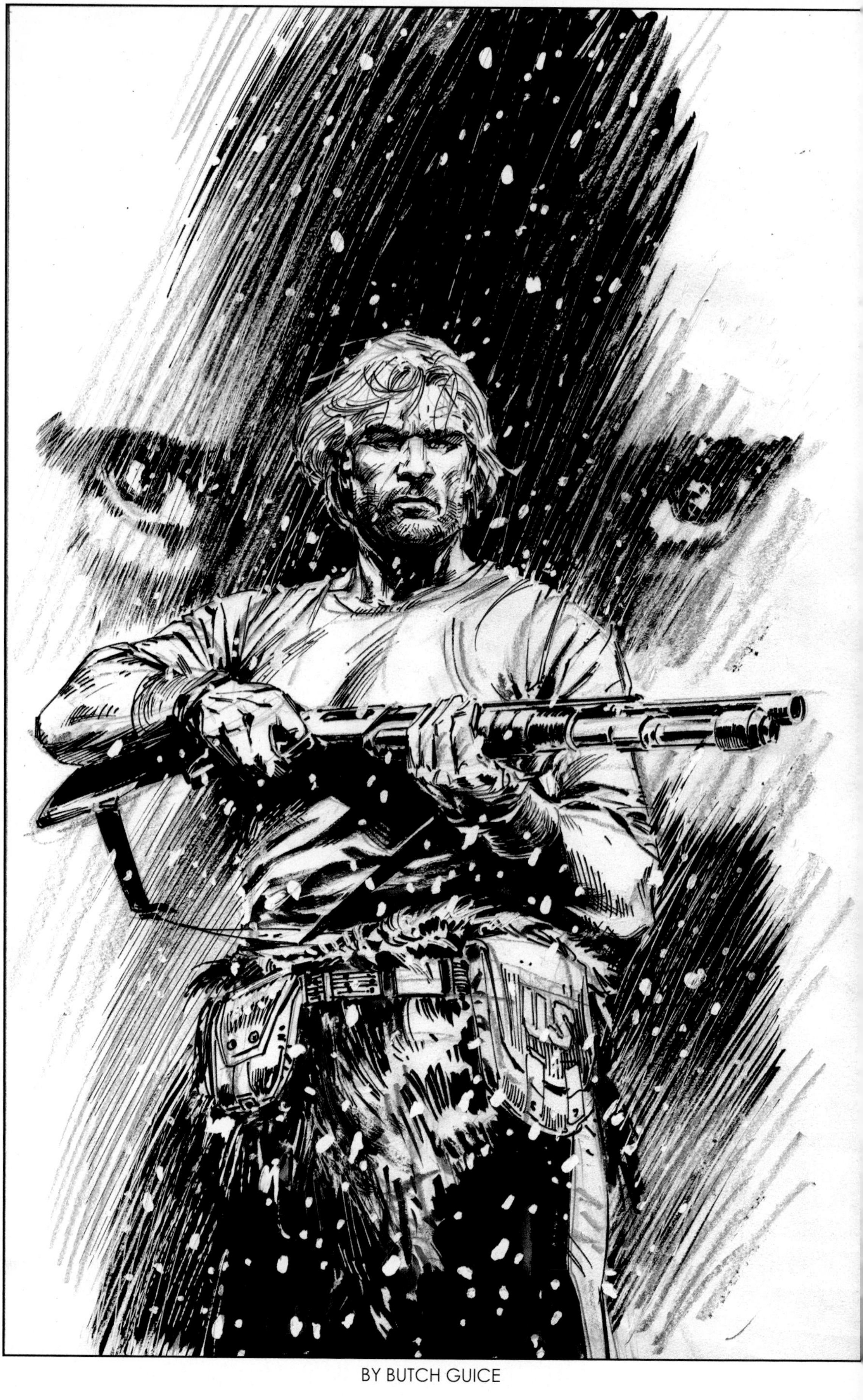

BY BUTCH GUICE

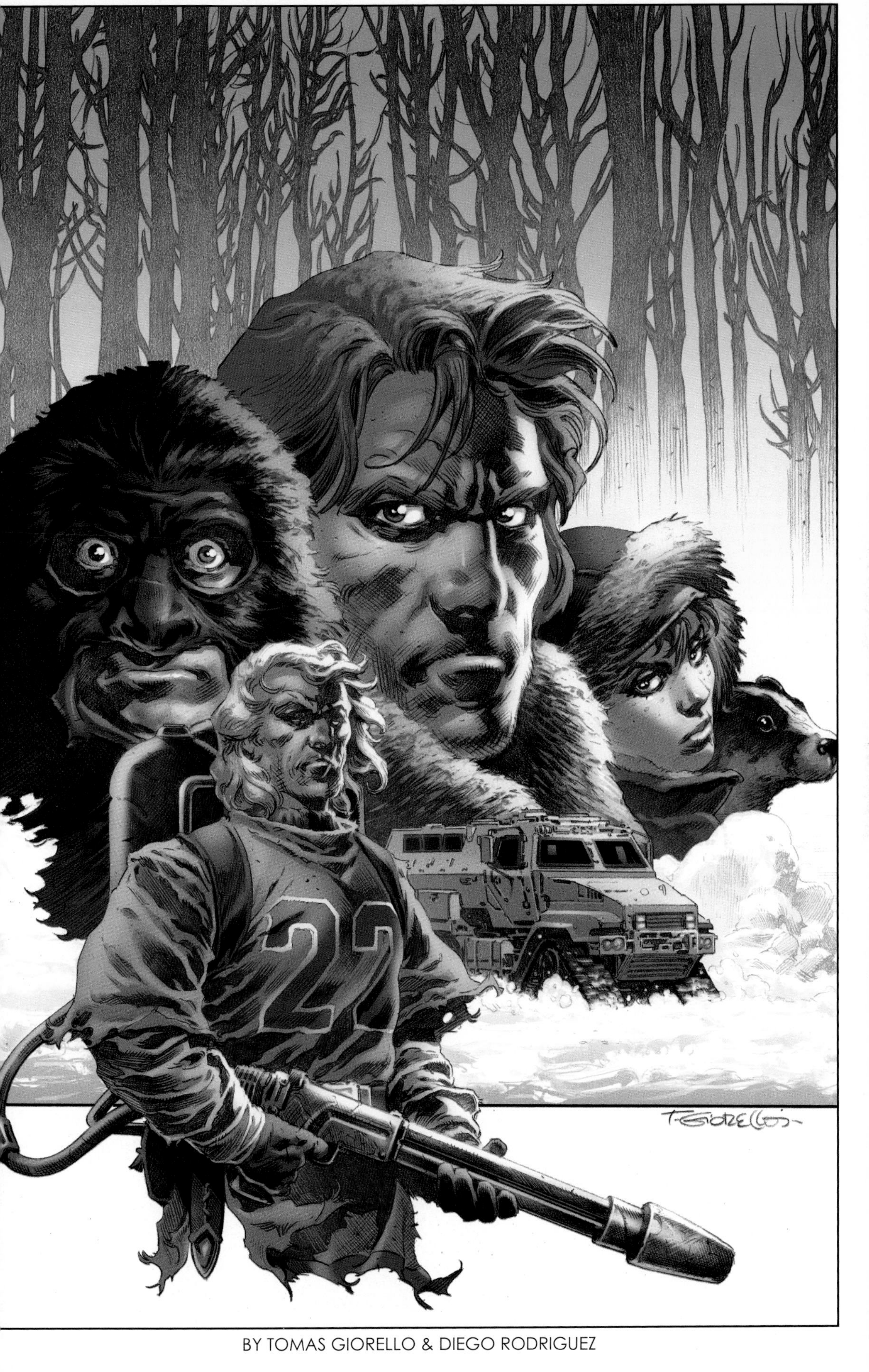

T-GIORELLO

BY TOMAS GIORELLO & DIEGO RODRIGUEZ

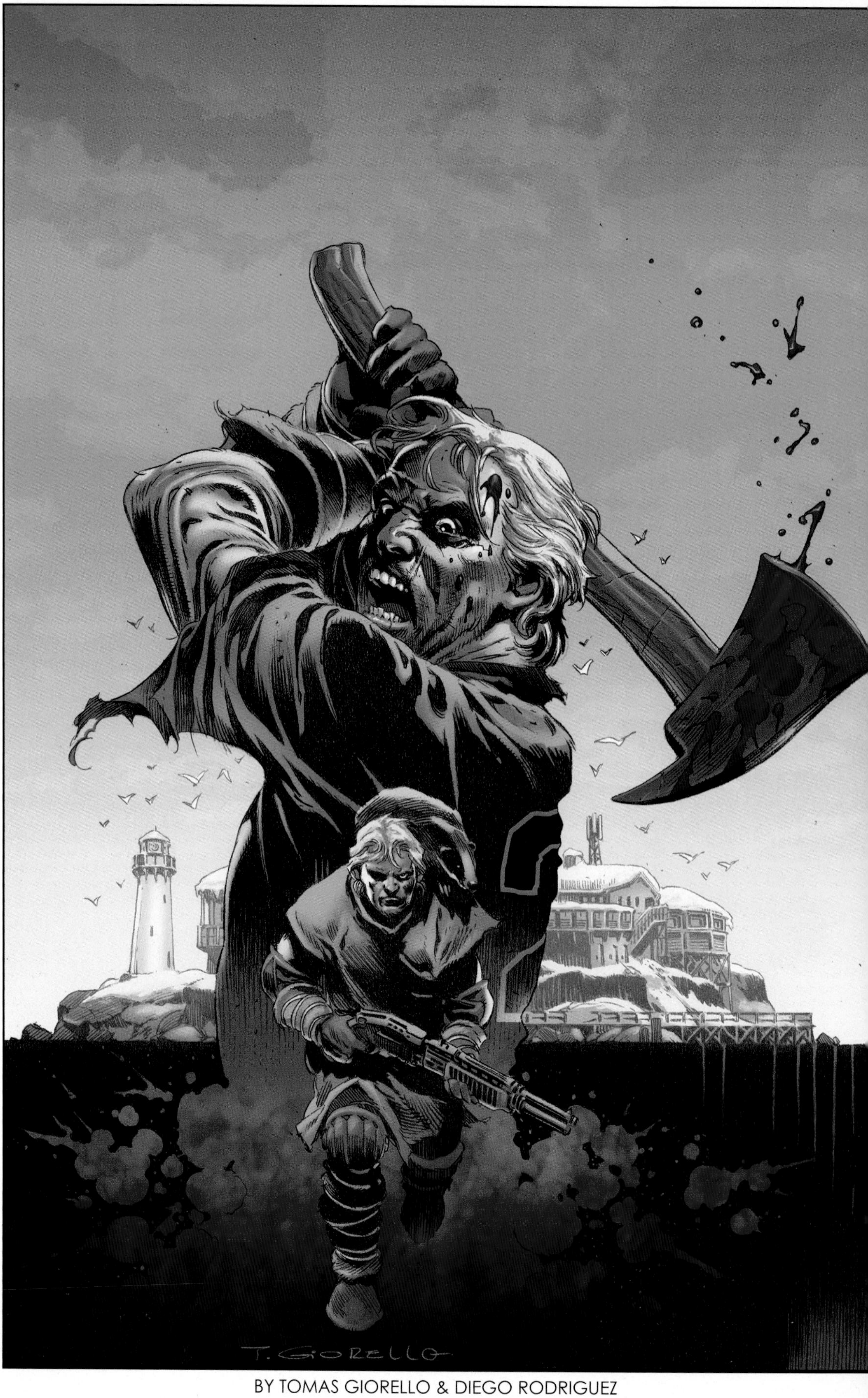
T. GIORELLO

BY TOMAS GIORELLO & DIEGO RODRIGUEZ

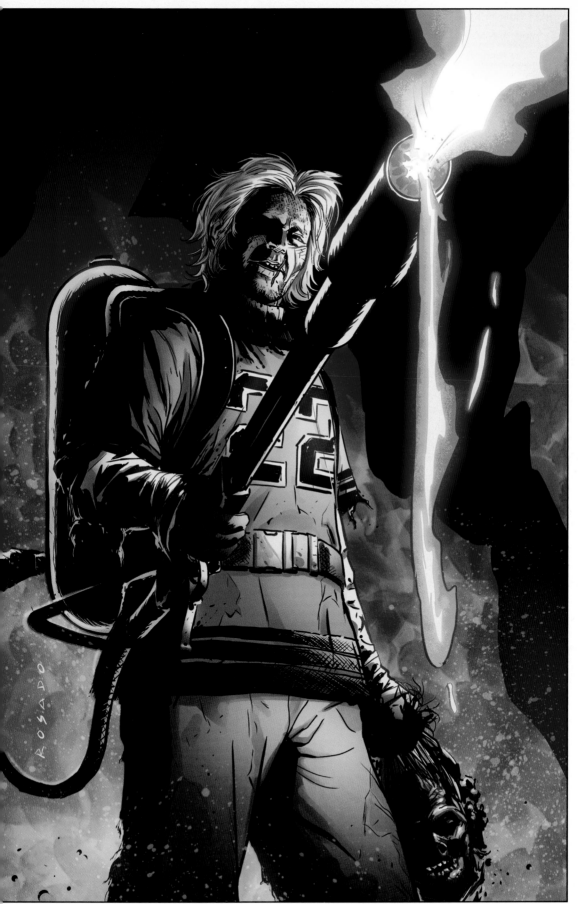

BY WILL ROSADO & DIEGO RODRIGUEZ

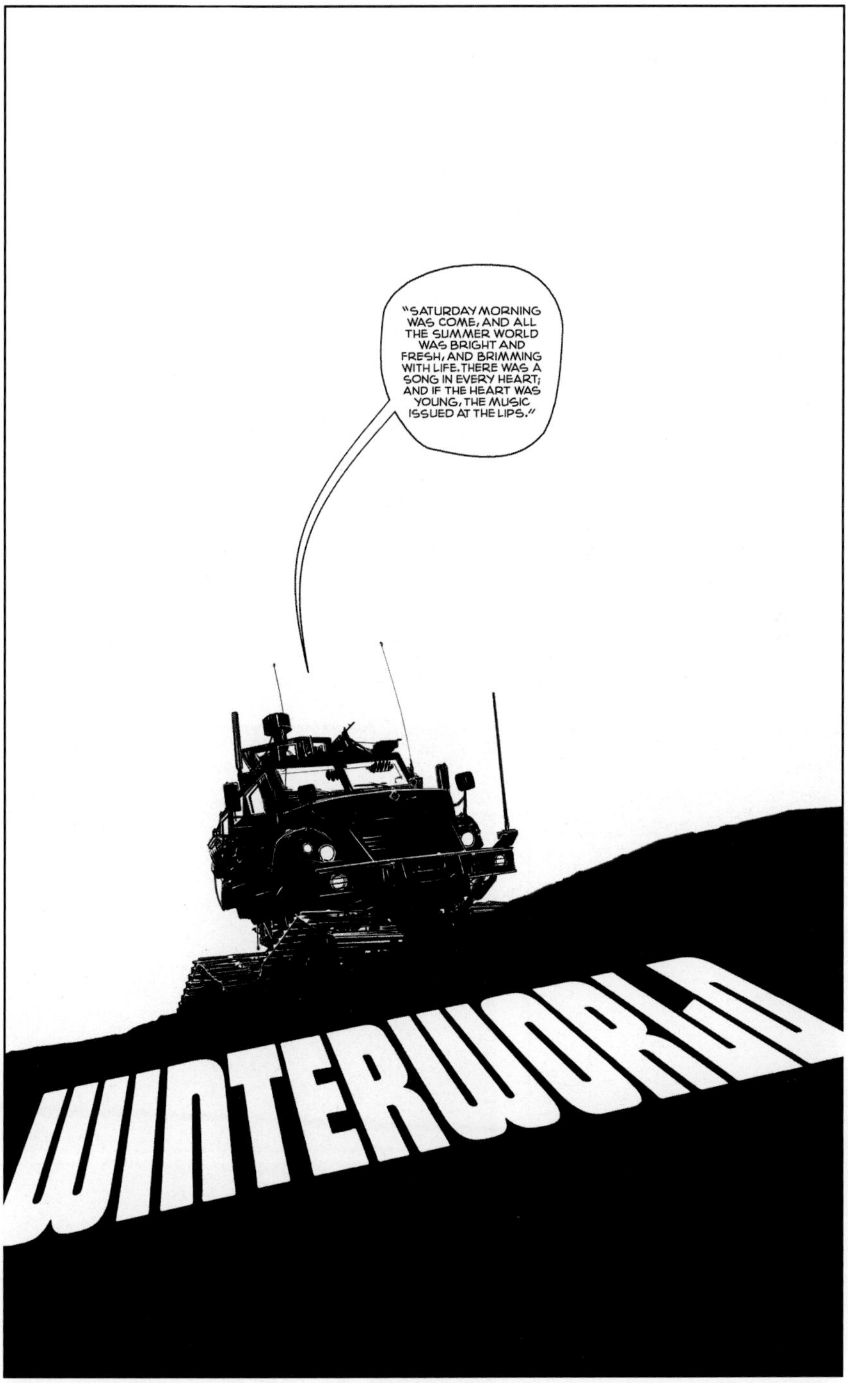
"SATURDAY MORNING WAS COME, AND ALL THE SUMMER WORLD WAS BRIGHT AND FRESH, AND BRIMMING WITH LIFE. THERE WAS A SONG IN EVERY HEART; AND IF THE HEART WAS YOUNG, THE MUSIC ISSUED AT THE LIPS."
WINTERWORLD

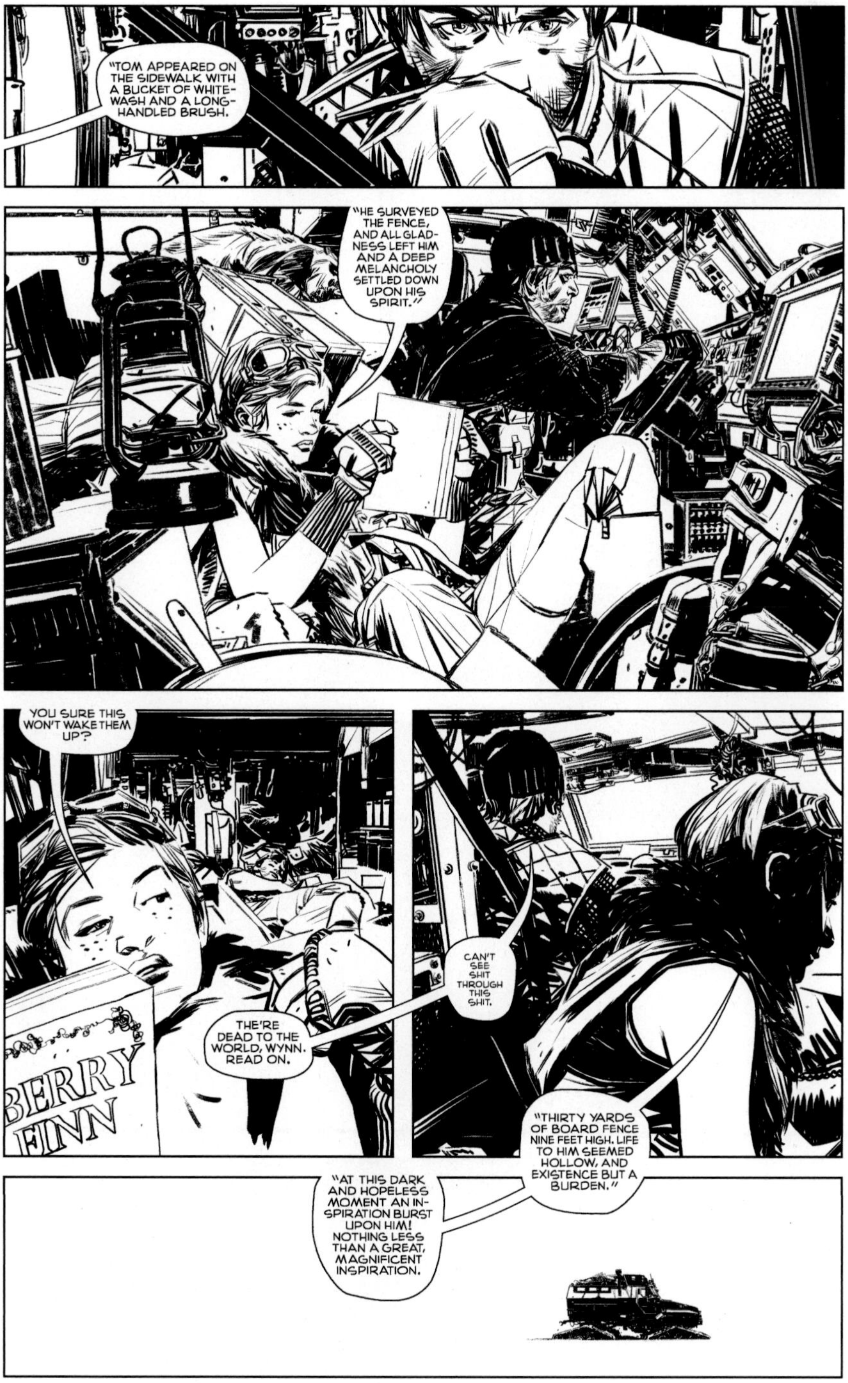
"TOM APPEARED ON THE SIDEWALK WITH A BUCKET OF WHITE-WASH AND A LONG-HANDLED BRUSH.
"HE SURVEYED THE FENCE, AND ALL GLADNESS LEFT HIM AND A DEEP MELANCHOLY SETTLED DOWN UPON HIS SPIRIT."
YOU SURE THIS WON'T WAKE THEM UP?
THE'RE DEAD TO THE WORLD, WYNN. READ ON.
BERRY FINN
CAN'T SEE SHIT THROUGH THIS SHIT.
"THIRTY YARDS OF BOARD FENCE NINE FEET HIGH. LIFE TO HIM SEEMED HOLLOW, AND EXISTENCE BUT A BURDEN."
"AT THIS DARK AND HOPELESS MOMENT AN INSPIRATION BURST UPON HIM! NOTHING LESS THAN A GREAT, MAGNIFICENT INSPIRATION.

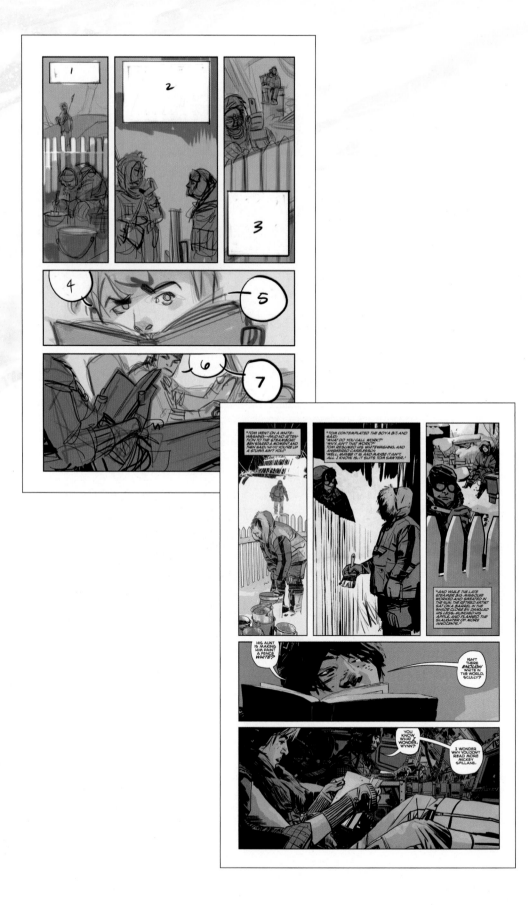

"TOM WENT ON A WHITE-WASHING--PAID NO ATTEN-TION TO THE STEAMBOAT. BEN STARED A MOMENT AND THEN SAID: 'HI-YI! YOU'RE UP A STUMP, AIN'T YOU!'"

"TOM CONTEMPLATED THE BOY A BIT, AND SAID:
'WHAT DO YOU CALL WORK?'
'WHY, AIN'T THAT WORK?'
TOM RESUMED HIS WHITEWASHING, AND ANSWERED CARELESSLY:
'WELL, MAYBE IT IS AND MAYBE IT AIN'T. ALL I KNOW, IS, IT SUITS TOM SAWYER.'"

"AND WHILE THE LATE STEAMER BIG MISSOURI WORKED AND SWEATED IN THE SUN, THE RETIRED ARTIST SAT ON A BARREL IN THE SHADE CLOSE BY, DANGLED HIS LEGS, MUNCHED HIS APPLE, AND PLANNED THE SLAUGHTER OF MORE INNOCENTS."

HIS AUNT IS MAKING HIM PAINT A FENCE *WHITE?*

ISN'T THERE *ENOUGH* WHITE IN THE WORLD, SCULLY?

YOU KNOW WHAT *I* WONDER, WYNN?

I WONDER WHY YOU DON'T READ MORE MICKEY SPILLANE.

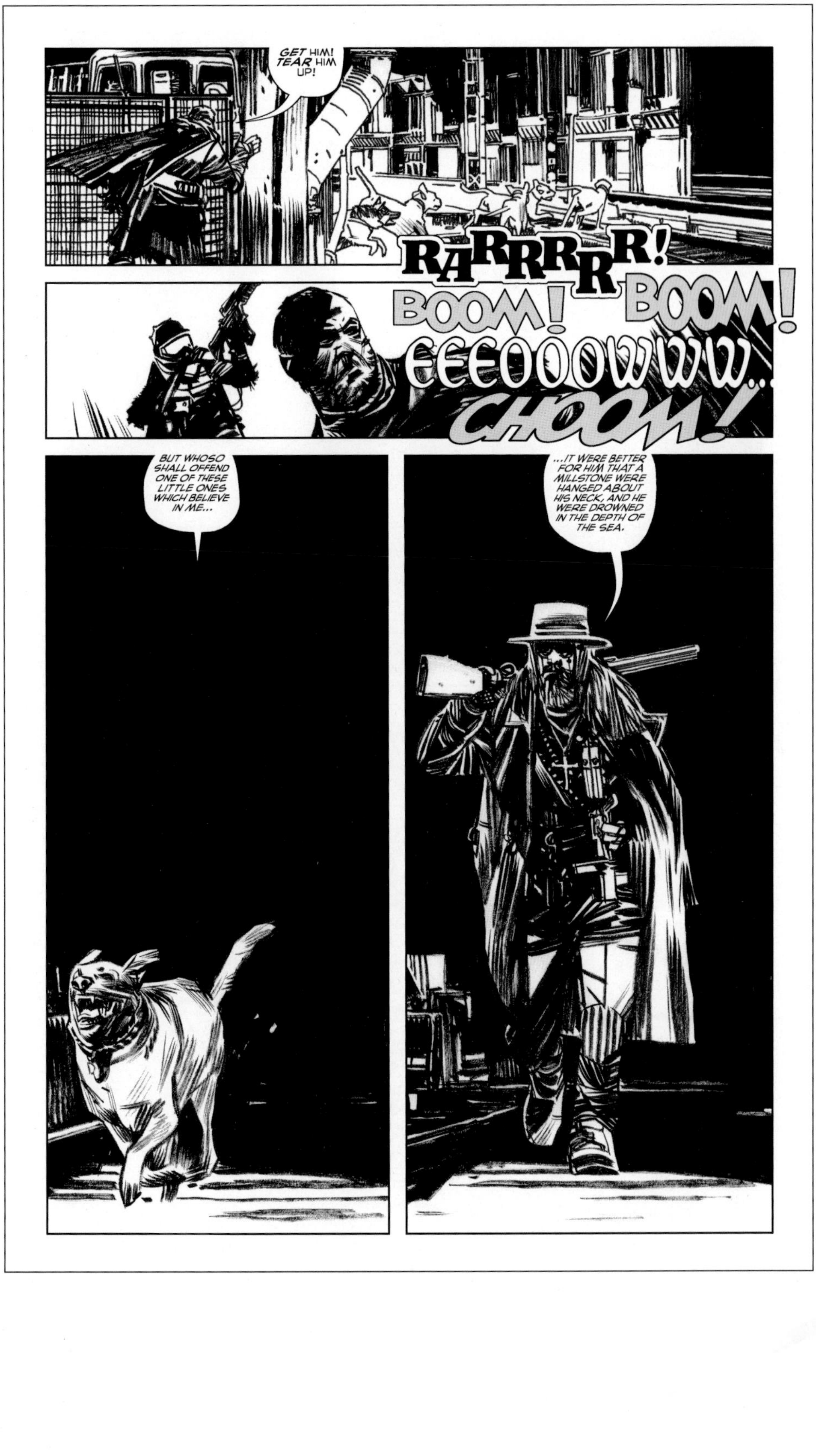
GET HIM! TEAR HIM UP!
RARRRRR!
BOOM! BOOM!
EEEOOOWWW...
CHOOM!
BUT WHOSO SHALL OFFEND ONE OF THESE LITTLE ONES WHICH BELIEVE IN ME...
...IT WERE BETTER FOR HIM THAT A MILLSTONE WERE HANGED ABOUT HIS NECK, AND HE WERE DROWNED IN THE DEPTH OF THE SEA.

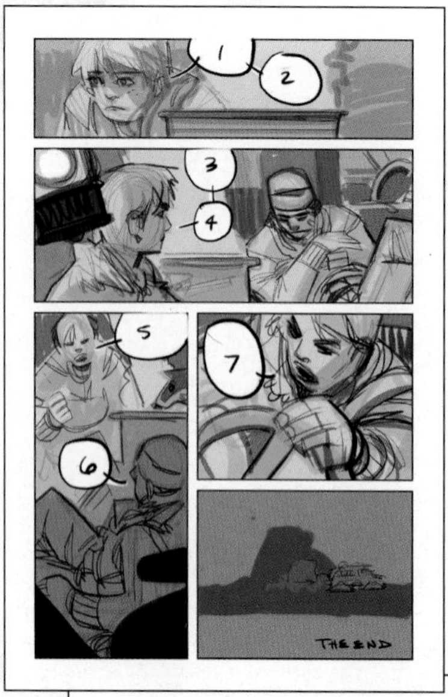
1
2
3
4
5
7
6
THE END

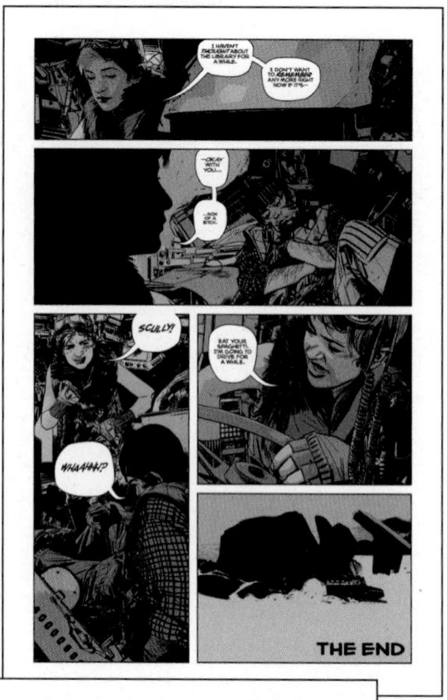
SCULLY!
WHAAHHH?
THE END

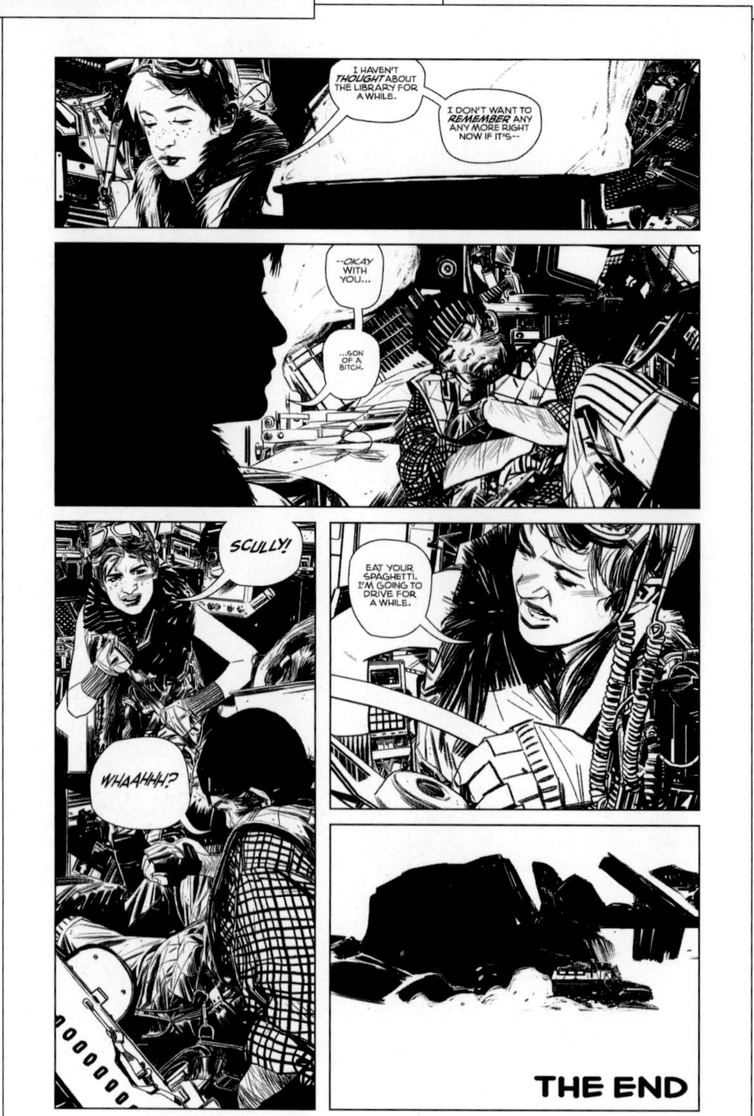
I HAVEN'T *THOUGHT* ABOUT THE LIBRARY FOR A WHILE.
I DON'T WANT TO *REMEMBER* ANY ANY MORE RIGHT NOW IF IT'S--
--OKAY WITH YOU...
...SON OF A BITCH.
SCULLY!
EAT YOUR SPAGHETTI. I'M GOING TO DRIVE FOR A WHILE.
WHAAHHH?
THE END